Audit Culture

'A visionary book. Two anthropologists piece together a global jigsaw: how for 25 years practices of accountability have been transforming almost every aspect of organisational and personal life. A brilliantly lucid, vigorously argued critique, clear-eyed about the structures that undermine us.'
—Marilyn Strathern, Emeritus Professor of Social Anthropology, University of Cambridge

'A new and compelling argument for why so many institutions continue to be spellbound by rankings and metrics – despite the cultural carnage they cause in schools, hospitals, universities, corporations and governmental agencies. How can we halt this "death by audit" craze that has swept through modern society like a deadly virus? In this thought-provoking book, the authors develop a radical agenda that will strike fear into number-loving technocrats around the world.'
—Peter Fleming, author of *Dark Academia: How Universities Die*

'The expansion of audits, indicators and rankings has become a pressing issue for governance and democracy. Cris Shore and Susan Wright build on decades of work to provide a powerful and definitive critical diagnosis of the effects of this audit culture on individuals, public organisations and society. Their book should be essential reading for scholars and policy makers.'
—Michael Power, Professor of Accounting, London School of Economics and Political Science

'If you want to go and see a film, choose a university or find the best restaurant, you are likely to consult some sort of ranking ... In this timely work, Shore and Wright ask us to question this contemporary common sense and the market managerialism that lies behind it. Can we imagine a world without audit, one in which our choices are not counted, and trust does not rely on numbers?'
—Professor Martin Parker, University of Bristol Business School

Anthropology, Culture and Society

Series Editors:
Holly High, Deakin University
and
Joshua O. Reno, Binghamton University

Recent titles:

Audit Culture

How Indicators and Rankings are Reshaping the World

Cris Shore and Susan Wright

First published 2024 by Pluto Press
New Wing, Somerset House, Strand, London WC2R 1LA
and Pluto Press, Inc.
1930 Village Center Circle, 3-834, Las Vegas, NV 89134

www.plutobooks.com

British Library Cataloguing in Publication Data
A catalogue record for this book is available from the British Library

ISBN   978 0 7453 3645 9   Paperback
ISBN   978 0 7453 4931 2   PDF
ISBN   978 0 7453 4930 5   EPUB

This book is printed on paper suitable for recycling and made from fully
managed and sustained forest sources. Logging, pulping and manufacturing
processes are expected to conform to the environmental standards of the
country of origin.

Typeset by Stanford DTP Services, Northampton, England

Simultaneously printed in the United Kingdom and United States of America

Contents

List of Figures

Abbreviations

BHS	British Home Stores
CIA	Central Intelligence Agency
CMA	Competition and Markets Authority
DHA	district health authority
EFA	Education Funding Agency
EU	European Union
EY	Ernst & Young
FRC	Financial Reporting Council
FSA	Financial Services Authority
FTSE	Financial Times Stock Exchange
GAAP	generally accepted accounting principles
GDP	Gross Domestic Product
GEAT	Australian Aboriginal land trust
GM	General Motors
GNH	Gross National Happiness
GPs	general practitioners
GWR	Great Western Railway
HMRC	Her Majesty's Revenue and Customs
IMF	International Monetary Fund
IT	information technology
MATs	multi-academy trusts
NAO	National Audit Office
NEF	New Economics Foundation
NGO	non-governmental organisation
NHS	National Health Service
NICE	National Institute for Clinical Excellence
NKS	Nya Karolinska Solna hospital (Sweden)
NPM	New Public Management
NSW	New South Wales (Australia)
OECD	Organisation for Economic Co-operation and Development
OfS	Office for Students
Ofsted	Office for Standards in Education, Children's Services and Skills

OMC	open method of coordination
PAC	Public Accounts Committee
PCAOB	Public Company Accounting Oversight Board
PCT	primary care trust
PFIs	private finance initiatives
PISA	Programme for International Student Assessment
PPs	performance points
PPPs	public–private partnerships
PwC	PricewaterhouseCoopers
QM	Queen Mary University
QS	Quantified Self
RAE	Research Assessment Exercise
REF	Research Excellence Framework
SCS	social credit system
SPV	Special Purpose Vehicle
TEF	Teaching Excellence Framework
THE	*Times Higher Education*
UN	United Nations
VW	Volkswagen
WEF	World Economic Forum
WHO	World Health Organization

Acknowledgements

We have received invaluable help from student research assistants at the Danish School of Education, Aarhus University. Notably, Iulia Iordache-Bryant did excellent research for Chapter 4 on global standards in education, and Safa Shahkhalili provided great insights through detailed research on audit in the UK health services for Chapter 5. Anna Sophie Mayland Boswell Bille helped with the final production by proofreading, checking references and following Pluto's style guide.

In addition, we would like to thank Jill Blackmore, Professor of Education at Deakin University, for reading and commenting on Chapter 4. Dr Graham Bickler, former Director of Public Health in England, provided valuable feedback on Chapter 5. Rachel Douglas-Jones, Associate Professor at the IT University in Copenhagen helped us with ethnographically based knowledge of the Chinese social credit system in Chapter 7, and Tom Stibbs, Principal Social Worker, provided background information on the reforms to child protection services that we developed in Chapter 8. Our thanks go to Isabel Shore for designing the figures in Chapters 3 and 7.

We would like to acknowledge the publications where we have published earlier versions of some of this work and thank the editors and peer reviewers for their comments and suggestions.

- Parts of Chapter 1 were published in our earlier article, 'Audit culture revisited: Rankings, ratings, and the reassembling of society', *Current Anthropology* 56(3): 421–444 (2015).
- An earlier version of Chapter 3 appeared in 'How the Big 4 got big: Audit culture and the metamorphosis of international accountancy firms', *Critique of Anthropology* 38(3): 303–324 (2018).
- An earlier version of Chapter 6 was published as 'The Kafkaesque pursuit of "world class": Audit culture and the reputational arms race in academia', in Sharon Rider, Michael Peters, Mats Hyvönen, and Tina Besley (eds) *World Class Universities: A Contested Concept*, pp. 59–76 (Singapore: Springer, 2020).
- Portions of Chapter 7 were published in a chapter titled 'Performance management and the audited self: Quantified personhood

beyond neoliberal governmentality', in Btihaj Ajana (ed.) *Metric Culture: Ontologies of Self-tracking Practices*, pp. 11–36 (London: Emerald Publishing, 2018).

The themes of the book were developed from many conference papers that we presented together, including at conferences of the European Association of Social Anthropologists, the American Anthropological Association, the Aarhus Institute for Advanced Studies, and Higher Education as a Research Object (HERO) at Uppsala University. We would like to thank the students at our universities, especially the Masters' students, who contributed insights and ideas while participating in the Anthropology of Organisations course at the Danish School of Education. Particular thanks go to the Helsinki Collegium for Advanced Studies and the Swedish Collegium for Advanced Studies for the fellowships which provided Cris Shore with time and space to work on this book and receive feedback from generous colleagues.

Not least, we would like to thank David Castle of Pluto Press for his unflagging support, encouragement and patience during the long gestation of this book.

Series Preface

As people around the world confront the inequality and injustice of new forms of oppression, as well as the impacts of human life on planetary ecosystems, this book series asks what anthropology can contribute to the crises and challenges of the twenty-first century. Our goal is to establish a distinctive anthropological contribution to debates and discussions that are often dominated by politics and economics. What is sorely lacking, and what anthropological methods can provide, is an appreciation of the human condition.

We publish works that draw inspiration from traditions of ethnographic research and anthropological analysis to address power and social change while keeping the struggles and stories of human beings centre stage. We welcome books that set out to make anthropology matter, bringing classic anthropological concerns with exchange, difference, belief, kinship and the material world into engagement with contemporary environmental change, capitalist economy and forms of inequality. We publish work from all traditions of anthropology, combining theoretical debate with empirical evidence to demonstrate the unique contribution anthropology can make to understanding the contemporary world.

Holly High and Joshua O. Reno

Preface

This book arises from our concern about the negative effects of audit culture on contemporary society. Audits are typically portrayed as objective instruments for promoting trust, accountability, transparency, and good governance but our research shows the opposite. As we demonstrate, the rise of audit since the 1980s, particularly in the public sector, has fuelled the spread of managerialism, marketisation and the development of new forms of capitalism. Rather than promoting efficient services that better serve the public interest, audit has produced a dysfunctional system that is undermining public sector organisations, destroying professional integrity and autonomy, and fostering new forms of audit capitalism while raking in enormous profits, particularly for the large accountancy firms. The key instruments of auditing – indicators, rankings, targets, numbers – appear to give people the power to make objective choices and rational decisions, but the development of audit processes has hollowed out democracy. We endorse the original purpose of audit to ensure financial probity, sound management of resources, the exercise of fiduciary responsibility, accountability, and trust. However, these principles have been progressively undermined as audit was untied from its original moorings, became instrumentalised as a tool of governance, and colonised ever increasing areas of everyday life. The aim of this book is to critique this audit culture, identify ways to curtail its spread, and suggest alternatives that will restore professionalism, public accountability and participatory forms of governance.

The book represents the culmination of research and analysis over thirty-five years. Our interest in audit culture began when higher education was undergoing profound changes variously labelled Thatcherism, New Public Management and neoliberalisation. We turned to our discipline, anthropology, to make sense of what was happening in our own university workplaces and to our profession. The 1985 Jarratt Report (Committee of Vice Chancellors and Principals et al. 1985) began the process of streamlining university management by converting vice chancellors into chief executive officers, personnel departments into 'human resource management', disciplinary departments into 'cost centres', and academics into 'units of resource'. Simultaneously, a raft of new auditing systems were implemented so that one year universities faced a Research Assessment Exercise, the next year a Teaching Quality Assurance audit (to ensure standards were being maintained despite rising student numbers and worsening staff–student ratios), and the third year an audit of the institution's financial and operational efficiency and standards.

We witnessed first-hand how the mission of the university was being undermined and recast in the alienating language of business and accountancy. Anthropologist Laura Nader (1972) has proposed 'indignation' as a valid motivation for critical research, especially if it provokes curiosity about the bureaucratic systems and hidden hierarchies that shape society. Indignation at the assault on our professionalism was our motivation for examining the often-opaque forces driving changes to our workplace, discipline, and profession. We began thinking and working together about these developments in the late 1980s through a series of workshops and conferences organised by UK's Group for Anthropology in Policy and Practice (GAPP). These events examined the transformations of public sector organisations and professions under Thatcherism. In a series of articles and chapters (Shore and Wright 1999, 2000, 2004, 2021; Shore et al. 2005), we mapped and monitored the rapid spread and mutation of audit-led managerialism. We continued studying these processes even after leaving the UK (Sue to Denmark and Cris to New Zealand). Projects conducted over many years in Europe, Australasia, and the Asia-Pacific region, explored how professions and organisations were transformed by policies aimed at driving competitiveness in the global knowledge economy.

There are strong elements of reflexivity and 'anthropology at home' in our critique of audit culture. Following Nader, we use our personal experiences as a springboard for 'studying up' and systematically study the way audit culture impacts on our own lives, livelihoods, and workplaces. This entails tracking the multiple actors, agencies, organisations, and political interests that are involved in audit processes. We research the genealogies of these issues by trawling the policy documents, briefing papers, parliamentary reports, newspaper articles, academic and grey literatures, and other materials produced by these actors and organisations. The statistics in these sources also often provide a basis for critiquing the way audit processes use numbers. We supplement this documentary information by interviewing key actors involved in the issues. In this sense, we have adopted an 'anthropology of policy' approach (Shore and Wright 1997, 2011), one that identifies the epistemic communities that form around policies and their implementation. This approach follows the way major events unfold and how contestations over keywords and practices associated with audit move through time and space and, in the process, transform the core concepts and values that define an organisation and how it is governed. The disciplinary and conceptual sources of inspiration for this approach are diverse. We owe much to the work of Foucault and governmentality theorists (Rose, Burchell, Miller, Dean) and equally to Gramscian and cultural Marxist approaches to the analysis of hegemony, ideology, language and contestation, as developed in cultural studies (Williams, Hall, Clarke). We also draw on the work of sociology and philosophy of science (Espeland and Sauder; Hacking), geographers (Harvey, Peck), political economists and critical accountants (Power) and, of course, anthropologists (Merry, Strathern, Scott).

Where this book differs from our previous work is in its broader, more comparative framework. We examine how audit works across different scales (from the global to the individual) and sectors (education, health, industry, the military). This bigger canvas enables us to theorise connections between audit, new forms of capitalism, and transformations in regimes of governance and power. This book is a warning about the dangers of audit culture and how it is shrinking the space for meaningful public discussion, reducing public accountability to a set of bureaucratic templates, and hollowing out democracy. On a more positive note, it also identifies ways to achieve whole-system reform, restore professionalism, reframe accountability, and renew public trust.

Cris Shore and Susan Wright
28 March 2023

1

Introduction: Audit Culture and the New World (Dis)Order

> Rankings are part of a global movement that is redefining accounta-
> bility, transparency, and good governance in terms of quantitative
> measures ... they diminish the salience of local knowledge and pro-
> fessional autonomy, they absorb vast resources, and they insinuate and
> extend market logic. (Sauder and Espeland 2009: 80)

Quantification, statistics and numerical ratings have long served as
instruments of state power. However, the past four decades have seen an
extraordinary rise in the use of numbers as performance indicators for
managing companies and governing organisations and populations within
and beyond the state. Modern management involves creating calculative
mechanisms that translate everyday activities into numbers and score
sheets, or what has been referred to as 'governing by numbers' (Porter
1996; Miller 2001). Anthropologists and theorists of power have long recognised that seemingly mundane routines can have the most profound
impact not only on how people are governed but on how they internalise
those external mechanisms of governance. Whether it is collecting points
to win the 'WAL-MART Employee of the Month' certificate, managers
using performance appraisals to 'stack rank' employees against each
other and weed out under-performing colleagues, universities counting
academic publications to brand themselves as 'world class', or the number
of emoticon smileys that a service department receives being used as a
measure of customer satisfaction, enumeration and classification lie at the
heart of such everyday forms of management. The use of indicators and
rankings has become pervasive; not only are they used as instruments in
the internal management of organisations but also in external representations of their quality, efficiency and accountability to the wider public. As
Sally Merry (2011: S52) noted, 'indicators are rapidly multiplying as tools
for measuring and promoting reform strategies around the world'. Their

use as instruments for monitoring and managing individuals' performance and their behaviour is also multiplying, as people are encouraged to think of themselves as calculating, responsible, self-managing subjects. There is also an element of gratification and pleasure, at least for those who perform successfully in terms of the chosen measures, and this gives these calculative regimes affective as well as disciplinary purchase. If the practices of modern accounting and financial control have long been integral to the world of corporate management, their widespread adoption and proliferation in other contexts, and their increasingly pervasive subjectifying effects on individuals and organisations represent a new phase in the development of neoliberal governance. These mundane practices provide critical insights into regimes of governance, the operation of power, and the rationality of auditing and assessment – which has become a fundamental organising principle of society. We term this rationality and its effects 'audit culture'.

In this book, we trace how the calculative principles and technologies of measuring, rating and ranking travelled from education to the military and industry and, despite appalling failures, were further translated into the public sector during the 1980s and beyond. As Nikolas Rose and Peter Miller observed in their seminal essay on power beyond the state, these 'calculative practices ... should be analysed as "technologies of government"' (1992: 183). That is, they are part of the machinery of modern bureaucratic power that helps to bind technical solutions to moral imperatives. As Rose and Miller argue, such calculative practices do more than simply provide solutions to the problematics of government: they also embody a particular kind of political rationality, one that has its own moral form and epistemological character (or understanding of the nature of the objects and subjects to be governed), as well as a particular language and set of idioms. Understood in the broadest sense, calculative practices are 'a kind of intellectual machinery or apparatus for rendering reality thinkable in such a way that it is amendable to political deliberations' (Rose and Miller 1992: 179). Indeed, one of the greatest achievements of audit culture has been to 'render thinkable' radically new ways of measuring, calculating and governing individuals and organisations for managerial purposes. While these calculative practices make government reforms operable, they also recast political programmes as mundane administrative and technical matters to be dealt with by experts, thereby masking their ideological content and removing them from the realm of contestable politics (Burchell 1993; Shore and Wright 1997a; Miller 2001). Since the 1990s, such political technologies have been expanded to become vehicles for assessing the quality and organisational effectiveness of municipal services, hospitals, schools, NGOs (non-governmental organisations) and businesses. Today, the creditworthiness of charities, utility companies, airlines, universities and even entire countries is measured and rated. All have been reduced to numbers and competitively ranked in league tables. Use of these technologies has intensified as governments and other organisations have sought to mobilise their assets to compete more successfully in the global knowledge economy. As a result, and as Chapters 2 and 3 illustrate, a vast new industry of profitable activities in measuring, accounting, ranking and benchmarking has emerged across numerous professional fields (see also Olds 2010; Robertson et al. 2012). Equally importantly, a new management-inspired language of governance has come to dominate organisations, one that typically 'confuses "accountability" with "accountancy" so that being answerable to the public is recast in terms of measures of productivity [and] "economic efficiency"' (Shore 2008: 281). Starting with an emphasis on the three 'E's of 'economy', 'efficiency' and 'effectiveness', these have been combined with new constellations of words like 'value for money', 'return on investment', 'innovation', 'transparency', 'responsibility' and 'quality'. The new semantic clusters that these concepts create when combined can be seen as the building blocks of contemporary neoliberal ideology (see also Bruneau and Savage 2002: 12).

To analyse these developments, we address six related sets of questions:

1. What can we learn about these audit practices by examining their origins and spread?
2. How should we theorise audit culture, analyse its effects and differentiate it from more conventional forms of 'governing by numbers'? How does audit relate to other trends that are reshaping the contemporary world, such as the uses of big data and algorithms, increasing concerns about risk, compliance and productivity, or debates over financialisation and the regulatory role of the state?
3. Who *are* the auditors and 'rankers' today and how do they operate? Who are the main actors that comprise this new industry, and what role do international auditing and accountancy firms and other ranking bodies play in shaping its development?
4. Why do governments, policy makers and managers continue to use these audit and accountancy practices despite evidence of their flaws?

What are the rationales that drive and legitimate their deployment, and how are they reshaping sectors such as public administration, education, and health and wellbeing?

5. What kinds of subjects do these calculative practices of audit assume or seek to create? How are organisations or individuals constructed as 'accountable' and 'free' agents who succeed by mobilising their resources to optimise 'what counts'?

6. Finally, we ask, where is this trajectory leading and is its relentless expansion inevitable? Just as Max Weber (2013 [1903]) warned about the 'iron cage of bureaucracy' as both a cause and effect of rationalisation and modernity, are audit's imperatives for accountability producing a new 'glass cage' of coercive transparency? How can we reclaim the professional autonomy and trust that audit practices appear to strip out of the workplace? Is it possible for professionals to sustain critical practice when what 'counts' in rankings no longer reflects the central role and purpose of a professional and public institution?

Towards a Theory of Audit Culture

The interaction of these contemporary processes of enumeration, ranking and governance, the economised and competitive relationships they create, and the new forms of performance and accountability these give rise to, can be usefully analysed and understood through the concept of audit culture. As we use the term, 'audit culture' refers to contexts where the principles, techniques and rationale of financial accounting have become dominant features of the way society is organised. This includes the ways to measure quality in the provision of public services, the 'quality of life' or the success of military interventions. From a theoretical perspective 'audit culture' should not be viewed as a type of society alongside alternatives such as 'feudal society', 'capitalist society', or 'post-industrial' society. Rather, it is a rationality of governance and corresponding set of dispositions and practices. It therefore refers to a *condition*, and to the constellation of processes that create that condition. This is similar to what Foucault (1980) called a 'formation' or *dispositif*. Put simply, audit culture refers to contexts where auditing has become a central organising principle of society, and where work and life are increasingly structured through the techniques, rationalities and language of accountancy (Shore and Wright 1999, 2000, 2015b). This set of processes and practices is dynamic and agentive, so the relations they create and the patterns they produce are never fixed or settled but are continually in-the-making.

Like many anthropological concepts, 'audit culture' combines both 'emic' (insider) perspectives and etic (external) perspectives: it is both an experiential phenomenon for those who have been made into 'auditees', or subjects of external scrutiny, and an analytical model that helps identify and theorise key processes and trends that are reshaping everyday social behaviour, cultural practices and power relations. In saying this, we are not suggesting that audit culture is either monolithic or uniform; audit and accounting work in diverse and complex ways and their meanings and ramifications shift according to context. For example, there is a world of difference between an audit of a company's consolidated financial statement and an audit of a hospital's clinical practices. Nor are we seeking to map or label a range of audit *cultures* as if each context constituted a discrete or bounded entity. Instead, we use the concept to refer to processes that have strong family resemblances in Wittgenstein's (1953) sense of the term; that is, where each incidence entails some forms of economic logic and some instrumental techniques of enumeration and commensuration. When combined, these form systems of accountability that are both individualising and totalising, but the precise constellation of features and how they work together vary, as do the politics of their adoption and resistance.

The expansion of auditing into new areas of work and life is more than simply 'policy transfer': audit brings with it a wholesale transformation in the ways in which individuals, organisations and even countries are managed and governed, what we term a 'domaining' process. The chapters in this book illustrate how such 'domaining' often produces unanticipated and even perverse effects on individuals and organisational behaviour, particularly when people are continually incentivised to compete and measure their performance according to decontextualised numerical targets. As Albert Einstein allegedly remarked, 'not everything that can be counted counts, and not everything that counts can be counted'. The important issue to probe is what audits and rankings bring into focus and what they render invisible or unsayable. This is where auditing and ranking also become questions of governance and power.

Audit Culture and New Forms of Capitalism

One of the first scholars to identify and analyse the rise of auditing and its effects on society was Michael Power, a professor of accounting and philosopher at the London School of Economics. Writing about Britain in the early 1990s and reflecting on more than a decade of radical Conservative governments under Margaret Thatcher and John Major, Power noted the extraordinary proliferation of formal auditing and monitoring systems. As well as traditional financial audits, the UK now had 'environmental audits', 'public spending audits', 'waste management' audits, 'democracy audits', 'technology and computing audits', 'teaching audits', 'academic audits', 'value for money' audits, 'land and water resource audits, media audits, medical audits – even stress audits' and 'audits of auditing systems' (Power 1994: 1). These trends continued under the New Labour governments of Tony Blair and Gordon Brown (1997–2010) and spread to many other countries, particularly those that embraced the doctrines of New Public Management and neoliberal policy goals. Power further developed this analysis in *The Audit Society* (1997), describing audits as 'rituals of verification' and noting their often contradictory effects. Paradoxically, these new instruments for ensuring good governance, transparency and trustworthy reporting often generated the opposite: poor governance, opaque decision making, increasing cynicism and mistrust. The replacement of practices based on professional judgement and autonomy by more transparent and formal systems of audit and inspection seemed to be producing a spiralling regress of trust (O'Neill 2002).

Audit culture is not only closely bound up with the introduction of New Public Management (NPM), it is also tied to the emergence of new forms of capitalism. As David Harvey (1989), Robert Reich (1991) and others have noted, the 1990s saw a major shift in capitalism from large corporations to more flexible and fluid forms of organisation. In place of multinational corporations with large, fixed costs in plant, land and labour, companies restructured around a small central management team which outsourced all aspects of the design, production and distribution of goods and services. Focusing on the production of a brand (best exemplified by the footwear and apparel company Nike), operations were reorganised through proliferating chains of contracts and subcontracts extending around the world. A company's central team managed these supply chains at a distance through contracts that set clear performance targets and output measures. How the subcontractors achieved these targets was not the company's responsibility or concern: all they required were minimal points of commensurability for the value chains to work (Tsing 2006). A further development entailed dividing companies into 'front office' and 'back office' and outsourcing the latter's activities to another company. That company further divided activities into 'front' and 'back' in an ongoing process of splitting and subcontracting – with consultants earning fees at every stage in forming these contract chains (Chong 2012). In short, a new approach to organising production and extracting 'value' emerged which provided a useful method that could be applied elsewhere.

These new forms of corporate management were translated into new ways to organise and govern the public sector and provided a model that was also echoed in the reorganisation of the state. In the UK in the late 1980s, Mrs Thatcher's government introduced a series of reforms, called the 'Next Step Initiative', to radically overhaul central government. Parts of the state bureaucracy were hived off as 'agencies' that were then contracted to provide the public services previously delivered by government ministries. These were managed at a distance through contracts with clear performance and output targets. In time, this process of what Pollitt et al. (2001) called 'agencification' was extended to local government and throughout the public sector. The government also engaged in public–private partnerships (PPPs) and private finance initiatives (PFIs) to build and run public infrastructure, including roads, hospitals, prisons and schools, while keeping the costs off the country's balance sheet (see Chapter 6). The terms of the contracts, however, often resulted in much higher costs to the public (Pollock 2004) through what were effectively state-guaranteed forms of rent extraction (Christophers 2020; see also Chapters 4 and 6) or what Wright (2008, 2016) calls years of 'taxpayer-funded risk-free capitalism'.

Agencification, privatisation and rent-seeking opened up new spaces of opportunity for private sector firms to extract value from public sector work. In contrast to the corporate model for outsourcing, where a large number of firms initially bidded for and won contracts to provide public services, over time a small number of increasingly large companies (including Serco, Tarmac, Group 4 and Carillion) came to dominate the field in the UK. For example, Serco, a FTSE 250 company listed on the London Stock Exchange, has contracts in the defence, justice and immigration, transport, health and citizen services sectors, and has used its UK experience to expand, with over 50,000 employees now working on some 500 contracts in Europe, North America, the Asia Pacific and the Middle East (Serco 2022). Having grown so large, some of these firms now hold a dominant position in the market for state services and are deemed 'too big to fail' – or at least, they cause chaos when they do fail. A good example of this is the UK construction company Carillion, which went into receivership in January 2018 leaving a £1.5 billion deficit and a £1 billion hole in its pension fund. This was one of the largest government contractors, responsible for numerous building projects for hospitals and roads, and for providing public services, including serving 32,000 school meals a day. The Big Four international accountancy firms (PwC [PricewaterhouseCoopers], KPMG, EY [Ernst & Young] and Deloitte) had collectively charged Carillion a total of £71 million for work carried out in the 10 years prior to 2018 (Marriage 2018a). KPMG had earned £29 million as the company's external auditor between 1999 and 2018, and had recently issued a clean bill of health for the company, despite the fact that at the time of the audit Carillion had allegedly been insolvent for two years. It had a current debt of £7 billion and just £29 million in cash (O'Dwyer 2023). Four months later, Carillion issued a 'catastrophic profit warning triggered by an £845m writedown', and nine months after that the company collapsed (Plimmer and Rovnick 2018). The government's response to the profit warning had been to issue three further contracts worth £1.3 billion in an attempt to save its hundreds of big projects (MacAskill 2018). These new contracts included helping build the government's high-speed (HS2) rail line to the north of England, and providing catering, hotel and mess services at 233 military facilities for the Ministry of Defence. KPMG's role in Carillion's collapse was subsequently investigated by the UK's Financial Reporting Council (FRC) which issued KPMG with a £14.4 million penalty – one of the largest fines in UK audit history – and a severe reprimand for misconduct (Budaly 2022). The tribunal concluded that the five senior KPMG managers who carried out the Carillion audit had 'acted deliberately and dishonestly in the creation of false documents and the making of false representations' to the FRC (O'Dwyer 2022b). KPMG had already been fined more than £34 million for misconduct in the UK in the previous four years, and had also settled a £1.3 billion negligence claim from Carillion's liquidators (O'Dwyer 2023). As Britain's former Labour Party leader noted, this outsourcing of contracts to private providers who are 'too big to fail' has 'done serious damage to our public services and fleeced the public of billions of pounds' (quoted in MacAskill 2018).

If agencification was a strategy for breaking up and outsourcing large public bodies to enable the private capture of public assets, the next step was to turn these agencies into profitable rent-seeking entities. Within this process audit has played an increasingly important role. As a principle, audit is supposed to 'serve the public interest by promoting trust and confidence' in the probity and integrity of the financial transactions of individuals, organisations and markets (EY 2021). It is also meant to provide an objective mechanism for ensuring the accuracy and reliability of accounting systems, financial reporting and legal compliance. Auditors themselves are expected to embody ethical standards covering their integrity, objectivity and independence. As the anthropologist, Marilyn Strathern put it, audits are where 'the financial and the moral meet' (Strathern 2000b: 1). Yet while the imperatives of audit have compelled private companies to demonstrate their compliance with formal requirements for accountability and transparency, as we show in this book, audit also provides a space where companies can evade public accountability and cover up their fraudulent and illegal activities. Indeed, the key claim for audit is that it promotes economy, efficiency and effectiveness and yet, as this book illustrates, every audited sector has experienced spectacular losses and financial collapses, often greeted with remarkable political and institutional indifference.

In mediating this relationship between public accountability, governance and new forms of capitalism, audit has come to take on a new role. The rise of systems of auditing and ranking has been accompanied and fuelled by the growth of international firms specialising in credit ratings and accountancy. These include, at one extreme, the various credit rating agencies that have now consolidated into the 'Big Three' firms of Moody's, Standard and Poor's, and Fitch. These agencies measure the creditworthiness of countries and organisations and their letter-grades, ranging from 'AAA' to 'D', communicate the agencies' view of the level of credit risk. These opinions affect the rates of interest at which a country can borrow money, sometimes with seriously deleterious consequences, as for example in February 2012 when Fitch downgraded Greece from 'CCC' to 'junk' status, thereby massively increasingly the country's already unsustainable level of national debt (Paphitis 2012). At a more micro level, credit reference agencies with Dickensian-sounding names such as 'Paydex', 'Experian Intelliscore', 'Dunn and Bradstreet', 'Equifax' and 'Call-Credit' score the creditworthiness of individuals to determine a person's eligibility for a mortgage, personal loan or credit card. In the field of banking, most banks and lenders today rely on the international 'FICO' score system to make credit issuing decisions (FICO being an acronym for the Fair Isaac Corporation, a measure of consumer-credit risk developed by engineer Bill Fair and mathematician Earl Isaac in the 1950s). Perversely, if someone suspects that their low credit rating is based on inaccurate information and requests a credit check, that check itself can result in a drop of up to five points, lowering their credit rating even further (Brown and Tarver 2021).

In the field of international accounting, four large commercial firms now dominate the market: Deloitte, PwC, EY and KPMG. Significantly, in 2011–12, a period of continuing financial crisis in Europe and the USA, the revenues of the 'Big Four' grew by an astonishing 6 per cent, netting a record US $110 billion thanks to their expansion into emerging economies (Big Four 2013). These firms have continued to grow and operate in over 150 countries. Between them they employed almost 1.5 million staff in 2022 (Statista 2023a), up from 1,148,505 in 2020 and, in 2022 alone, they generated staggering combined revenues of US $189.44 billion (Statista 2023c). More importantly, these companies have also helped to pioneer a new form of business entity that is not a multinational corporation, nor a global partnership, nor single firm. Instead, these companies act as coordinating entities for a network of global affiliates, who are to be unified around 'brand', 'risk', 'quality', 'values' and 'ethics' by adhering to a common code of conduct (EY n.d.; KPMG 2015a). The expansion of the Big Four has been fuelled by their diversification beyond auditing into consultancy and a host of other services. This often leads to conflicts of interest because, as we illustrate in Chapter 4, a Big Four firm can be employed to audit a company's accounts while another part of the same firm is employed to provide the company with financial advice and consultancy services that include aggressive tax avoidance strategies. At the same time, a rapid 'revolving door' has developed between the Big Four and government, whereby the firms advise government on developing tax policies and later use that information to advise their commercial clients on how to navigate loopholes in the legislation (Brooks and Hughes 2016). In this way, these audit firms occupy a pivotal point between the development of new systems of governance, emerging forms of capitalism, and transformations in the state.

Tracing the Spread of Audit: From Education and the Military to Corporations and Back

There is nothing new about the use of quantitative measurements and performance indicators. However, what is distinctive about these audit technologies today is the scale of their diffusion and the extraordinary extent to which they have been embraced, endorsed and normalised

(Strathern 2000b). As Michael Power (1994: 41) observed three decades ago, 'we have lost the ability to be publicly sceptical about the fashion for audit and quality assurance' to the extent that they have come to appear as natural and benign solutions to the problems of productivity, management and governance. Power's analysis suggests that audits and indicators may be part of the problem of accountability rather than the solution. Their declared aim is to enhance organisational trust and transparency, but their effects are often the very opposite as they typically promote gaming behaviour, opacity and mistrust. They also result in the reshaping of institutions according to the criteria and methods used to measure them, and the transformation of organisations and people into 'auditable' entities whose energies are focused on doing what 'counts' rather than what is socially beneficial or accords with their professional ethics. How did this situation arise and where did these calculative technologies for measuring and enhancing performance stem from? Significantly, as a study by Hoskin and Macve (1988) illustrates, universities and academies were themselves early pioneers in turning complex social processes into numbers (Wright 2012).

In 1817, the new principal of the West Point Military Academy, Sylvanus Thayer, instituted an educational system, which he borrowed from the École Polytechnique in France, based on arithmetic grading. Thayer established a hierarchical structure at the academy, down which rules and regulations passed to the students, and up which flowed regular and systematised reports including students' grades. The authors of this study explain:

> This is a total accountability system, where all aspects of performance, academic and behavioural, are constantly measured, evaluated and recorded in a joint numerical-linguistic language which is also a currency. (Hoskin and Macve 1988: 49)

According to Hoskin and Macve, every student's subject knowledge was tested daily, weekly and half-yearly, and marked according to a standardised 7-point numerical scale. Students' aptitude, study habits, and whether their conduct was sufficiently 'military' were also recorded in weekly, monthly and half-yearly reports, and given a grade on a 7-point descriptive scale from 'excellent' to 'indifferent'. Both sets of reports went up the hierarchy. The marks were used to divide each year into four graded classes. Each student knew his place and what he had to do to move up the ranking. This was:

> an exhaustive hierarchical reflexive system of command and commu-
> nication ... which (ideally) made every individual in the institution
> constantly visible and accountable for his behaviour. (Hoskin and
> Macve 1988: 59)

The West Point students were made into calculative, self-disciplined selves. They learnt the norms against which they were marked, and they knew what they had to do to improve their grades. Their final mark determined how prestigious their first appointment would be, and their record accompanied them throughout their military career and beyond.

This system produced the best civil engineers in the country. It also produced some of the best managers of the armouries, the railroads and the newly forming industrial corporations. They imported into these organisations a hierarchy down which passed meticulous regulations and up which passed written reports with number-based, normalising judgements. These reports graded each employee's productivity and were the currency for comparing units, so that every employee 'felt and often remarked that the eyes of the company were always on them through the books' (Chandler 1977: 267–8, quoted in Hoskin and Macve 1988: 67). In short, the organisation of corporate America relied heavily on the West Point graduates' reflexive knowledge about how to create a system of organisation and discipline that turned managers and workers into calculative, accountable selves.

This method of accounting was further refined by Frederick Taylor's (1913) theory of scientific management, which analysed workflows in order to improve labour productivity. Taylor's ideas were influential in the organisation of domestic industries during the First World War and taken up in the 1920s as part of the Scientific Management Movement. Shortly before his death in 1915, Taylor visited the automobile factory in Michigan where Henry Ford had been developing his own principles of modern mass production and automation that paralleled Taylorism. Initially, Ford's success derived from dividing the car manufacturing process into standardised small elements, then costing and measuring every aspect of production to achieve efficiencies, while carefully maintaining oversight of the assembly line's coherence and flow. But fragmenting the production process also had negative consequences. During the 1940s

Henry Ford II employed ten 'whiz kids' from the army air force's statistical team to create further productive efficiencies. One of these, Robert McNamara, became president of the Ford Motor Company in the 1950s. As president, he used the new IBM computers to feed numbers into spreadsheets to turn what had been a family company into 'an omniscient operating system', albeit one that he later admitted he would 'go out of my way to discourage my son from working in' (Starkey and McKinlay 1994: 980, quoted in Martin 2010: 16). The manager of each section was given targets and their performance was measured by a higher bureaucracy. This created a task-driven, fiercely competitive culture, in which each section competed with every other, and gamed the system to advance their own institutional position. This became counter-productive and dysfunctional when concern for internal competition and intrigue far outweighed any overall vision of the quality of the car or the satisfaction of the customer. Situations arose in which, as one manager confessed, supervisors were only concerned with 'meeting output targets ... even if it meant subverting Ford's quality control systems' (Martin 2010: 16–17). Tom Peters, co-author of the famous management book *In Search of Excellence*, complained: 'Start with Taylorism, add ... a dose of McNamaraism, and by the late 1970s, you had the great American corporation that was being run by bean counters' (2001: 88).

When he was appointed US Secretary of Defence under President Kennedy, McNamara transferred this system to the running of the Vietnam War. Military victory, he maintained, would be achieved through the meeting of measured, objective, quantitative targets. But he later admitted that 'body counts' proved a disastrous substitute for 'our profound ignorance of the history, culture and politics [of Vietnam]' (McNamara, quoted in Martin 2010: 16). In his autobiography, *My American Journey*, Colin Powell, former Secretary of Defense under President George W. Bush, recounted his personal experience of McNamara's quantitative measurement system while serving in Vietnam:

While I was in the Be Luong base camp [Defense] Secretary McNamara had made a visit to South Vietnam. '... every quantitative measurement,' he concluded after forty-eight hours there, 'shows that we are winning the war.' Measure it and it has meaning. Measure it and it is real. Yet, nothing I had witnessed in the A Shau Valley indicated we were beating the Viet Cong. Beating them? Most of the time we could not even find them. McNamara's slide-rule commandos had devised precise indices to measure the immeasurable ... This conspiracy of illusion would reach full flower in the years ahead, as we added to the secure-hamlet nonsense, the search-and-sweep nonsense, the body-count nonsense, all of which we knew was nonsense, even as we did it. (quoted in Natsios 2011: 16)

If McNamara's handling of the Vietnam War exemplifies the perverse logic of governing by numbers and the 'conspiracy of illusion', another example from the automobile industry highlights the 'banality of evil' that may result from the marriage of cost accounting with the single-minded pursuit of profit that is the driving force and legal mandate behind the modern corporation. Joel Bakan (2005) describes the story of Patricia Anderson's multibillion-dollar liability lawsuit in the *Anderson v. General Motors Corporation* case. On Christmas day 1993 Anderson, her four children and a family friend were driving home from Christmas Mass when the back of her car, a Chevrolet Malibu, was struck by a drunk driver. The Malibu's gas tank exploded on impact. The adults were able to escape but the four children were trapped in the back seat and suffered terrible second and third-degree burns. The plaintiffs filed their lawsuit on the grounds that to save costs, the fuel tank had been dangerously positioned, just 11 inches from the back bumper, with no metal brace to separate the fuel tank from the rear of the car. A company directive had recommended that fuel tanks be at least 17 inches from the rear bumper and during the trial Anderson's lawyers obtained General Motors (GM) internal memos that the company had blocked in previous lawsuits. These revealed a damning 1973 report written by GM engineer Edward Ivey, which concluded that it would be cheaper to maintain the current fuel tank than design a tank that did not explode in a crash. Ivey's report estimated there would be 500 fatalities related to accidents with fuel-fed fires and that each fatality would cost $200,000 in compensation. He then calculated that since there were 41 million General Motors automobiles on the road, the cost per car to GM would be $2.40. On the other hand, the cost of designing a non-exploding fuel tank would be $8.59 per car. Hence, the company stood to 'save $6.19 ... per automobile if it allowed people to die in fuel-fed fires rather than alter the design' (Bakan 2005: 63).

Although it is not clear whether anyone in senior management had seen Mr Ivey's report, the judge described GM's behaviour as 'morally reprehensible and against applicable laws because it had put profits above public safety' (Bakan 2005: 63). The court awarded Anderson and her children compensatory damages of $107 million and unprecedented punitive damages of $4.9 billion. A Los Angeles Superior Court later reduced this to $1.09 billion. To the US Chamber of Commerce this was an 'illegitimate result' on the grounds that manufacturers' use of cost-benefit analyses in the design of products is 'a hallmark of corporate good behaviour' and the 'logic underlying it is unimpeachable' (Bakan 2005: 64).

The same 'unimpeachable' logic of numbers and calculation trumping ethical concerns continues to inform how the world's leading car manufacturers operate. In 2014, for example, Toyota was fined $1.2 billion for concealing safety problems in its vehicles, including 'sticky' accelerator pedals and floor mats in its luxury Lexus model, a design fault that resulted in an estimated 89 deaths and 52 injuries. Initially, Toyota attributed these incidents to driver error, claiming that people hit the gas pedal when they meant to apply the brake. Even after issuing recalls to address the problem of accelerators becoming pinned down by floor mats, the company still hid a further flaw in the design of the accelerator pedal that caused the same problem. As US Attorney Preet Bharara put it:

> In its zeal to staunch bad publicity in 2009 and 2010, Toyota misled regulators, misled customers, and even misstated the facts to Congress. Even while giving unequivocal assurances that it had fully addressed a grave safety problem, Toyota knew full well that the problem of unwanted acceleration persisted. (quoted in Muller 2014)

More recently, in 2017 the German car manufacturer Volkswagen (VW) was ordered by a US District Judge to pay a staggering $2.8 billion criminal penalty for cheating on diesel emissions tests (Associated Press 2017). Following an investigation by the Environmental Protection Agency in 2015, VW admitted installing illegal cheat software into the engines of 500,000 US vehicles and 11 million vehicles worldwide. These so-called 'defeat devices' enabled diesel engines to detect when they were being tested, changing the performance accordingly to improve results. Why did VW take this extraordinarily illegal and unethical action? According to its chair Hans-Dieter Pötsch, this was not a corporate decision but a pragmatic solution concocted by its engineers. The US had introduced new emissions standards and VW's engineers could not find a technical solution within the company's 'time frame and budget' (Goodman 2015). Other reasons include the company's system of performance bonuses coupled with authoritarian management structures and a work environment that eschewed debate and dissent. As workers told *Newsweek* journalists, VW has a 'highly centralized hierarchy that expects them to perform, no matter what the demands' (Goodman 2015). However, the idea of 'management by performance' and setting performance targets is by no means unique to VW or private corporations.

Obsessive Counting Disorder: From Private Industry Back to Public Sector

Regardless of these regulatory failures and flawed calculative logics in both industry and the military, the idea of applying cost-benefit analysis techniques and financially driven performance indicators in order to turn organisational activities into numbers was transposed to the public sector in the 1980s as a core feature of NPM.

As Andrew Natsios puts it, 'Washington's Obsessive Measurement Disorder (OMD) spread like an infection with the adoption of this RAND-based approach to measurement-based decision making and policy analysis' (Natsios 2011:15).* But it was not only in the US that this disorder took root. As we have documented elsewhere (Shore and Wright 1999, 2000), in Britain the work of schools, hospitals, municipal government, provision for the elderly, and most other public services were reduced to numerical score sheets and ranked in competitive and hierarchical league tables. These new regimes of accountability were justified in the name of 'efficiency' and 'transparency'. The performance of players at the top of the league tables were distilled and decontextualised as 'best practice' to be spread to the others, notably those 'named and shamed' at the bottom. These reports were then published and widely disseminated among the professional health and teaching organisations in what were to become 'rituals of public humiliation' for those whose performance failed to meet the target (Shore 2008: 286). Key performance indicators (KPIs) were devised as measures of the quality, efficiency and value for money of virtually all public services. Typically, performance was expressed in economic figures and, while claims were made that these numerical indicators were only 'proxies' for quality or effectiveness, in reality monetary value became

---

*   Natsios (2011: 3) defines Obsessive Measurement Disorder (OMD) as 'an intellectual dysfunction rooted in the notion that counting everything in government programs (or private industry and increasingly some foundations) will produce better policy choices and improved management'.

the dominant measure. In this way, quantification and scientific management were married to an ethics of accountability shaped within a new project of marketisation and 'economisation' (Çalışkan and Callon 2009).

A new period in the evolution of this system of governing through numbers started with its introduction into universities. Britain, Australia and New Zealand were early pioneers in the 1980s (Olssen and Peters 2005; Wright et al. 2014). First, Britain developed a national evaluation of university research called the Research Assessment Exercise (RAE). The research output of each department was read by a committee of peers from the relevant discipline and, reminiscent of the West Point system, was graded on a 7-point marking scale. While initially each institution received a standardised amount of funding per researcher, in the course of successive RAEs, governments used these grades to concentrate funding on those at the top of the league table and to withdraw funding from those at the bottom. By 2001, 75 per cent of research resources were concentrated on the top tier of departments. This method of 'rewarding success' and 'punishing failure' ensured that those universities lower down the scale were denied the resources that might enable them to pull themselves up. The same competitive and punitive model was applied to the national school system, with similar effects (see Chapter 2). Such systems of grading and ranking have 'skewing effects', as academics also know from the literature on 'teaching to the test' and the 'washback effect' of any examination system (Cheng et al. 2004). The skewing effects of systems of measuring and grading universities' research output are now so familiar they have acquired their own terminology such as 'salami slicing' (cutting research results into small chunks, each published as a separate journal article), 'rushing to press' (publishing partial results as soon as they are available rather than making a mature and considered analysis) and the 'star player' syndrome (hiring high-profile researchers just before an RAE) (Wright 2009; Shore and McLauchlan 2012: 282). The UK's House of Commons Science and Technology Committee called the RAE a 'morass of fiddling, finagling and horse trading' that was 'starting to lack credibility' (House of Commons 2004: 21). Similarly, a British Academy Policy Centre report warned of the perverse effects of using aggregated measures and rankings punitively to name and shame, rather than developmentally to internally diagnose and remedy problems (Foley and Goldstein 2012; see also Chapter 6). Regardless, these exercises in measuring, ranking, and differentially rewarding universities have been extended from the

Research Excellence Framework (REF) to a Teaching Excellence Framework (TEF) and, from 2021, a Knowledge Exchange Framework (KEF).

With the multiple borrowings of these ranking systems – from the French École Polytechnique to West Point Academy and the management of private corporations, and from there to the public sector including universities – important shifts occurred both in the assessment technologies and their effects. These 'omniscient operating systems' became ever more 'individualising and totalising' (Foucault 1977) in that they simultaneously worked across scales to order a whole population or sector while also rendering individual military cadets, factory workers and university students as calculating and 'calculable' subjects. At the same time, these ranking technologies also radically reshaped institutions in their own image, for, as is well known, when a feature of an organisation is measured, that measure becomes a target. This is often referred to as 'Goodhart's law' after the adviser who warned Britain's Conservative government in the 1970s against trying to conduct monetary policy on the basis of targets (Goodhart 1981). Michael Power has noted that audit procedures 'transform the environments to which they are applied', effectively colonising and 'permeating the auditee organisation totally' (1997: 90, 97). The effect is that organisations reshape their operations and values around that which is measured. Equally importantly, individuals are interpellated as 'auditees', whose behaviour is expected to align with the rationality of audit (Power 2005: 335).

Audit Effects: A Framework for Analysis

The examples in the previous section highlight wider theoretical points which, building on the work of Timothy Mitchell (1999) and Sally Merry (2011), we call 'audit effects'. We identify five of these that are of particular importance: 'domaining effects'; 'classificatory effects'; 'individualising and totalising effects'; 'governance effects' and 'perverse effects'. We elaborate briefly on each of these in turn.

Domaining effects are where the introduction of audit and ranking into a new organisational context radically reshapes that environment in ways that mirror the values and priorities embedded within the audit technologies. These may undermine professional values and practices. The application of audit to environments for which it was never originally designed can often produce a 'runaway effect' when the newly created systems and modes of operating gather their own momentum, as illustrated earlier, where McNamara's competitive accounting model at Ford spiralled out of control. The introduction of the evidence-based imperatives of audit into counselling and psychotherapy is another example of the domaining effects of audit on professions whose therapeutic practices rely on more holistic or conversationally based practices (King and Moutsou 2010).

Classificatory effects highlight the fact that indicators and statistics are never neutral. Like other systems of measurement, in the field of international development, audit produces knowledge by 'announcing what it measures, such as "rule of law" or "poverty"' (Merry 2011: S84) and hailing into existence the subjects it categorises and labels. The way that institutional systems classify and order populations has been amply documented by Foucault (1980) and others. However, audit changes the values, priorities and practices of organisational subjects in subtle and often unnoticed ways such that their subject positions are transformed. This is what Ian Hacking (2004) has elsewhere termed 'dynamic nominalism' or the 'looping effect'. Hacking (2006) exemplifies this with reference to the invention of medical categories such as 'multiple personality disorder', 'IQ' and 'obesity', but it is equally evident in the classification of 'failing schools', 'lowest ranking cadet' (such as the 'West Point's goat'), and the US business magazine *Fortune*'s 'most admired' human resources department.

The way these classifications and rankings simultaneously order both individuals and entire populations is captured by the 'individualising and totalising effect'. Key to the success of this process is the neat, simple and efficient way in which it achieves its effectiveness – at minimal cost and effort to the organisation. For example, when the international standing of universities is turned into a performance indicator, and that indicator is used to allocate funding, this simple mechanism has effects across three scales: the whole sector is reorganised in pursuit of competitive advantage; each organisation is re-purposed around the targets and incentives, and every individual is impelled to concentrate on 'what counts' (Wright 2014). For example, US law school deans have been unable to contest the 'individualising and totalising' effect of law school rankings as these determine their position in the market and ability to attract income from student fees (Sauder and Espeland 2009). Governance through numbers, as these examples show, creates ranking regimes that operate across multiple scales, producing a 'total accountability system' (Hoskin and Macve 1988) that is sometimes opaque and Kafkaesque even to those situated within it, as Chapter 6 illustrates.

'Governance effects' are a corollary of these individualising and totalising mechanisms. Performance indicators, benchmarks, and best practice are instruments designed to make organisations more 'accountable' to funders, government, stakeholders, consumers and the public. While they render individuals and organisations more 'legible' to external experts, there is a coercive dimension to that accountability: organisations must represent themselves according to the narrow, predetermined script of expert assessors. This is what Marilyn Strathern (2000a) calls the 'tyranny of transparency', what Don Brenneis terms 'coercive commensurability' (Brenneis et al. 2005) and what James C. Scott (2008 [1999]) and Michel-Rolph Trouillot (2001) call 'seeing like a state'. These ways of opening up organisations for scrutiny and inspection provide an ideal vehicle for enacting and extending the presence of the state and its capacity to exert its control over individuals and populations.

Finally, the idea of 'perverse effects' highlights the ways in which governing by numbers and metricised management through the use of performance indicators and measurement of outputs, when taken to extremes or misapplied, not only fails to deliver what is promised but may result in policy making that is amoral or outcomes that are *immoral*, as in our examples of the Vietnam War and automobile industry. One dimension of this is the increasing stress and anxiety that rankings produce among individuals who are placed under pressure to constantly monitor and improve their own performance (King and Moutsou 2010; Wright 2011; see also Chapter 7). As a result, those individuals often resort to gaming tactics or outright fraud, such as the headteacher of a school in southern England who was jailed for forging his pupils' national Standard Attainment Tests (SATs) because 'he felt pressure from the publication of league tables and financial difficulties at the school', which poor results would have made worse (see Shore 2008: 285–6). As the old saying goes, 'weighing the pig does not make it grow fatter'. Yet constantly measuring an individual's performance has all kinds of other effects – social, political, subjectifying and managerial. For Espeland and Sauder (2016), these systems of measurement and rankings are 'engines of anxiety', in which stress is a necessary bi-product of more intensified work productivity. This phenomenon is poignantly captured by the director Ken Loach in his films *I, Daniel Blake* and *Sorry We Missed You*. A tragic example was that of Ruth Perry, a 53-year-old headteacher of a primary school in Reading, who, in January 2023, took her own life after being informed that her school was to be downgraded from 'outstanding' to 'inadequate' by Ofsted inspectors.

One parent told the inspectors, 'I am impressed with how happy my child is at the school. The staff are brilliant and caring, inspiring them to be the very best they can be' (Ofsted 2022: 3). The report itself echoed this view:

> Pupils' behaviour in lessons is exemplary. They love to learn and they relish the challenges that teachers provide. Pupils who struggle with their behaviour benefit from the pastoral care they receive from leaders and staff ... Leaders provide pupils with extensive opportunities for personal development. They are passionate about making sure that every pupil has access to the wide range of visits, visitors, clubs and events that are available. Personal, social, health and economic education is well sequenced and ensures that pupils are ready for their move to secondary school. Pupils have a strong understanding of democracy and show respect for other people's points of view. They learn how to stay healthy both physically and mentally ... Staff are supportive of senior leaders. They feel respected and appreciate the consideration leaders place on well-being and workload. (Ofsted 2022: 3)

The school was marked 'good' on every category but 'inadquate' on leadership and management. The grounds for this were that, although 'staff know how to identify concerns about pupils and to report these to the appropriate leader', 'records of safeguarding concerns and the tracking of subsequent actions are poor' (Ofsted 2022: 3). Ruth Perry knew that this failure in the audit trail would inevitably inflict long-lasting damage on the school. According to her sister, 'this one-word judgment is just destroying 32 years of her vocation – education was her vocation – 32 years summed up in one word, inadequate'. She said, 'it just preyed on her mind until she couldn't take it any more' (Sinmaz 2023).

Ofsted's audit judgements are based on a snapshot but elsewhere systems of auditing performance and outcomes are integrated minute-by-minute into the working day. This was highlighted in a BBC *Panorama* investigation into the employment conditions at one of Amazon's UK warehouses (BBC 2013). They found intensified time-and-motion techniques were taken to new levels. Amazon gave its 'pickers' handsets, which told them what to collect from the shelves. It allotted 33 seconds to find a product, then a timer counted down until the next product was retrieved. A manager oversaw this electronic data-flow to ensure all the pickers kept up to speed throughout their ten-and-a-half-hour shifts that involved up to 11 miles of walking. Professor Michael Marmot, a leading expert on stress at work, argued that these conditions greatly increased the risk of mental and physical illness (BBC 2013). For example, Amazon's serious injury rate in 2021 was 6.8 per 100 workers, more than twice the average in the general warehousing industry (Sainato 2022). Amazon's working conditions also result in high staff turnover. Before the Covid pandemic Amazon was losing 3 per cent of its workforce weekly, or 150 per cent annually, which is three times the annual turnover in comparable industries. Jeff Bezos, Amazon's founder, originally welcomed such high turnover, as he associated long-term employment with a 'march to mediocrity'. However, a leaked internal memo in 2021 warned that the 'company was in danger of exhausting its entire available labor pool in the Phoenix, Arizona, metro area by the end of that year, and in the Inland Empire region of California by the end of this year' (Sainato 2022). This labour turnover was estimated to cost Amazon US $8 billion in annual global revenues in 2022 (O'Sullivan 2022). By autumn 2022, the post-pandemic downturn in online retail resulted in Amazon's lowest growth for 20 years, a hiring freeze and job cuts (Jasy 2023). By now the first Amazon warehouse to be unionised had begun to organise against even greater intensification of their work (O'Sullivan 2022). Despite these perverse effects, this is the kind of 'omniscient operating system' that McNamara sought to achieve and the 'efficiencies' it delivers are ones to which many other corporations aspire.

Audit, Rankings and the (Re)Ordering of Society

As the chapters that follow illustrate, audit culture takes a diversity of forms in the different settings in which it operates, yet there are striking similarities in its effects. Measurement and ranking fulfil a number of economic, managerial and governmental purposes. First, they appear to provide a more rational way of controlling institutions through new configurations of knowledge and power. Second, they are extremely effective in opening up for external scrutiny the inner worlds of organisations and they render commensurable and controllable all kinds of disparate individuals, institutions and objects with vastly diverse features. Third, numerical rankings exert a curiously seductive power (Porter 1995: xi). Indicators are assumed to be objective and unambiguous because of their association with science and the 'pure and constant rules of mathematics' (Merry 2011: S90). They typically reduce complex situations to simplistic, easily graspable numbers whose apparent facticity can lure people into thinking that they are making decisions based on rational, objective and fair criteria. This often deters people from questioning the methods and assumptions underlying the production of such numbers. As Strathern (2000b:8) puts it, 'an aura has come to surround numbers and, despite the caveats of professional auditors, it is those unfamiliar with financial auditing who tend to sanctify them'. Significantly, the people who are enamoured by numerical rankings 'tend to be those most distant from their production' (Sauder and Espeland 2009: 72).

Our fourth observation is that the digital revolution and new social media technologies have enabled individuals to produce numbers for monitoring themselves and their own routines, movements and bodily practices. When these are combined with ever more powerful and sophisticated devices for harvesting that personal data, the relation between the producers and users of those numbers becomes increasingly distant and blurred. The result is a self-reinforcing and potentially dangerous combination of self-auditing that creates big data which is then used to try and influence and manage people without their knowledge or consent. As we argue, this 'big-data governance' (Fuchs and Chandler 2019) through 'data colonisation' (Couldry and Mejias 2020) is intimately tied up with new and emerging forms of authoritarianism, surveillance capitalism, and projects of managerial control (Zuboff 2019; see also Chapter 7).

The institutionalised processes of measuring and ranking, and their spread across organisations and in everyday domains of life, reveal the emergence of a new type of governmentality based on an economic calculus; an instrumental, results- and target-driven normative order which governs by numbers and, more importantly, *through* the subjectifying effects of numbers. While not confined to neoliberal polities, its characteristics include many of the features commonly associated with neoliberal thinking, including 'governing at a distance'; a relentless pursuit of economic efficiency; deregulation, outsourcing and privatisation; marketisation and the privileging of competition over cooperation; increasing separation between an empowered managerial elite and a de-professionalised workforce; and the objectification of human labour combined with an increasing emphasis on calculative practices aimed at promoting individualisation and responsibilisation. In this way, the political technologies of financial cost accounting wedded to the project of management have been highly effective in producing accountable and transparent subjects that are simultaneously docile yet actively self-managing.

These arguments are developed throughout the chapters of this book in a stepwise and systematic fashion as follows.

Chapter 2 ('Rankings as Populist Project: Governing by Numbers and Hollowing Out Democracy'), begins by detailing the explosion in the use of indicators and rankings, and the extraordinary range of new forms of auditing and assessment this has given rise to. We explore some of the seemingly more bizarre features of this 'index mania' and the curious new domains of enumeration and classification that it is creating, from the ranking of literacy rates and the quality of customer service to indexes that measure freedom, biocapacity and the 'state of the future' (Glenn and Florescu 2017). From here we track the links between indicators and populism and the way that competitive rankings have become a populist project. We explore some of the political and ideological aspects of this trend, including how numerical evaluations are used to prepare the way for restructuring and outsourcing organisations, and to legitimise programmes to break up the public sector and facilitate the capture of public assets for private gain in what are often disguised forms of asset-stripping and corporate raiding. We turn to the UK to illustrate these points, taking as our case study the rise in government-sponsored academy schools.

Chapter 3 ('The Big Four Accountancy Firms and the Evolution of Contemporary Capitalism') examines some of the key actors behind the increasing spread and institutionalisation of these calculative systems of auditing and ranking. While this includes various global players, many of them in the finance and IT industries, this chapter focuses on the Big Four international auditing and accountancy firms, EY, PwC, Deloitte and KPMG. We track the history of their rise to prominence, particularly their post-1970s metamorphosis from relatively small auditing firms to giant global companies and the expansion of their business model into a vast array of advisory, management and tax consultancy services. We also investigate some of the inevitable conflicts of interest that these multiple roles create. This provides a wider lens for examining broader questions about the relationship between audit, ethics and accountability, and the problems of audit failure, fraud and corruption that these increasingly entangled webs of relations are producing.

Chapter 4 ('Global Governance through Standards, Seduction and Soft Power') explores the power of statistics beyond the state by examining the expansion of international systems of audit and assessment and analysing the global ranking organisations that produce them. More specifically, we focus on the way these indicators and rankings travel and settle in new domains, and how these numerical scoresheets get translated and institutionalised into policy and practice. Our case studies include Transparency International's Corruption Perception Index, the Organisation for Economic Co-operation and Development's (OECD) Programme for International Student Assessment (PISA) and the *Times Higher Education's* 'World University Rankings'. We also explore the politics around the production and consumption of these rankings, and especially the OECD's and the European Union's (EU) open method of coordination (OMC) as a technology for producing standardisation in various sectors.

Chapter 5 ('Metrics, Managerialism and Market Making: Unlocking Value in Healthcare') reflects on the way the rationales and practices of audit and accountancy have been introduced into the health sector and the effects this has had on the delivery of health services. As a laboratory for radical neoliberal policy reforms, the UK over the past two decades again offers instructive case studies. We focus on the complex and multiple ways that audit has been used to reform the UK's National Health Service (NHS) and how audit laid the ground for subsequent attempts to promote privatisation in the NHS, encourage the development of a series of disastrous PFIs, and catalyse the global spread of PPPs. Originally conceived as instruments for raising off-balance-sheet funds for new public investments spurred by expertise from the private sector, the net result of these PFI and PPP schemes has been to impoverish the public sector and provide risk-free, taxpayer-funded profits for private corporate investors.

Chapter 6 ('Reforming Higher Education: The Kafkaesque Pursuit of "World-class" Status') examines the way the introduction of new regimes of audit and accountability changes the nature of organisations. Drawing on examples from higher education, we show how activities become increasingly focused on the measures by which performance is judged. Espeland and Sauder (2016) have illustrated the powerful coercive and domaining effect of numerical measures, and how their transposable templates are used for managerial control and new forms of remote surveillance. We focus in particular on the effects of these new management models and performance metrics on academic subjectivities and social relations. The chapter shows how managerial demands aim to produce calculative, responsibilised selves whose behaviour and performance are driven by imperatives for continual self-assessment, self-monitoring and self-improvement. As we illustrate, these management models have numerous perverse effects and provoke interesting and novel strategies of engagement and resistance.

Chapter 7 ('The New Subjects of Audit: Performance Management and Quantified Selves') considers the experiential and subjectifying effects of audit culture and its impact on individuals and their behaviour, and on the way people conceptualise and understand themselves in relation to others, including the state. These regimes of audit create the categories into which people are invited to rethink themselves. Those who sell and operate these systems see this 'classificatory effect' as delivering positive outcomes, but critics might point to the other ('individualising and totalising', 'governance' and 'perverse') effects and draw different conclusions. A key aspect of this process of subjectification is the rise of the Quantified Self movement and the popularity of personal devices for tracking and monitoring one's activities and daily routines, which many claim offer new possibilities for self-awareness and empowerment. By contrast, critics argue that these technologies represent a new form of subordination and enslavement, and pose challenging questions about who actually owns personal data of the kind offered up to big corporations such as Facebook and Google. We argue that these debates can be usefully addressed by placing them in a more global and comparative context. We therefore turn to explore some of the new regimes of audit and accountability that are being developed in other, non-Western contexts, particularly in China where big data can create spaces for new forms of authoritarian governance. While Western critics have condemned China's system of social credit as an Orwellian nightmare, we suggest that the marriage of big data and corporate interests in Western countries constitutes an equally dangerous trend, as shown by the controversy around UK tech firm Cambridge Analytica's harvesting of private Facebook data to influence the US presidential elections and Brexit referendum.

In Chapter 8 ('Conclusion: Repurposing Audit – Restoring Trust, Accountability and Democracy') we raise questions about what is to be done and how people might take back control to reassert democratic forms of governance. By this we mean finding ways to reverse audit culture's alienating effects and restore the capacity of people, as employees and citizens, to exercise autonomy and meaningful participation in the decisions that affect their lives. We ask how we might generate new forms of accountability and audit that empower and enable rather than disempower and oppress. As our case studies show, the spread of numerical performance indicators has been highly instrumental, not only in distinguishing a new class of technocrats (data analysts, managers, accountants, administrators, human resources officers, and executive leaders) but in creating a new industry of measurement, self-monitoring, data harvesting and human resource management. This industry is tasked with the job of controlling the workforce (or company, or citizenry) to ensure that individuals or organisations 'perform' in the ways deemed appropriate by those in power, or meet the pre-set targets.

One effect of this has been to undermine the authority of other professions – teachers, lecturers, nurses, health and social workers, to name just a few encountered in this book. Measures for audit and performance are often at variance with these professions' values and undermine their capacity to exercise professional judgement. We draw on specific examples to show where certain sectors have succeeded, to some extent, in developing alternative ways of organising and acting based on their professional values and judgements. First, in higher education we offer examples of individual academics working with students to create alternative educational spaces, albeit only at a local level. Second, child protection in Britain has been reimagined in ways that foreground professional values and competencies, and our example shows how this has been part of a wider, whole-system reform that encompasses the management, governance and auditing of the sector. Our third example concerns the audit industry itself. Numerous reports from government, parliamentary committees, political parties and academics have clearly identified the systemic failures in the audit industry and how they can be remedied. However, lack of political will has meant these reforms have yet to be implemented. Finally, building on the critique of the effects of audit culture on democracy, we draw on academic research that proposes alternative methods of auditing. Rather than audit continuing to promote the proliferation of managerial regimes of top-down inspection and surveillance based on the logics of free-market capitalism, these academics are experimenting with participatory and qualitative methods to generate more meaningful kinds of public trust and accountability.

In this book we argue that audit culture is the vehicle through which society is being colonised by the logics of managerialism and the predatory interests of finance capitalism whose steady advance is crushing public institutions and democracy. The four examples in our conclusion highlight the changes needed to prevent this and to develop alternative forms of accountability. These changes have to span the whole range of scales, from the individual professional and the organisation of a sector, to the regulation of the global audit industry and the concept and practice of democracy itself.

2

Rankings as Populist Project: Governing by Numbers and Hollowing out Democracy

> In our brave new world, it seems that a single final criterion of value is recognized: a quantitative, economic criterion. All else is no more than a means. And there is a single method for ensuring that this criterion is satisfied: quantified control. (Lock and Martins 2011)

Introduction: From Index Mania to Reshaping Governance

One of the striking features of our times has been the extraordinary growth in the use of performance indicators and ranking systems as instruments of management and governance in the public sector as well as private companies. Benchmarking, scorecards and league tables that purport to measure or rate the qualities and merits of particular phenomena have proliferated and become a populist project of global proportions applied to all aspects of life, from goods and services, commercial products and sports teams, to the standing of organisations and the qualities of individuals. In Western societies, this index mania is more than simply a proxy for assisting consumer choice or an expression of popular culture; it is also creating the conditions for a new form of governance to flourish, one that uses numbers and ratings as technologies to extend managerial control, reshape institutions, and align individual subjectivities to suit neoliberal policy agendas. One effect of the popularisation of this kind of governing by numbers is to narrow dramatically the public space for democratic debate and exclude citizens from participating in decision making regarding the policies and services that affect their lives. These technologies of ranking play a major role in hollowing out democracy and eroding the fabric of public life, or as Wendy Brown put it, 'undoing the demos' (Brown 2015).

In what follows, we first briefly outline how indicators and rankings now pepper a vast range of domains in public life, civil society and the commercial sector. We argue that seeing the world in terms of indicators and competitive scorecards and league tables, whether in television game shows, restaurant and hotel rankings or Facebook 'likes', represents the populist end of a more profound neoliberal project of audit-driven social transformation, or what is sometimes called 'governing by numbers' (Porter 1995; Shore and Wright 2015a). In the second part we trace the development of that neoliberal project through the reform of the public sector in Britain, Denmark and other European countries. We ask, how are these seemingly mundane technical instruments of audit and ranking reshaping public institutions? How are these measurements instrumental in creating new ways of knowing and governing populations and economies? And how does the normalisation and popularisation of rankings-driven competition affect democracy? To address these questions we turn, in the third part of the chapter, to a detailed case study of the rise of academy schools in Britain from the late 1990s onwards. This highlights the way popularised measurements and rankings have been used to roll back local authority control in education, open up school governance and assets to new private sector and civil society interests, and place schools beyond the reach of local public oversight.

Rankings as a Populist Project

Measurements and tables are integral to modern science and its project to know and classify the natural world. From the periodic table and Linnaeus's system of biological taxonomy, science has sought to name, label and order phenomena into categories and classes. Similarly, in government and administration, taxonomies constructed through statistical measures have long been used to order individuals and whole populations. These numerical forms of governance often operate as what Foucault (1982: 777–79) termed 'dividing practices'. Using the examples of health (1994), punishment (1977) and sexuality (1979 [1976]), Foucault showed how the state in early modern France divided populations into different categories (for example, the mad and the sane, the sick and the healthy, the criminals and the 'good boys') that objectified subjects and established what was normal and what was deviant. These practices provided the parameters by which modern states could govern whole populations and the individuals within them, while setting out the norms by which subjects should govern themselves. Though often construed as negative and punitive, these technologies can also act in positive ways as instruments of undoubted social benefit. Such measurement systems can be valuable tools for reducing poverty, improving health outcomes, and minimising risks. These include absolute and relative measures of poverty and inequality, such as the Joseph Rowntree Foundation's (2021) annual UK poverty statistics reports or the calculation of inequality using the Gini coefficient. They also include standard blood tests for measuring haemoglobin and sugar levels, the Richter Scale for gauging earthquake intensity, Geiger counters for measuring radioactivity, and indexes for measuring air pollution, the pH acidity of soils or the rate at which polar icecaps are melting. In this respect, statistics and expert classifications can be valuable tools for addressing societal problems as well as instruments of management, governance or statecraft.

However, in recent decades, there has been a massive expansion of systems for turning aspects of everyday life into numbers and competitive rankings that cover all kinds of phenomena that were previously considered unquantifiable. These phenomena include everything from customer satisfaction, hospital waiting times, ambulance and fire service response times and household carbon footprints to indexes of corruption and risk, and dashboards of 'fear and greed'. For example, US college students are invited to 'Rate My Professor' on the grounds that this will help other students to select the best courses and teachers. Based on the responses of 19 million students' ratings of over 1.7 million professors and 7,500 universities, the website constructs 'Top Lists' of the 'Highest Rated Professors' and 'Top U.S. colleges' (RateMyProfessors 2019). In another example, Baptist churches in the US have developed a tool for individuals to gauge their 'Spiritual Growth Assessment Process'. Six criteria are investigated through ten questions each, and the answers plotted on a 'Discipleship Wheel'. The tool purports to measure how individuals are growing in 'Christlikeness' and to enable them to develop an 'Annual Spiritual Growth Plan' (LifeWay 2021: 2).

People have become increasingly accustomed to reading the numbers generated by such indicators and often would not think to question the basis upon which they are calculated. These indicators, as Jelena Brankovic (2022: 2) points out, have 'further helped to institutionalize the imaginary of the modern world as a stratified order, whose actors are being imagined as *continuously striving* to overtake those they are compared with'. In short, they serve to normalise the hegemonic view that competition is natural and beneficial. They also work to reinforce the cultural imperative that people should think of themselves as autonomous and discerning agents who must constantly improve themselves (Gershon 2011) and perform '*better than others*' (Brankovic 2022: 2).

A plethora of apps and online services have been developed (typically by US companies) to enhance competition and consumer choice by ranking the qualities and merits of particular goods and services such as restaurants, bars and coffee shops (Yelp), hotels and tourist attractions (Tripadvisor), fast-food delivery and order pickup (GrubHub) and films and television programmes (Rotten Tomatoes and IMDb). To watch television or listen to news bulletins is to be saturated by a world of rankings and numbers, from the 'health' of markets and national currencies to the changing position of sports teams in the national and international leagues and which films are in line for an Oscar or which songs have a chance of winning a Grammy award. There seems to be an insatiable public appetite for rankings and ratings, but the use of indicators has also become a populist project. It is a key ingredient of reality TV, epitomised in programmes like *America's Got Talent*, *Big Brother*, *The X Factor*, The Bachelor, *Love Island* and, one of the most popular TV shows in the UK, *The Great British Bake-Off*. All of these programmes invite panellists and audiences to score contestants and cast their votes to rank the winners and losers. In this way, these programmes are a training ground for people to become discerning citizen-consumers who are capable of rating products and exercising choice (Slater 1997; Rose 1999). These subjectifying techniques are constitutive of a wider form of governance that involves popularising auditing practices and combining them with privatisation and market making.

Other examples have commercial interests at heart. For example, US global television sports channel ESPN compiled a much-cited 'Degree of Difficulty' table for different sports. This gives the highest scores to boxing, ice hockey and American football, and the lowest to fishing and snooker (Topendsports 2019). Condom manufacturer Durex conducted a 26-country 'sexual wellbeing survey' in 2011 that purported to measure how many people had weekly sex and with what level of satisfaction. Its online survey revealed that Russians had the most sex (80 per cent) but only 42 per cent were satisfied. Among Americans, 53 per cent had weekly sex and 48 per cent were satisfied, whereas 34 per cent of Japanese had weekly sex but only 15 per cent were satisfied (Durex 2011). Other indexes focus on the commercial prowess of individuals and companies. Examples here include the Martin Prosperity Institute's 'Global Creativity Index'

(GCI) and *Fortune* magazine's 'Most Admired Companies' for their human resources practices.

From a non-commercial perspective, there is a long history of organisations seeking to develop indexes of global development and wellbeing. Gross domestic product (GDP), 'the world's most powerful number' (Fioramonti 2014), was first developed by economist Simon Kuznets in 1934. This measure of the value of goods and services produced within a country proved a useful indicator for the US government to steer its recovery from the Great Depression and to develop top-down management of economic production during the Second World War. During the Cold War, GDP also served as a useful propaganda tool to highlight US economic supremacy over the USSR. Today it is widely used to measure and compare the economic health of all countries in the world. However, GDP is widely criticised for what it does *not* make visible, including economic inequalities within a country and, as Kuznets himself acknowledged, how a narrow focus on production has human costs in terms of health or wellbeing (Costanza et al. 2014). GDP measures mainly market transactions, output and spending, or as Robert Kennedy famously put it, 'everything except that which makes life worthwhile' (Costanza et al. 2014: 283). Even the OECD acknowledges its limitations:

> It measures income, but not equality, it measures growth, but not destruction, and it ignores values like social cohesion and the environment. Yet, governments, businesses and probably most people swear by it. (OECD 2005)

Another aspect of GDP is that it gives extraordinary power and authority to technocrats and economists (Fioramonti 2014: 13).

For all these reasons, many people and organisations have sought to develop alternatives to GDP and to calculate the wealth of nations based on different measures to those of classical economics. For example, the 'Global Innovation Index' (GII) is co-published by Cornell University, the business school INSEAD in France, and the World Intellectual Property Organization (WIPO), an agency of the United Nations (UN). Recognising innovation as a driver of economic growth and prosperity, the *GII Report* ranks national innovation capabilities by drawing on indicators that go beyond the traditional measures of research and development (Global Innovation Index 2019). The New Economics Foundation's 'Happy Planet Index' measures sustainable wellbeing for the non-governmental organisations (NGOs) Friends of the Earth and the Soil Association. It also produces the 'Green Grin-o-meter', a survey which asks children about 'how they feel, and what they do in their day-to-day lives', on the basis of which it 'calculates scores in terms of their health, footprint and happiness, and provides advice on how they can better achieve good lives that don't cost the Earth' (New Economics Foundation 2018). The Gross National Well-being Index, developed by the International Institute of Management in the United States, is a secular econometric model that is designed to measure global development across seven dimensions: economic, environmental, physical, mental, work, social, and political (IIM 2005). The OECD produced a Better Life Index in 2011, based on eleven topics the organisation identified as essential for material living conditions and quality of life, but its interactive website invites users to make their own ranking and share their views on what makes for a better life (OECD n.d.a, 2017). A self-described 'global nonprofit based in Washington, DC' called the Social Progress Imperative launched its Social Progress Index in 2013, which tracks changes to society over time by measuring 51 indicators along three broad dimensions of social progress: Basic Human Needs, Foundations of Wellbeing, and Opportunity.

An even more ambitious project is the Bhutan government's 'Global Gross National Happiness Index' (GNH Index), which proclaims the value of collective happiness as the goal of governance. Gross National Happiness was incorporated into the Constitution of Bhutan in 2008, and in 2011 the UN unanimously adopted a General Assembly resolution, introduced by Bhutan with support from 68 member states, calling for a new economic paradigm and a 'holistic approach to development', aimed at promoting sustainable happiness and wellbeing as a fundamental human goal (OPHI 2019). The GNH Index uses surveys and objective measures across nine domains: psychological wellbeing; health; time use; education; the preservation of culture and cultural diversity; good governance; community vitality; environmental conservation, ecological diversity and resilience; and sustainable and equitable socio-economic development and living standards (Ura et al. 2012). Societies are graded as 'unhappy', 'narrowly happy', 'extensively happy' or 'deeply happy'. According to the *World Happiness Report 2018*, Bhutan itself came 97th out of 156 countries (Sachs et al. 2018). Critics, including Human Rights Watch, suggest this is because before democratic government began in 2008, in the name of cultural preservation, Bhutan had expelled a sixth of its population who were non-Buddhists, ethnic Nepalese or of Hindu faith, and most of the remaining 900,000 population lived in grinding poverty (Frelik 2008).

Many US cities and states have used versions of Bhutan's GNH Index and several companies have been inspired by it to implement sustainability practices in business. The UN Sustainable Development Network produces an annual 'World Happiness Report', which for the past five years (2018–22) has ranked Finland as the happiest country in the world (Pohjanpalo 2022).

These performance indicators and audits have become increasingly widespread as ever more areas of life are indexed, measured and ranked. A striking aspect of this phenomenon is their popularity and the extraordinary enthusiasm with which people have uncritically embraced and endorsed them. As Michael Power (1994: 41) observed for the term 'quality' – another keyword of contemporary management – 'we seem to have lost our ability to question or be publicly skeptical about the fashion for quality assurance' to the extent that it has come to appear a natural and benign solution to the problems of performance, accountability and governance. The power of these technologies lies less in compulsion or coercion, and more in their incitement to act and take on certain identities and pleasures: in short, in the affect or anxiety that they provoke or reinforce (Foucault 1980). In this respect, the popularity of these rankings helps individuals, organisations and entire countries to recast themselves as auditable, compliant subjects and prepares the ground for the expansion of audit culture as a new kind of governance. The naturalisation and taken-for-grantedness of these numerical indices, and their application to ever-increasing areas of life, changes the way people see themselves: not as equal participants, citizens or members of a shared enterprise, but rather as subjects of competition, divided, individualised and ranked against each other. This is not so much the classical figure of *Homo Economicus* but rather a new species of *Homo Aemulatio*, the competitive emulator.

Indicators, Rankings and New Forms of Governance

While many of the examples above may seem outlandish and bizarre, these same techniques have been cultivated and used in a political project that aims to change the nature of the state, how its institutions operate, and the manner in which its citizens are expected to conduct themselves. Turning competitive measurements and rankings into an accepted aspect of popular culture helps to cultivate an environment in which new forms of governance-through-audit can be established. Part of the appeal of these numerical indicators is that they make decision making easy and provide quick solutions to the problems of governance. However, as Michael Power (1997) argues, audits and indicators are increasingly part of the problem rather than the solution: their aim may be organisational transparency, but they end up being opaque, they reshape institutions according to the criteria and methods used to measure them, and they transform organisations and people into 'auditable' entities that focus their energies on doing what 'counts' rather than what is necessarily moral or right. How did this situation arise and where did these calculative technologies for measuring and enhancing performance stem from?

The UK offers one of the clearest examples of how this transition towards audit-based governance occurred. As mentioned in Chapter 1, much of this project was spearheaded by Mrs Thatcher's Conservative government in the 1980s as part of its attempt to introduce efficiency savings through a raft of reforms commonly referred to as 'New Public Management' (NPM). The blueprint for these reforms was set out in a series of reports published in the late 1980s in what became known as the 'Next Step Initiative' (Jenkins et al. 1988; NAO 1989; Gay 1997). This aimed to reshape the civil service around new norms of economy, efficiency and service delivery, and has subsequently been widely used as a model for restructuring the operations of the state in other countries. Written by members of the government's 'Efficiency Unit', the *Next Steps* report had far-reaching implications. It recommended hiving off the delivery functions of Whitehall into autonomous arm's-length agencies, which would involve transferring around 75 to 95 per cent of the existing civil service to these agencies. Second, it recommended changing the skills and management of what remained of the Whitehall machine. Third, it recommended retaining a unit in the centre of government to keep up the institutional pressure for reform. Together, these implied fundamentally changing the 'bone structure' of Whitehall and transforming the way officials conceived of their core functions and responsibilities (Panchamia and Thomas 2014: 2).

Each of the new arm's-length government agencies was treated as a separate cost centre, with its own performance indicators and annual objectives. The reforms replaced descriptions of work with numerical measures. The Conservative minister Michael Heseltine summed up the rationale for this approach:

> When the literacies of the Civil Service and the generalities of their
> intentions are turned into targets which can be monitored and costed,
> when information is conveyed in columns instead of screeds, then
> objectives become clear and progress towards them becomes measura-
> ble and far more likely. (Heseltine 1987, cited in Pollitt 1993b: 58)

The next move was to outsource public service functions to private
companies, NGOs, or newly privatised parts of the bureaucracy. This
equivalent of the outsourced industrial supply chain was based on what
Pollitt et al. (2001) termed 'agencification', and the idea that the gov-
ernment-as-purchaser of services should be separated from providers in
a quasi-market. Contract management was central to the art of governing these outsourced public services. These contracts were to be managed
through a small handful of carefully selected indicators and performance
measures. However, quite quickly the outsourced agencies turned the
measures into targets and narrowed the focus of their operations down
to meeting key performance indicators (KPIs) rather than improving
overall service delivery. This conversion of measures into targets typically
provoked three responses. One was to keep moving the assessment goalposts so that people would not know what the criteria would be in the next
round (sometimes justified as preventing those assessed from 'gaming
the system'). A second was to increase targets to cover as many aspects
of the outsourced service as possible. For example, a 2015 report found
that UK health services were so micro-managed through indicators that
hospital managers were consumed by a 'terror of targets' and were failing
to address frontline problems because they were too 'busy collecting information on how they are doing each week to satisfy regulators, NHS bosses,
health commissioners and politicians' (Meikle 2015).

A third response entailed breaking up professional work into a series
of performance objectives, tasks and checklists. This occurred across all
sectors but particularly in education. Pre-school teachers in England,
for example, had to keep a 'learning journal' for each child to assess and
shape their development. One example that we have seen was divided
into seven sections, each of which involved assessing every child against
checklists containing specific criteria. For example, Understanding the
World involved 42 criteria; Personal Social and Emotional Development
59 criteria, while Communication and Language had 66 and Physical
Development had 79. The manager's introduction insisted that these per-

formance indicators were 'crucial for igniting children's curiosity and enthusiasm for learning' yet we heard that many teachers found it had the opposite effect and complained they no longer had time to care for children according to their own professional standards.

Similar trends occurred in other countries. For example, Denmark's Ministry of Finance established an agencification process in the 1990s. Contracts were based on a selection of strategic performance indicators so that service providers could minimise the time spent on reporting and focus their energies on improving services. However, as in England, the number of indicators and measures proliferated. Instead of liberating time and energy, professionals were overwhelmed by the burden of reporting. Many organisations could only cope by hiring additional administrators to deal with the reporting requirements. Even the civil servants who first formulated contract steering publicly protested against the system they had helped to create. Writing in a Danish national newspaper, their article was entitled, 'Forgive us – we knew not what we did' (Gjørup et al. 2007). As one lamented, contract steering was based on in-built mistrust of professionals, and had shifted power to managers and 'brutally side-lined' professional judgement (Nissan 2007).

In the UK, this undermining of professional judgement also occurred though other initiatives designed to empower 'users', now variously constructed as 'taxpayers', 'citizens', 'consumers', 'clients', 'stakeholders' and 'the public'. As prime minister Tony Blair proclaimed:

> We are proposing to put an entirely different dynamic in place to drive our public services; one where the service will be driven not by the government or the manager, but by the user – the patient, the parent, the pupil and the law-abiding citizen. (Blair 2004, cited in Clarke et al. 2007: 1)

Each of these labels implies a different set of relationships between people and the state, as government increasingly sought to implement strategies for 'governing at a distance' and to outsource responsibility for managing the population to individuals, NGOs and the private sector. Business interests acquired growing influence over the governing boards of public organisations such as university councils, hospital trusts and school governing bodies, and the performance of professionals came to be measured according to a bewildering array of indicators and rankings.

Transforming Education: Academy Schools in England

A good example of the processes described above is the reform of the education system of England carried out by British governments since 2010 in their attempts to promote 'academy schools'. This project was described as 'one of the most radical and encompassing programmes of school reform seen in the recent past amongst advanced countries' (Eyles and Machin 2015: 1). It entailed breaking up and outsourcing public education to enable the expansion of for-profit providers. It also illustrated clearly how rankings and performance measures were used instrumentally both to move away from centralised control and accountability, and to open up public sector schools for capture by private interests. In this process, as we highlight below, numbers were not only used to *identify* under-performing schools. They were also used to construct certain schools as 'inadequate' and 'failing', thereby legitimising draconian 'special measures' as a stepping-stone to enforced transition to academy status.

Academies are state schools in England that are directly funded by the Department for Education, unlike ordinary 'maintained schools', which are regulated and supported by their elected local authority. Academies have more freedoms than maintained schools, for example in determining their own curriculum and setting their own staff pay and conditions. They are not required to comply with a national employment agreement and can even employ staff who have no formal teaching qualifications. Each academy has a 'sponsor', often a local entrepreneur or faith organisation that sets up the academy as a company limited by guarantee and as a self-governing, non-profit charitable trust (with all the tax exemptions that status entails). The sponsor is responsible for appointing the school's governors, who set its curriculum, define its ethos, and decide on its specialisms. These freedoms are in return for bringing in private investment to rebuild the school. Initially, the sponsor contributed 10 per cent of the capital costs up to a maximum of £2 million (but later even this requirement was removed) and the government paid the other 90 per cent of the rebuilding costs as well as providing the running costs thereafter. Academies were also free to subcontract for services, whereas maintained schools have to go through regulated processes involving their local authorities.

The first academy schools were introduced in 2000 by Tony Blair's Labour government. Their idea was to turn around poorly performing city secondary schools by granting them independence and support from an experienced sponsor. Whereas the initiative was initially limited to 200 schools, the Conservative–Lib Dem coalition government in 2010 massively expanded the conversion of maintained schools into academies. It was claimed that such freedoms and independence would assist in 'spreading high standards', 'school improvement' and 'reducing unnecessary complexity' (NAO 2018a: 15), but it was also a way to remove schools from local authority control and increase private sector influence. In 2010 the Secretary of State for Education invited every headteacher in England to opt out of local authority control and convert to academy status. He also announced plans to open up the academies programme to primary schools and special schools. In 2016 there was a mass conversion of all the remaining schools into academies so that, in the words of Prime Minister David Cameron, 'local authorities running schools is a thing of the past' (Cook 2016). That same year the Education and Adoption Act gave the Secretary of State a 'duty to compel inadequate maintained schools to become academies by issuing directive academic orders [and it] placed a statutory duty on governing bodies and local authorities to comply with these orders' (NAO 2018a: 17). The number of academy schools rose dramatically, from 203 in August 2010 to nearly 2,000 in 2012 (Department for Education 2012: 11; 2014). By January 2018 the number had almost trebled again (NAO 2018a: 7) and by 2020, 77 per cent of secondary schools and 35 per cent of primary schools had undergone conversion to academy status (Politics.co.uk 2020).

There were several financial incentives to make the academy programme attractive. Initially, failing schools that became 'sponsored academies' were required to specialise in particular areas such as business, computing, engineering, arts or sports, and for each specialism they received additional funding of £130,000 per annum, but this was removed in 2010. To bring about the massification of academies, the Department for Education spent £81 million on converting schools to academies, including payment of one-off grants of £25,000 towards the costs of schools becoming academies without a sponsor, or grants of £70,000 to £150,000 if they had a sponsor. Significantly, local authorities incurred costs when their maintained schools became academies (of between £6,400 and £8,400 per school) and they retained any accumulated deficits of maintained schools that converted with a sponsor (averaging £5,400 for primary schools and £120,300 for secondary schools) (NAO 2018a: 10). In short, the rapid conversion to academies entailed massive transfers of public schools' assets and annual revenues to private sponsors and their trusts, leaving local authorities with only the financial deficits. As a result, local authorities can no longer exercise oversight and maintain the coherence of an increasingly fragmented educational system.

A further development was the creation of multi-academy trusts (MATs), which is when one trust takes over the running of several academy schools. Some of these are large, with 40 or more academies; most are smaller, having between 1 and 10 schools. When individual academies have run into difficulties and lost their sponsor, it becomes the responsibility of the Department for Education to 're-broker' them by instructing them to join a MAT. In 2016–17, 165 of the 6,500 academies were re-brokered (Perraudin 2017a) and this number surged to 307 by 2019 (Ford and Jack 2020). In 2016–17, 64 academy schools, with roughly 40,000 students, were waiting to find a new sponsor after being abandoned by, or stripped from, the trust originally managing them (Perraudin 2017a). By 2019 there were 93 schools with some 53,000 students in this position (Chakrabortty 2019). These have been labelled 'zombie academies' because while they exist in this state of limbo they are unable to make long-term planning decisions, hire new permanent staff members, or organise pay rises. Not only were individual academies facing severe financial problems, but, in 2018, 6 of the top 10 MATs that operate hundreds of schools across the country issued warnings that they had unsustainable deficits (Mansell and Savage 2018). A year later, nearly half of all MATs included at least one school that was failing financially (Ford and Jack 2020).

These problems have been exacerbated by serious incidences of fraud and corruption. A particularly egregious case was that of the King Sciences Academy in Bradford, one of the first of the new Conservative government's 'free schools' in Britain, founded by local Bradford entrepreneur and Oxbridge graduate Sajid Hussain Raza. Hailed by Education Secretary Michael Gove as a 'flagship school', it was completed in 2012 at a cost of £10.5 million. The then prime minister, David Cameron, visited the school and described it as 'innovative and inspiring'. Yet in October 2013 a report into the school's finances found that it had 'serious failings', including the disappearance of tens of thousands of pounds, false invoicing, and questionable staff appointments and payments. Subsequent investigations by the Department for Education's auditors revealed that its principal, Raza, his sister (one of the teachers), and the former finance director and teacher had defrauded the academy of £150,000. Passing down jail sentences on all three defendants, the judge declared:

they are called free schools because of the way they were set up, entrusted with funds as a trust, a non-profit making organisation. They were set up to educate children. They were not set up to be a vehicle for making money by those who ran them. (Press Association 2016)

Yet despite their status as 'non-profit organisations', many other academy schools have been implicated in financial scandals. The Perry Beeches Academy Trust is a case in point. This academy chain, lauded by Prime Minister David Cameron, who had officially opened one of its schools, was responsible for five secondary schools in Birmingham, England's second largest city. However, in 2016 an Education Funding Agency (EFA) report found evidence of serious financial misconduct. Its investigations revealed that the trust had funnelled £1.3 million to a private company owned by Liam Nolan, its accounting officer and 'superhead'. Nolan also received a second salary of £160,000 over two years, on top of the £120,000 annual salary he made as head (Staufenberg 2018).

Another case is the Wakefield City Academies Trust. In 2015 the trust was named as one of five 'top-performing' academy sponsors by the Education Secretary and given £500,000 to improve schools in the north of England. The trust took on 14 schools in 'special measures' over three years – a period 'where the academy system felt like the wild west, with big personalities coming in and changing things with little educational justification', according to Professor Becky Francis, director of the Institute of Education at UCL (University College London) (quoted in Sodha 2018). An investigation by the EFA in 2016 determined the trust was in 'an extremely vulnerable position' with 'inadequate governance, leadership and overall financial management'. It found 16 breaches of official guidance. The trust's interim chief executive, businessman Mike Ramsay, had paid himself £82,000 for 15 weeks' work, despite not having an employment contract. The trust also paid almost £440,000 to IT and admin companies owned by Ramsay and his daughter (Sodha 2018). Ramsey received double the approved mileage rate and the trust even spent £1,500 on a pen for his dogs. The trust had instructed all 21 schools to transfer their funds to a centralised account. These funds totalled over £1.5 million and had been raised by parents and volunteers at Christmas markets and other events to support the children's educational activities (Perraudin 2017b). Meanwhile, headteachers begged for funding for crucial electrical and plumbing work, and one had to buff her school's floors herself because she lacked funds for a cleaner (BBC 2019). One headteacher complained that the trust 'was run more like a business for profit' and '200 children were impacted because of the austere regime' (BBC 2019). One trustee was sacked after raising such concerns. Teachers and parents protested about the management but there was no accountability to them and the trust spent more than £1 million of public money to sack staff just before it went into liquidation (BBC 2019). In September 2018, two days after the start of the new school year, the Wakefield City Academies Trust announced it was divesting itself of its schools and asked the Department for Education to transfer them to new sponsors (Perraudin 2017b). The asset-stripped academies were left as 'zombie schools' and lacked resources for teaching in the current term. Deloitte was paid £200,000 out of public funds to wind up the trust, equivalent to the cost of a year's education for 43 children (BBC 2019). None of the funds were returned to the 21 schools. Wakefield City Council called in the police to investigate the trust's finances, but they found that no crimes had been recorded (BBC 2018). Despite the fact the trust had broken 16 regulations, the public authorities seemingly had no mechanisms for recouping misspent funds or seeking redress. Not only had the school's assets been stripped, but parents, teachers and headteachers had no voice in the running of the trust and no one was being held responsible for the damage to children's education. In short: democracy and accountability had also been stripped.

Conclusions: Populism, Performance Measurement and the Break-up of the Public Sector

The story of academy schools in England highlights several key points about performance measurement and populism.

School Rankings as a Populist Project

As with many other areas of contemporary society, the competitive ranking of schools is part of a wider project to transform the state sector through the outsourcing and privatisation of public assets. This project combined neoliberal policy prescriptions with a populist rhetoric that sought to capitalise on 'anti-elitist' and anti-system sentiments and claimed to speak for the common people (and in this case, parents, faith groups and local entrepreneurs).* In England, parents have long used rankings created by the

* For example, Sir Peter Vardy, a Christian car dealer and evangelist, was the sponsor who set up the Emmanuel Schools Foundation, a multi-academy trust which permitted the teaching of creationism.

schools' regulator, Ofsted to decide on the best school for their children. These Ofsted rankings are used in advertisements by estate agents to raise house prices for those looking to move into the 'catchment zones' of highly ranked schools. This perversely helps to promote educational elitism, selectivity and inequality. Because these performance measures and league-table rankings have become so accepted as common sense, parents focus on the numbers and rarely question the details of their production. Few really know how to contextualise and analyse their meaning. As a result, these rankings have provided government with an extremely convenient tool for breaking apart the public sector and opening it to predatory financial interests and other non-traditional providers – all behind the spurious claim to be raising standards and giving parents greater choice.

Do Academy Schools Herald a New Form of Governance?

The proliferation of academy schools in England is important to our argument about shifting forms of governance for several reasons. It showcases the Conservative government's agenda for 'rolling back the state' by ending local authority control of schools and outsourcing the latter to private providers (under the rubrics of 'driving up quality' and promoting 'freedom and choice'). It also illustrates how numerical scores, rankings and 'quality assurance' agencies are being mobilised to justify and promote this privatisation project. Journalist Aditya Chakrabortty's article about Waltham Cross primary school in Essex vividly highlights this. It was forced to become an academy following an Ofsted report that classified it as 'inadequate'. That verdict ran counter to the views of the school's principal and teachers, as well as most of its parents, who waged a protracted campaign against this forced academisation. Their evidence demonstrated the school's success and alleged conflicts of interest and bias in Ofsted's reporting. Nevertheless, Essex County Council announced the school's transfer to a non-local trust called 'Net Academies'. Yet two of the Net Academy Trust's schools in Warwickshire and Reading were also ranked as 'inadequate' and, according to an Education Policy Institute report, 'Net Academy Trust was the sixth worst primary school group in England, falling below even the collapsed Wakefield City Academies Trust' (Chakrabortty 2018).

The forcing of academy status on schools was an ideological project of market making, part of the Conservative government's 'all-out war' on mediocre education. This aim was used to justify the forced academisation of schools over the heads of its pupils, parents and teachers, and opened the door for the capture of state-funded schools and their assets by predatory private providers. Despite copious evidence of systemic failure in the academy school model, which even auditors highlighted, the project of academisation continues.

Accumulation through Dispossession and Hollowing Out Democracy

This new class of education entrepreneurs who take up lucrative leadership positions in these chains of 'failing' schools highlights what David Harvey (2004) termed 'accumulation by dispossession'. Academies are supposed to be non-profit organisations and conversion to academy status is typically portrayed as a philanthropic contribution of entrepreneurs who are meant to lend their experience to improve the efficiency, effectiveness and rankings of schools. However, academies provide bountiful opportunities for entrepreneurs to 'release' the taxpayer-funded assets that are supposedly being 'freed up' from erstwhile state schools.

As we have noted, one key effect of this forced conversion to academy status has been a steady removal of local authority control and local democratic oversight. Academisation has disempowered teachers and parents, excluded them from decision making and given them no vote on whether or not they wish to turn their school into an academy. Moreover, if a maintained school becomes an academy and is then dropped by its trust, there are no legal mechanisms for it to return to local authority control. Even when malpractices have been identified, public authorities seem to have no effective means of enforcing regulations, recouping lost monies or seeking redress. The 'zombie schools' produced by this privatised educational system are emblematic of the way democratic institutions are being dismantled to create new opportunities for rent-seeking entrepreneurs and venture capitalists.

3

The Big Four Accountancy Firms and the Evolution of Contemporary Capitalism

Introduction: Accounting and Society

> The calculative technologies of accountancy do more than transform the capacities and attributes of the self. They also construct the calculable spaces that individuals inhabit within enterprises and organisations by making visible the hierarchical arrangement of persons and things. (Miller 1994: 253)

> Fortunes have been made and lost through the reinterpretation of financial categories; heroic entrepreneurship and criminal embezzlement may be distinguished by no more than a subtle point enunciated ... by the regulatory agencies. (Porter 1995: 97)

Given that statistical thinking, mathematical reasoning and resource management have been integral to processes of governing since at least the seventeenth century, what is new about the current 'world of numbers'? How has the nature of accounting changed, and what are its implications for organisations and society, and for theorising shifts in what Foucault (1991) called the 'art of government'? An important way into these questions is to ask *who* are the producers and designers of these numerical measures and who decides what counts? This chapter addresses these questions by focusing on the changing nature of the accounting profession and, in particular, the rise of the Big Four international audit firms: Deloitte, PricewaterhouseCoopers (PwC), Ernst and Young (EY) and KPMG. The history of these companies, which dominate the international accountancy sector, highlights key moments and trajectories in the transformation of contemporary capitalism.

The concept of audit culture offers a useful framework for analysing these developments and, more specifically, for revealing the economic and cultural logics that underpin them. As we have argued in Chapter 1, audit culture embodies a rationality and a set of processes that exert power by making particular dispositions and financialised forms of governance appear normal and natural. Audit culture draws attention to the increasingly important link between enumeration and financialisation that is central to contemporary capitalism. The Big Four accountancy firms have been at the forefront of initiatives to create new forms of surplus value by using numbers and indicators to disaggregate and disembody phenomena – for example, student loans, securities, financial derivatives and subprime mortgages – and then reassemble them in packages that are tradeable (Tett 2009; Smith 2014; 2015).

This chapter has three parts. First, we trace the development of the Big Four auditing companies through three historical phases from their nineteenth-century origins to the present. In particular, we highlight their link to emerging forms of capitalism since the 1990s. Second, we explore some of the consequences and tensions arising from their expanded remit and changing profile, particularly the shift from traditional accounting to consultancy. We focus on the conflicts of interest and the proliferation of fraud that arise when there is a blurring of the boundaries between audit companies' role as watchdogs serving the public good and their commercial interest in serving their clients. As Theodore Porter (quoted in the epigraph) highlights, there is a thin line between heroic entrepreneurship and criminal embezzlement. What are the implications for auditor independence and accountability when professional accountancy 'gamekeepers' turn 'poachers' and then 'gamekeepers' again in a revolving door between governments and accounting firms? Finally, we examine some of the internal drivers of these processes including the changing priorities, values and career trajectories of audit company personnel. We ask how the professional formation of the chartered public accountant – a figure traditionally steeped in the disciplines of financial probity and detailed number checking – is transformed when they become a manager and entrepreneurial partner in the audit firm. We draw on ethnographic studies of the professional formation and 'habitus' of employees of international accounting firms. These studies offer novel insights into the tensions and dynamics arising from changes in the professional practices and managerial subjectivities of these companies and their systems of governance.

From Joint Stock Company Auditors to Global Value Creators: A Brief History of the Big Four

Look up at the central business district of almost any major city today and four names – or global brands – dominate the skyline: Deloitte, PwC, EY and KPMG (Figure 3.1). These Big Four audit companies are typically seen as single firms, but they actually comprise a network of independently owned and managed companies. This global network of legally independent professional accounting companies coheres around a common name, brand, intellectual property, and quality standards. As noted in Chapter 1, the Big Four employed nearly 1.5 million staff in 2022 (Statista 2023a), operated across 150 countries and generated a massive US $189.44 billion in revenues (Statista 2023c). These firms dominate the market and since the 2008 global financial crisis have steadily increased their grip over the global accounting, tax preparation, bookkeeping and payroll services industry. In 2011, they collectively audited over 80 per cent of all Japanese public companies and 97 per cent of all US public companies with sales between US $250 million and US $5 billion (Pai and Tolleson 2012: 85). In 2021 they audited all of the UK's FTSE 100 and some 90 per cent of the FTSE 250 companies (FRC 2021). Even the smallest of the Big Four, KPMG, is larger than the next four accounting firms combined (*The Economist* 2014). A striking feature of their revenues has been the rapidly

Figure 3.1   Artist's impression of the Big Four dominating the city skyscape

Source: Isabel Shore.

growing percentage of income that comes not from traditional auditing but from consulting and from financial advisory, tax and legal work. Whereas in 2012 most of Deloitte's US $31.2 billion income came from audit and assurance (*The Economist* 2012b), by 2020 this accounted for only US $15.5 billion (32.6 per cent) of its US $47 billion global revenues (Statista 2021). This combination of market dominance and the shift of *modus operandi* towards financial and management services creates major tensions and conflicts of interest that have long been recognised but are far from resolved.

From the Roots of the Profession to Post-war Expansion: 1880s–1970s

As most histories of accounting note, modern auditing in the UK began with the development of the joint stock company in the mid-nineteenth century. The 1844 and 1845 amendments to the British Companies Act required public companies to conduct an annual audit with an auditor selected by shareholders. Notably, the Great Western Railway's (GWR) stock price slumped in 1849 resulting in William Welch Deloitte's appointment as the independent auditor of the company (Coffee 2005: 208). According to Deloitte (2022a), GWR directors found his work so helpful that a boom for people skilled in understanding and solving complex business problems resulted.

Whereas in the UK the eponymous ancestral heroes of the accounting profession originated in private-sector auditing, in the US the myth of origin is in public-sector accounting. In the US case, the rise of accounting occurred in 1893 against a background of economic decline and worries about government inefficiency. Accountants Haskins and Sells were appointed to investigate, department by department, how the US government carried out its work. They simplified the operations, increased efficiency, improved quality and saved the government what was then a hefty sum – $600,000 a year. Furthermore, the 1913 amendment to the US Constitution that allowed income tax to be levied on US citizens for the first time meant that people had to prepare statements of income and expenditure, which heralded a new era of expanded work for public accountants (Deloitte 2022a). It was not, however, until the 1933 Securities Act that US legislation made it mandatory for public corporations to have independent audits done by disinterested, certified public accountants. This occurred in the wake of the 1929 Wall Street crash, as it was thought that proper accounting practices could have prevented some company bankruptcies. The point emerging from these origin stories is that, initially, auditors were appointed for their independence, accounting skills and fearless probity, but they were also seen to generate advice on how to improve organisational efficiency. According to these stories, no tension existed between these two roles.

These individual accountants, while setting up firms in London or New York, soon also opened branches in countries that were the destinations of capital flows. They were therefore international from a very early stage, operating largely across the Atlantic between London, many US cities, Canada and Brazil. In the post-Second World War period, one of the main drivers of change was the application of new data-processing technologies to automate bookkeeping. For example, Touche Ross pioneered the early use of computer technology for audits for leading corporations and government agencies. This freed up accountants to start focusing more on the way clients managed their firms and heralded the later move towards the expansion of consultancy.

Expansion, Mergers and Acquisitions: 1970–1990

From the 1970s, a new style of management came to prominence as corporations sought synergies and economies of scale through mergers and acquisitions in order to become larger, multinational and global. According to the way that the Big Four narrate themselves, at this time corporations began looking to their accountants not just for audit and tax skills, but for expertise as business consultants, to help them expand their enterprises and assets through mergers and acquisitions, new technologies, financial services and business strategies (Deloitte 2022a). As accountancy firms increasingly recast themselves as management consultants, their role also expanded to cover advising companies on their global operations and strategies.

At the same time, these accountancy firms were themselves engaging in an unprecedented wave of mergers and takeovers worldwide, which resulted in the emergence of the so-called 'Big 8' (see KPMG 2015b; PwC 2022a; EY 2015; Deloitte 2022a). For example, Touche Ross and Deloitte Haskins Sells merged to form Deloitte and Touche in 1989. The company's leaders, J. Michael Cook and Edward A. Kangas, 'shared the belief that successful accountants of the future would combine strong professional abilities with a deep understanding of their clients' industries, situations and needs' (Deloitte 2022a).

Just as in the earlier era, while one strand of accountancy was developing in the private sector, another was being pioneered in the public sector through the new opportunities being created by privatisation and managerialism. During the 1980s, particularly in the UK, the remit of the auditing firms was massively expanded through the Thatcher government's policies to revolutionise and rein in the public sector, as we described in Chapter 2. The aim was to create an 'enterprise culture' through a sustained programme of cost cutting, competitive tendering, creating internal markets and turning each government department into a cost centre with performance targets. Employees and professionals were recast as 'units of resource' whose performance was to be managed, measured and incentivised through targets and regular performance appraisals.

Audit became an even more prominent profession and increasingly visible instrument of political rule in the UK with the creation of the national Audit Commission, an institution established by the Local Government Finance Act of 1982. Initially, this body was just responsible for auditing local authorities. Later its remit was extended to include a vast range of other public services, including the National Health Service (NHS), the fire and rescue services, social benefits and social housing. The Audit Commission was to be 'a driving force in the improvement of public services' and in the process of fulfilling that remit the meaning of audit itself expanded from scrutinising the accounts and ensuring financial regularity to promoting 'good government'. The language of audit also began to embrace terms such as 'monitoring performance', identifying 'best practice', 'improving value for money' and 'ensuring the effectiveness of management systems' (Audit Commission 1984: 3). When it was launched, the Audit Commission had 500 staff, a quarter of whom were drawn from the major private accountancy firms Price Waterhouse, Touche Ross, Coopers & Lybrand, and Peat, Marwick, Mitchell. When the Audit Commission was finally disbanded in 2012 its work was transferred to four private-sector firms. While Ernst & Young and KPMG won five contracts between them, the largest single share (four contracts) went to Grant Thornton, at that time the world's sixth largest audit firm, which also took on over 300 of the Commission's former staff (Jones 2012; Reed 2012).

The key point of this account is that during this period a new market was created as a result of the government's privatisation of the public sector and requirement that all public bodies and newly formed organisations be annually audited by accredited private accountancy firms. This guaranteed market enabled the audit companies to become exceptionally large organisations. At the same time, they expanded the scope of audit from governing *of* numbers in company and public accounts to governing *by* numbers and the financialisation and measurement of governance itself.

Going Global: 1990s–Present

Against the backdrop of the collapse of the Soviet Union, the end of the Cold War, the expansion of the European Union and rising economic powers in the Asia-Pacific, corporations demanded sophisticated knowledge of international business, ever more complex trade agreements, and integrated cross-border services. Accounting firms rose to this challenge by expanding their remit, creating deeper knowledge of particular industrial sectors and markets, and developing expertise in the specificities of accounting requirements and company law in different countries. The larger audit companies engaged in radical restructuring as they sought to become global brands and one-stop shops providing everything their clients needed for their global operations.

This is the period when audit companies shifted from large corporate structures to more flexible forms of organisation. This typically entailed creating themselves as new entities that, rather than providing their own services to clients, allowed independent firms to use their 'brand'. This move was consistent with their globalisation strategies that also entailed outsourcing of contracts to legally independent local firms. As PwC (2022b) acknowledged, '[I]n many parts of the world, accounting firms are required by law to be locally owned and independent.' Responding to these new constraints and opportunities, Deloitte's professional staff – which by 2022 numbered almost 412,000 (Statista 2023b) – were employed in independent firms, each of which became a registered member of Deloitte Touche Tohmastu Ltd (also known as Deloitte Global), each of which was a private company incorporated in England and Wales and limited by guarantee, and serviced a specific geographical area. These member firms and their related entities (each a 'Deloitte firm') provided audit, business consulting, financial advisory, risk management and tax advice to clients in their area (Deloitte 2015) while providing access to the resources, recognition and reputation of the wider network that forms the Deloitte organisation. Deloitte Global itself does not provide services to clients, nor does it direct or control the decisions Deloitte firms make with respect to the clients they serve. This model means that each affiliated firm 'operates

within the legal and regulatory framework of [the] particular jurisdic-
tion(s)' of its nation state (Deloitte 2022c). This structure, it is claimed,
'allows Deloitte to be an industry leader at all levels – locally, nationally
and globally' (Deloitte 2022c), but it also means that Deloitte can remain
aloof if an affiliate is indicted for malpractice. In some respects, the Big
Four have helped to pioneer a new form of business entity that is neither
a multinational corporation, nor a global partnership, nor a single firm.
Their role, instead, is to act as coordinating entities for their network of
global affiliates, who are ostensibly unified around 'brand', 'risk', 'quality',
'values' and 'ethics' by adhering to a common code of conduct (EY 2020;
KPMG 2021). Deloitte (2022c) coordinates its affiliates as 'separate and
independent firms that have come together to practice under a common
brand and shared methodologies, client service standards, and other professional protocols and guidelines'. The latter includes 'Deloitte's Shared
Values' – to 'lead the way, take care of each other, foster inclusion, collaborate for measurable impact and serve with integrity' (Deloitte 2022b).

The New Audit Regime: Issues, Effects and Case Studies

In the context of the increasing globalisation of capitalism, the new organisational model of the Big Four was designed to make the firms more
flexible and responsive to their globalising clients and able to capture
new markets. It also made them increasingly vulnerable to fraud, malpractice and dangerous levels of risk-taking. This was evidenced in the
spate of high-profile scandals and national court cases involving fraud,
false accounting, manipulation of share value, money laundering, tax
evasion, and corruption. For example, KPMG failed to warn directors of
the Canadian company Hollinger about violations of fiduciary standards
that investigators described as 'corporate kleptocracy'. Its founder, Lord
Conrad Black, was found to have syphoned off US $400 million from
1997 to 2003, which was more than 95 per cent of Hollinger's adjusted net
income (Somers 2006; Coffee 2005: 207). In India's biggest ever accounting fraud, the chair of the computer services firm Satyam confessed in
2009 to falsifying the company's accounts by a massive US $1.47 billion.
Because the auditors were five Indian-based affiliates of PwC (Lovelock &
Lewes, Price Waterhouse Bangalore, Price Waterhouse & Co. Bangalore,
Price Waterhouse Calcutta, and Price Waterhouse & Co. Calcutta), the
case went to the US Securities and Exchange Commission (SEC). The SEC
found that these companies had repeatedly conducted deficient financial

audits that had allowed this massive accounting fraud to go undetected for several years. They also found that the audit failures 'were not limited to Satyam, but rather indicative of a much larger quality control failure throughout PW India' (SEC 2011). PwC's offending affiliates received a US $6 million penalty fine and a prohibition on accepting any new US-based clients for six months while they retrained their staff and revised their audit procedures.

Another case of massive fraud involved the Japanese company Olympus, whose executives stole US $1.7 billion from the company, resulting in the company's shares losing half their value. An independent report criticised the auditors, KPMGAZSA and Ernst & Young ShinNihon, for failing to expose the fraud at the company (Tabuchi and Bradsher 2011). Another case involved the theft of millions of dollars by trustees of the Australian Aboriginal land trust (called GEAT). KPMG and Deloitte were sued in the Northern Territories Supreme Court for undisclosed millions for failing to detect substantial 'irregularities' in the trust's accounts between 2010 to 2012. In this case, KPMG auditors *did* identify the misuse of funds. They told the trust members immediately to cease diverting money intended for community members and stop spending it on cars (US $2.4 million in one year), boats, casino gambling, purchasing property for friends, and inflating their own wages. Yet the auditors failed to take action to stop these irregularities. They argued that their company had no responsibility and no 'contractual duty to prevent loss to the trust of trust money or other property by fraud or breach of trust' and that 'any losses arising from KPMG's actions were caused by false, misleading or incomplete information given to the firm by GEAT's trustees' (Wild 2014).

In the UK, the Big Four have been mired in a series of high-profile scandals involving audit failures at major companies including Carillion, Tesco, Rolls-Royce, Patisserie Valerie, Conviviality and British Home Stores (BHS). The latter is a particularly egregious example of the lax standards, incompetence and regulatory failure that all too often is associated with the work of these firms. BHS was a British retailer listed on the FTSE 100 until 2000, when retail tycoon and billionaire Sir Phillip Green bought it for £200 million. Within four years Green had taken out £422 million from the company and paid it to his family. By the following year, BHS had been transferred to the Arcadia Group, which belonged to Sir Phillip's wife, Lady Tina Green, who was based in Monaco. She then received an even bigger dividend of £1.2 billion. When BHS started to fail, Green offloaded the company for just £1 to former racing driver and twice-declared bankrupt Dominique Chappell and his company 'Retail Acquisitions Ltd'. Within twelve months, Chappell had taken out £25 million in fees and loans for himself and his fellow company directors. The following year (2016) the company collapsed with £1.3 billion of debt, a £571 million pension deficit, and the loss of some 11,000 jobs (Jack 2016). PwC had been BHS's auditors for the previous seven years and had signed it off as a going concern just days before it was sold off to Chappell. After concluding its investigations, the Financial Reporting Council (FRC) fined PwC £6.5 million for misconduct. Steve Denison, a senior PwC partner since 1982, was fined £375,000 and barred from operating as an auditor for 15 years (Farrell 2018).

Richard Murphy (2018), a professor of accounting at Sheffield University, describes the BHS scandal as a shocking example of negligence, incompetence, fraud and systemic failure. Following his close reading of the FRC's report he calculates that the PwC team spent just 154.5 hours auditing BHS. While Green's Taveta Group paid an audit fee of £355,000 to PwC, the firm received some £3 million in non-audit fees; in short, it earned over five times more for its consultancy work. Moreover, Murphy calculated that the average charge per hour for the auditing work was £2,297, even though most of this was done by very junior staff. As Murphy (2018) observes, the £6.5 million penalty imposed by the FRC was less than 1 per cent of PwC's profit: 'It was a cost of doing business at more than £2,000 an hour. An inconvenience if the rest of the show can stay on the road.' Murphy is highly critical of the FRC for its failure to act. As he notes, PwC provided 'no value added', just a 'veneer of service' to cover its rent-seeking behaviour, which the FRC failed to deter (Murphy 2018). The BHS scandal is one among a parade of examples where the Big Four have committed serious audit failure. As Sikka et al. (2018: 2–3) point out, the regulatory authorities have failed to check these predatory practices, improve audit quality, mount speedy and thorough investigations, apply effective sanctions or develop any schema for public accountability of the auditing firms. Instead, in a situation where the regulators appear to have been captured by the auditing industry, poor quality of audit work is the inevitable outcome (Sikka et al. 2018: 3).

Perverse Incentives and Conflicts of Interest

The conditions for these illicit behaviours were largely created by the internal reorganisation of the auditing companies and their growing emphasis on consulting services. The Big Four not only reorganised themselves into affiliations of independent firms but, within those companies, each partner had his or her own clients and, where large firms were concerned, a partner often became a 'one-client' practice (Coffee 2002: 1410). During the 1990s, as the audit activities of the firms became less important than the consulting arm, the (then) Big Five learned 'how to cross-sell consulting services and to treat the auditing function principally as a portal of entry into a lucrative client' (Coffee 2002: 1410). Significantly, 'the typical large public corporation now pays its auditor for consulting services three times what it pays the same auditor for auditing services' (Coffee 2002: 1411). This created a dangerous set of interdependencies between auditee and auditor. As Coffee argues, should an auditor refuse to endorse a client's 'aggressive accounting policy', the company executives could threaten to end their consulting contract and the partner would be out of a job.

The most dramatic illustration of this conflict of interest and its implications for the probity of auditing occurred with the collapse of Arthur Andersen, at that time the largest audit firm, following the Enron Corporation scandal of 2001. Through the manipulation of accounting loopholes, so-called 'special purpose entities' and poor financial reporting, Enron's chief financial officer and other executives were able to hide billions of dollars in debt from failed deals and projects. They deceived Enron's board of directors and audit committee about their high-risk accounting practices. They were able to persuade Arthur Andersen to ignore the issues largely because one of the Arthur Andersen partners relied on Enron as his 'one-client practice'. A subsequent court case found Arthur Andersen guilty of shredding evidence and obstructing justice, a conviction that led to the collapse of the firm and reduction of the Big Five to the Big Four. These scandals led the US Congress to pass the 2002 Sarbanes-Oxley Act, a piece of legislation designed to protect shareholders and the general public from business accounting errors and fraudulent practices. In an attempt to address the problem of the conflict of interest, the act limited the consulting services that a US accounting firm could offer to an audit client and improved the accuracy of corporate disclosures.

The response of the leading audit firms to such scandals is often to blame offending individual partners, portraying them as 'rotten apples' whose behaviour traduces the company's values and code of conduct. However, the passage of the Sarbanes-Oxley Act pointed to systemic failures. These audit firms have been complicit in almost every major financial crisis since the 1970s and have played a key role in creating fraudulent offshore tax shelters to assist clients evade government taxes (Sikka 2014). While they are supposed to perform a public service by detecting financial malpractice, their record of regulatory failure is dismal. For example, in 2008 both Lehman Brothers and Bear Stearns (America's fifth largest investment bank) received unqualified audit reports only months before their collapse (Sikka 2009: 869). The catalogue of failures also includes KPMG's admission of criminal wrongdoing in creating fraudulent tax shelters to help wealthy clients dodge US $2.5 billion in taxes, for which they were fined a mere US $456 million in penalties (IRS 2005). A US Senate investigation documented that one KPMG professional had urged the firm to ignore Internal Revenue Service (IRS) rules on registering tax shelters:

> He 'coldly calculated', a Senate report said, that the penalties for violating the law would be no greater than $14,000 per $100,000 in fees that KPMG would collect. 'For example', he wrote, 'our average ... deal would result in KPMG fees of $360,000 with a maximum penalty exposure of only $31,000'. (Hudson et al. 2014)

Nothing more clearly illustrates the calculating logics of governing by numbers in a financialised world of audit and accounting, or the cavalier attitude such companies have towards compliance with government legislation. After the collapse of Arthur Andersen, the Big Four soon realised that governments were reluctant to get too tough with them. For example, in the KPMG tax shelter scandal mentioned above, KPMG's lawyer made clear that 'the company could probably survive a tax fraud charge, but an obstruction charge would kill us'. The US government only charged the company on the lesser count of tax fraud and then quickly dismissed the charge under a 'deferred prosecution' agreement that allowed KPMG to put the criminal case behind them with a mere fine. It seems the US government feared that criminal charges leading to the collapse of one of these firms would turn the Big Four into an even more powerful oligopoly of three. As with the banking scandals that precipitated the 2008 global financial crisis, the Big Four are seen as 'too big to fail' (Hudson et al. 2014: 7).

While the Big Four may appear to stand above elected legislators, they also go out of their way to inform themselves about – and influence – forthcoming legislation. For example, when the US Public Company Accounting Oversight Board (PCAOB) was considering changes to the regulations to compel companies to regularly change their auditors, the Big Four deployed their lobbying resources and orchestrated 260 letters that poured into the PCAOB. They regularly devote large sums of money to lobbying on Capitol Hill (as in Figure 3.2). In 2019, they spent $10.5 million lobbying lawmakers and regulators from the Federal Reserve to the SEC, although this declined in 2020 because the Covid-19 pandemic limited in-person contact with lawmakers (Iacone and Skolnik 2021). In addition, these four firms' employees target campaign money directly at members of Senate and House of Representatives committees that oversee the industry. For example, the chair of the House Financial Services Committee, which oversees the PCAOB, accepted $370,000 in contributions from the accounting and audit industry during his career (Ingram and Aubin 2012).

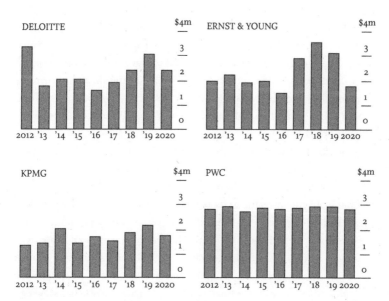

Figure 3.2   Annual spending by the 'Big Four' accounting firms to lobby Congress

Source: Bloomberg Industry Group analysis based on Senate Lobbying Disclosure Reports (https://lobbyingdisclosure.house.gov; https://news.bloombergtax.com/financial-accounting/big-four-cut-back-federal-lobbying-amid-pandemic).

Revolving Doors between Government and Audit Firms

The power of the Big Four is also facilitated by the proximity of private audit firms' staff to government legislators and the 'revolving door' between them. The term 'revolving door appointment' has long been used in US politics to describe the way senior government officials move from the public to the private sector – and vice-versa – and the collusive relationships that this creates between government and business. This is particularly notorious in the areas of food regulation and defence contracting (Wilks-Heeg 2015: 135), but our own research indicates it is equally prevalent in the areas of finance and tax. In France, the tradition of retiring senior government officials taking up lucrative positions in private companies is referred to as *pantouflage* (literally, 'putting on slippers'), while in Japan a similar phenomenon is termed *amakundari* ('descent from heaven'). In the UK this phenomenon was less common, as traditionally it was considered a breach of public service rules for civil servants to take up lucrative appointments in the private sector until at least three years after retirement. However, during the 1980s this changed as a result of Mrs Thatcher's programme to bring the state and business closer together, and the trend continued under Tony Blair's New Labour government. Since 2008, dozens of former UK ministers and senior civil servants have left government posts for jobs with the Big Four. Blair himself, after retiring as prime minister, combined being 'Middle East envoy' with a £2.5-million-a-year (US $3.27 million) advisory role with the JP Morgan Chase bank (Gapper 2013).

In the US, the revolving door phenomenon has become both normalised and extensive. For example, in 2014 KPMG announced that the former deputy director of the US Federal Reserve, Deborah Parker Bailey, had become managing director in its regulatory risk service network (KPMG 2014). During her tenure in the Federal Reserve, she was responsible for stress-testing the 19 largest US banks' holding companies and reporting directly to its chair, Benjamin Bernanke. KPMG understated the value of her knowledge and networks when it commented that she would 'provide strategic insight' for KPMG's financial service clients. KPMG has also been proactive in cultivating ties with the PCAOB itself, the body responsible for examining accounting firms for deficiencies in their audits. In 2014 a PCAOB report on its inspections of KPMG audits showed that 23 out of 50 audits (or 46 per cent) were deficient. One of KPMG's measures to improve its results was to hire Brian Sweet, former PCAOB Associate Director with responsibility for conducting internal inspections of KPMG audits, as a partner in its Department of Professional Practice Group. Before joining KPMG, Sweet allegedly 'copied from an internal PCAOB database to his office computer various confidential inspection-related materials he believed might help him at KPMG' (Levine 2018: 2). This included the confidential list of KPMG audits which the PCAOB were planning to inspect in 2015.

In the UK, lack of knowledgeable staff sometimes compels the Treasury to second staff from the Big Four, who have a much greater range of expertise. The House of Commons Public Accounts Committee (PAC) was shocked to learn that Deloitte, Ernst & Young, KPMG and PwC had provided the government with expert accountants to draw up its new tax laws and then used that knowledge to exploit loopholes for commercial purposes. In a video interview with the *Guardian* newspaper, the chair of the PAC, Labour MP Margaret Hodge (2013), explained the committee's concern:

> What was particularly galling to us was to see this 'poacher-turned-gamekeeper-turned-poacher' syndrome. It came out with KPMG. They had put somebody into the Treasury to help advise on how to write the law on a new tax relief. This was a tax relief to encourage businesses, who invented new products, to commercialise them. It's called the 'Patent Box'. The guy who wrote the law immediately left Treasury, went back to KPMG and wrote a brochure saying, 'Patent Box – What's In It For You?', and sold it as a tax avoidance scheme to KPMG's clients. And that is just not on. This 'poacher-turned-gamekeeper-turned-poacher' syndrome really should be stopped by government.

As Hodge went on to note, it is fine for government to listen to stakeholders when drafting new laws, but:

> What is *not* on is to allow your stakeholders to be so closely involved in writing the law that they then know how to exploit it as a tax avoidance scheme. And it's quite a simple thing for Treasury to do. They can punish KPMG for doing that, or they can have a code of practice that if you are asked in to help government devise a new policy or write a new law, you will *not* engage then in using that law to help your clients avoid tax. (Hodge 2013)

The problem, as Hodge illustrates, is that audit firms have exercised institutional capture; they have gained undue influence over those areas of government intended to regulate their conduct and have been able to commercialise their insider knowledge of legislation and its loopholes.

The case of Dave Hartnett, former head of tax at Her Majesty's Revenue and Customs (HMRC), provides a clear illustration of the way the UK's revolving door phenomenon works to cement collusive relation-ships between government and business. Under Hartnett's leadership, HMRC struck several highly controversial deals that allowed Starbucks and Vodafone to avoid paying billions of pounds in corporation tax. Deloitte was heavily involved in Vodafone's acquisition of the German telecoms operator Mannesman. Between 2006 and 2010 Hartnett held over 47 meetings with Deloitte's UK chair, David Cruikshank, to resolve Vodafone's tax dispute with HMRC. Vodafone eventually made a settle-ment payment of a mere £800,000 (US $1,046,536), with an additional £450,000 (US $588,676) spread over five years. A year after retiring from HMRC, in 2013 Hartnett joined Deloitte as a specialist adviser (Sikka 2016: 264). Another example is that of Sir Hector Sants, the former head of the Financial Services Authority (FSA), who was responsible for reg-ulating the banks during the global financial crisis. In 2012, six months after retiring from the FSA with a knighthood for his public service, Sants joined Barclays Bank to lead its '1,300-strong compliance department and repair fraught relations with regulators' (Treanor 2013). That same year Margaret Cole, ex-head of enforcement of the FSA, joined the executive board of PwC (MacMillan 2012). This movement of former public servants into the financial sector, and especially the Big Four, is matched by the even greater movement of former government ministers into lucrative positions in the various health, defence, transport or building companies with whom they dealt while in office (Brooks and Hughes 2016). This revolving door between public and private sectors helps create the con-ditions for poachers to become gamekeepers and then poachers again, which enables the emergence of a new class of entrepreneurs. These indi-viduals are adept at gaming the opportunities that arise from the blurring of state and private boundaries in ways that recall the patronage ties and collusive brokerage relationships that facilitated the rise of the Sicilian Mafia in the nineteenth century (Shore 2021) or, more recently, the US neocons, whose manoeuvrings through 'flexible networks' enabled them to exploit the newly created market opportunities in post-Soviet Eastern Europe (Wedel 2009).

Factors Driving the Rash of Financial Irregularities and Fraud

One of the problems with the new regime of audit arises from the relax-ation of the rules around what mandatory auditing entails. In the past an audit was expected to certify that an organisation was conducting it financial affairs with probity. An audit was supposed to provide assurance that statements were correct. Today, a company audit offers only a 'reasonable assurance' that, in the opinion of the auditors, the company's statements are in conformity with generally accepted accounting principles (GAAP). As *The Economist* noted:

> GAAP is a 7,700-page behemoth, packed with arbitrary cut-offs and wide estimate ranges, and riddled with loopholes so big that some accountants argued even Enron complied with them. (*The Economist* 2014)

The Sarbanes-Oxley Act required auditors to report to an audit committee set up by company shareholders rather than to the company's managers. This aimed to ensure that the audit process was fully independent and not influenced by managers. The act asserted that the auditors must have no 'material relationships' with the listed company, meaning no 'commercial, industrial, banking, consulting, legal, accounting, charitable and familial relationships'. However, it also acknowledged that '[i]t is not possible to anticipate, or explicitly to provide for, all circumstances that might signal potential conflicts of interest, or that might bear on the materiality of a director's relationship to a listed company' (Gorman 2009). *The Economist* (2014) considered that misaligned incentives built into auditing all but guarantee that accountants will not adequately meet investors' needs.

In the US, if a company's accounts are found to be incorrect, it is required to present a 'financial statement restatement'. In the 1990s, there was a crescendo of such restatements, mainly due to what is euphemistically termed 'improper revenue recognition'. The number continued to rise to a peak of 1,784 in 2006, although by 2009 the number had fallen to 711 and remained at around that level until 2012. The numbers peaked again in 2016 with 1,800 restatements and were falling away before spiking once more in 2021 with 1,470.

The effect of financial statement restatements on company employees and shareholders is severe. They often result in SEC enforcement proceedings, and in the 1990s the stock price of the companies affected, on average, dropped by 10 per cent within three days, and by 25 per cent within 120 days of restatement (Richardson et al. 2002). Over the first decade of the twenty-first century on average, the stock price fell by 1.5 per cent in reaction to restatements, although the stock price fell by 6.8 per cent if the restatement involved fraud (Scholz 2014: ix).

Figure 3.3   Financial restatement trends
Source: Audit Analytics (2022: 5).

Driving this rapid increase in the number of restatements, in many instances, was 'premature revenue recognition' (Coffee 2005: 204). In other words, managers 'stole' earnings from future periods or invented revenues that did not exist to create a spike in their company's reported revenues. A major reason for this was the abrupt shift, in the 1990s, from cash-based to equity-based remuneration for CEOs. In 1990 the median CEO made US $1.25 million, 92 per cent of which was in cash and 8 per cent in equities; in 2001 the median CEO made US $6 million, of which 34 per cent was in cash and 66 per cent in equities (Hall 2003). The point here is simply that managers' stock options increased in value as the company's share price rose and they could sell them off before the fraud was detected and the company's share price fell. As Coffee notes, this 'creates incentives for short-term financial manipulation and accounting gamesmanship' and 'absent special controls, more [stock] options mean more fraud' (Coffee 2005; 202–3).

One of the biggest financial statement restatements in history, which exemplified many of the points raised above, involved the Federal National Mortgage Association (FNMA), colloquially known as Fannie Mae. In 2006, three of its directors were accused of manipulating earnings to maximise their bonuses. A few years later, the SEC found that KPMG knew and approved of misleading statements claiming the companies had minimal exposure to subprime loans at the height of the home mortgage bubble. KPMG had been Fannie Mae's auditor for over 30 years and in the period 2001–2003 it was paid $28 million for both auditing and providing consultancy advice to Fannie Mae (including on how to comply with new accounting rules and auditing its compliance with those same rules). The SEC found Fannie Mae's financial statements 'riddled with errors' and declared that it was 'not even on the page' when it came to complying with the new accounting rules, for which it was fined $400 million (Hilzenrath 2006). As the same *Washington Post* article notes, 'KPMG rubber-stamped Fannie Mae internal accounting decisions in defiance of KPMG's professional obligations and the purpose for which it was hired.' Fannie Mae's restatement erased $6.3 billion from the company's profits, and it cost a further $1 billion to re-do its books for those years.

The case studies outlined above highlight at least three main problems with the new audit regime. First, the organisational architecture of the flexible, globalised audit companies and their independent affiliates has in-built tendencies that are not adequately constrained by the common company codes of practice. Second, the revolving door between government and private-sector companies almost invites institutional capture. Third, despite bodies that can investigate cases and fine companies, such as the US SEC, the companies are able to calculate that the costs of penalties are relatively insignificant compared to the consultancy fees they are likely to earn.

Changing Professional Habitus of the Accountant

The proliferating stories of accounting irregularities, fraud and corruption beg the question of how a profession once renowned for its accuracy and probity came to be so mired in scandal? If one set of factors involved the changing political economy of the sector and the lucrative new opportunities and incentives created through consulting and advisory work, another involves the changing professional habitus of the chartered accountant. As Spence and Carter's (2014: 3) ethnography of partners in the Big Four shows, two institutional logics shape the accounting profession; one technical and bureaucratic, the other commercial and entrepreneurial. They argue that while technical proficiency is essential for entry into the profession, rising to the top of the company hierarchy requires a very different skill set, one that combines salesmanship, commercial savvy, leadership, coaching, and networking client relationships. Above all, the successful partner must be convivial, able to win work, and cross-sell services to other business functions – and do all this without exposing the company to legal risk (Spence and Carter 2014: 10). They quote a retired managing partner from one of the UK-based firms:

> To be a partner in a Big 4 firm these days ... you have to be a hunter, a killer and a skinner. That means that you have got to be able to go out, get the new work in, identify the opportunities, secure them and also you have to be able to do the work, so that is the skinning part of it. (Spence and Carter 2014: 9)

Not only are partners expected to be dynamic, personable, 'hunter-killers' and team leaders, it is the *individual partner's* contribution to the bottom line that counts:

> Traditional professional rhetoric about serving the public interest and acting with integrity and in accordance with ethical principles was notable only by its absence in the talk of our interviewees. (Spence and Carter 2014: 10)

The key point of their analysis is that to rise to the position of partner requires employees to transcend their original, narrow professional identity based on technical excellence and adopt the suite of dispositions associated with a commercial-professional logic.

These findings are supported by other empirical studies (Covaleski et al. 1998; Kornberger et al. 2011). As Kornberger et al. demonstrate, the transition from accountant to commercial partner occurs at the level of the manager, a role that they analyse as a 'rite of passage' in the traditional anthropological sense. In that ritual process, managers experience a destabilisation of their previous professional identity and acquire a new set of skills (performing, game playing and politicking) that run contrary to the previous disposition of adherence to fixed procedures and rules. Now they have to compete with each other, become entrepreneurial, take risks, rely on their own judgement, sell themselves, and learn a new set of unwritten rules in which 'personal performance' and 'real performance' do not necessarily coincide' (Kornberger et al. 2011: 528).

The point that all these authors stress is that staff in the organisations have little choice but to engage in this transformation of their professional identity. Standing still is not an option: employees must go up the hierarchy or exit the organisation (Kornberger et al. 2011: 521). As they ascend the hierarchy, employees both distance themselves from, and show disdain for, the dull 'bean counter' disposition of the conventional chartered accountant (Carnegie and Napier 2010: 364).

These trends were already evident in the 1980s and 1990s when Covaleski and his colleagues interviewed 180 individuals from the then Big Six. As they noted, practices such as management by objectives (MBO), mentoring and performance review 'exemplified techniques aimed at transforming autonomous professionals into business entrepreneurs by duplicating the organization within the individual' (Covaleski et al. 1998: 294). These ethnographic studies of professional staff in the big audit firms highlight the coercive nature of an audit culture. The rationality of a new political economy was translated into political technologies designed to reshape the professional ethos of individuals so that they became risk takers whose focus was to 'grow the business' rather than conforming to standards and procedures. Or at least, it reshaped the professionalism of those staff members who joined in the compulsory competition to rise through the company's hierarchy where the only choice was 'up or out'.

Conclusions: The Accounting Industry and Capitalism

This chapter has illustrated how the growth of audit culture is closely tied up with the expansion of the accounting industry and modern forms of capitalism. Our analysis shows how historical changes in political economy are reflected in the business practices of accounting firms and their clients and the way these are instantiated in new organisational forms with drivers and incentives. These incentives are producing the conditions for remaking professional identities and rationalities of conduct. As our cases show, accountancy has long been associated with forms of capitalism, ever since the railroads and the first joint stock companies in the 1840s, and the rise of large American multinationals in the 1950s and 1960s. Similarly, audit has long been engaged in international flows of capital and investment, and is intimately connected to the current, more flexible forms of globalisation. The extent of this change is perhaps captured by the popular image of the archetypical chartered accountant in the 1880s and the 1980s. The Big Four's websites represent the nineteenth-century roots of accounting in heroic ancestral figures such as George A. Touche, William M. Lybrand, Adam A. Ross, Arthur Young, Alwin Ernst, Charles Haskings, William Welch Deloitte and Samuel Lowell Price. They epitomise the ideal of the upright, conservative warrior of integrity and financial probity. In contrast, in the 1990s, the ideal accountancy partner had become an indi-vidualistic, entrepreneurial risk taker, dedicated to 'growing the business' by using audit as an entrée for selling all sorts of consultancy services (Carnegie and Napier 2010). Changes in accounting practices thus both map and mirror changes in contemporary capitalism.

Social scientists, echoing Max Weber, have often argued that the rise of bureaucracy associated with quantification, enumeration and cap-italist modernity would produce ever greater forms of legal-rational organisation. However, these cases suggest that, rather than the dead hand of bureaucratic routine and conformity, the current shift towards entrepreneurialism, financialisation and ever more pervasive systems of governing by numbers has produced organisational behaviours that are far from legal-rational, rule bound and routine. A major problem with the current model of auditing is that it generates conflicts of interest and blurs the boundaries between the private audit firms and the companies they are supposed to audit. As Prem Sikka puts it:

> The auditing firms are capitalist enterprises and are dependent upon companies and their directors for income. The fee dependency impairs claims of independence and has the capacity to silence auditors ... It poses fundamental questions about the private sector model of auditing which expects one set of capitalist entrepreneurs (auditors) to regulate another set of capitalist entrepreneurs (company directors). (Sikka 2009: 872)

The post-1980s integration of audit firms into the capitalist operations that they are supposed to stand apart from and hold to account creates the conditions for institutional capture and a complicit silence (Sikka 2009). This situation produces a tension between two interacting forms of 'governing by numbers'. On the one hand, as our examples show, company managers paid in stock options are incentivised to inflate company earnings and create artificial spikes in share prices to boost their personal income. On the other hand, auditors – whose position may depend on selling ever more lucrative consulting services – are vulnerable to pressure from their clients, who may threaten to end their consulting contracts if financial accounts are not approved. If the calculative practices of accountancy are central to modern forms of audit, they also work to transform accountancy firms themselves into calculative entities that straddle the increasingly fine line between criminality and entrepreneurship. Ethnographies of accounting firms show us how these financialised logics and behaviours have been institutionalised in perverse forms of 'governing by numbers'.

The UK government has long recognised this problem, yet has signally failed to address it, despite three independent reviews of the audit industry since 2018 and a lengthy public consultation. The Big Four auditors have lost their status as impartial custodians of the capitalist market because they have become so deeply embroiled in the fraud of the companies whose books they audit, as has been illustrated in the high-profile scandals surrounding Carillion, Ted Baker, Rolls-Royce, BT, Sports Direct and many other well-known companies. Yet two decades on from the Enron scandal, the same problems continue: the audit market is dysfunctional, has been captured by an oligopoly of firms who effectively set the rules for auditing standards. They treat audits as commodities to be sold to clients who are required to commission audits from private firms by law. As Sikka (2013) notes, competition, consumer pressure and threats of liability are supposed to be the key drivers for improving standards in market economies yet the market for auditing is state-guaranteed and new players cannot easily enter it. Moreover 'it is almost impossible to sue auditors for negligence, as in general they owe a "duty of care" to the company only, rather than to any individual shareholder, creditor, employee or any other stakeholder' (Sikka 2013). Hence, there is no meaningful process by which citizens can hold these companies to account. As Oxford University Professor of Business and Public Policy Karthik Ramanna (2018) points out, those who choose the auditors are not the ones who need their reports: 'Auditors are effectively chosen by management and the board. But management and the board have access to inside information and, perversely, the incentive to cover up things that have gone wrong.' Following repeated threats by government to force the Big Four to split their tax reporting and audit services from their consultancy, so far only EY has announced it will stop offering advisory services to audit customers in an attempt to restore public confidence in the industry.

Little else has been done to date to reform the audit industry (White and Miller 2020). This is a theme we will return to in the concluding chapter.

4

Global Governance through Standards, Seduction and Soft Power

> Some critics expressed concern (even fear) that a non-educational organization is assuming a global standardizing role in the name of accountability despite a lack of accountability to any of its members or affiliates ... the very meaning of public education is being recast from a project aimed at forming national citizens and nurturing social solidarity to a project driven by economic demands and labor market orientations. (Meyer and Benavot 2013: 10)

The dramatic way that audit culture is spreading globally is largely due to the work of international organisations such as the Organisation for Economic Co-operation and Development (OECD). American analysts of educational governance Meyer and Benavot (quoted in the epigraph) highlight this in their book on the OECD's Programme for International Student Assessment (PISA). They examine how the OECD has developed new expertise in measuring and comparing the educational performance of 15-year-old school children across the world. Whereas measurement of educational standards was previously the prerogative of national governments, today international organisations like the OECD play a key role in defining and shaping school standards. Yet the OECD has no formal mandate or powers in the field of education. What is at stake in this transition from national to international standard setting is far more than simply a jumping of scale: through the construction of global indicators and rankings, non-government organisations (NGOs) and think tanks are pioneering new forms of 'soft power' (Nye 1990) and global governmentality (Larner and Walters 2004). These have important implications for policy, governance and public accountability.

Previous chapters asked what is driving the global spread of audit culture, how can we explain the move toward ever more intrusive and competitive systems of rankings, and who are the key agents behind these proliferating ranking systems? This chapter takes up these questions by examining global ranking organisations and the new forms of knowledge and power they are creating.* We explore the ways these standardised forms of measurement and comparison are created, disseminated and used to produce rankings, and how these numerical scores are institutionalised and translated into practice. We also investigate why policy makers in different countries and regions appear to be seduced into actively participating in the generation, promotion and spread of these global regimes of governance. Given that international ranking organisations such as the OECD, the World Economic Forum, Transparency International and the *Times Higher Education* have no formal authority, legal competence or democratic mandate to set policy, how are they able to wield such global influence? Why are their indicators and rankings taken up so widely? How are these systems reshaping policy agendas and what are their epistemological or world-making effects? If 'what is measured is likely to become what matters' (Burnstein et al. 1992), then those who do the measuring hold a position of exceptional power in society. But whose interests and agendas do these measurements serve?

The Globalisation of Audit: International Ranking Organisations

The indicators and rankings produced by international organisations have acquired an astonishing influence and global spread. Some of these organisations such as the OECD, the World Economic Forum, the Cato Institute and the Millennium Project, are 'think tanks'; others, including Transparency International, Reporters Without Borders, Amnesty International and Index on Censorship are international NGOs, while others such as the Economist Intelligence Unit, *Times Higher Education* and U.S. News & World Report are commercial businesses.

These organisations share a common feature in that all were established by just one well-placed and highly motivated individual operating as a cultural entrepreneur or broker. For example, Transparency International (TI) was founded in 1993 by Peter Eigen, a German former World Bank official following his encounters with corruption in Kenya. TI, which now ranks as one of the world's most influential NGOs with chapters in 100

---

* We would like to thank Iulia Iordache-Bryant for her research assistance for this chapter.

countries, produces the Corruption Perception Index (Sampson 2005; Anderson and Heyward 2009). The World Economic Forum (WEF, previously the European Management Forum), was established in 1971 by Klaus Schwab, a German engineer, economist, entrepreneur and former professor of business policy. WEF describes itself as 'The International Organization for Public–Private Cooperation' and produces annual Global Competitiveness Reports and Global Risk Reports. The *Times Higher Education* (*THE*) produces the 'World University Rankings', which is another example of a small unit inspired by just one individual, the British journalist Phil Baty. *THE* describes itself as 'the company behind the world's most influential university ranking'. It began producing the 'World University Rankings' in 2004 and by 2021, the list had grown to include over 1,500 universities across 93 countries. It had also diversified into a series of more specialised rankings (for example, of universities under 50 years old, universities in specific regions of the world and 'university impact rankings' as measured against the United Nations' [UN] Sustainable Development Goals). The OECD's PISA was started by the German-born statistician and education researcher Andreas Schleicher. Thirty-two countries took part in the first PISA study in 2000 and by 2022 this number had nearly tripled, with 90 participating members.

A second feature of these ranking organisations is that each has created an extensive capillary network of voluntary participants who assist in the processes of designing, conducting the necessary surveys and disseminating their rankings. These assemblages are fashioned into epistemic communities who mutually participate in constructing its discursive framings through a series of meetings, events and consultations (see Wright 2020). For example, the OECD's secretariat attracts and attaches to its activities a vast range of actors from public and private research centres, experts, OECD professionals, politicians and policy makers, technicians, high-level civil servants, academics and teachers. For its PISA studies, they help to develop the concepts and convert them into the design of its survey instruments. When the survey results are available these data are amplified into a range of documents involving a further network of experts and external researchers, other international agencies, national policy-making teams, educational experts and teachers (Carvalho 2014: 66). This strategy is powerful in that the OECD's secretariat not only 'in-sources' much of its work from voluntary contributions but, in the process, it also creates extensive networks of experts, influencers and decision makers spanning different social worlds. Through their involvement, many of them acquire a sense of connection or belonging to the organisation and a commitment to disseminating and using its results. This process of 'attracting and attaching' (Carvalho 2014: 66) draws wide networks of actors into the OECD's policy orbit and reassembles them into a loose yet coherent epistemic community. These transnational webs and networks around rankings and standards exercise, as we illustrate below, an affective form of 'soft power'.

The *THE* employs a similar soft-power strategy of enticing people into its ambit. *THE* holds several regional and world summits each year, which bring together 'thought leaders' and critics to discuss its ranking methodology. Phil Baty, who convenes these meetings, portrays himself as the 'franker ranker' (Lim 2016), because of his emphasis on making the methodology transparent and open to discussion. These meetings also draw in leading university vice chancellors and ministers to show how the rankings are used productively in their own institutions. These meetings help legitimise the rankings, promote their value and create ambassadors who will further champion and extend their use.

The WEF has developed this approach on a much larger scale. The forum's annual gathering of world leaders in the exclusive Swiss ski resort village of Davos, addresses the world's most pressing problems, from global poverty to climate change and the refugee crisis, and is widely reported in the world's media. In keeping with its multi-stakeholder approach, WEF invites foremost business leaders, politicians, entrepreneurs and academic experts to Davos where they mingle with each other over cocktails and in the company of selected celebrities such as Elton John, Kate Blanchett, Pharrell Williams, Bono and Yo-Yo Ma. To be chosen to join these earnest discussions is a badge of honour and recognition of status which few people refuse (see Garsten and Söborn 2018). Being invited to this exclusive club – to see and be seen among the rich, the powerful and the glitterati – creates its own a self-reinforcing 'prestige economy'.

Ahead of the annual Davos meetings, WEF publishes two main reports. Its Global Risks Report results from a network of leading experts and decision makers across the world and a Global Risks Perception Survey, in which nearly a thousand experts and decision makers 'assess the likelihood and impact of 30 global risks over a 10-year horizon' (WEF 2018a). WEF's Global Competitiveness Report is based on the rankings and data profiles of 140 countries that feature in its Global Competitiveness Index. Each year WEF expands its range of expertise and in 2021 it produced a 'Stakeholder Capitalism Metrics' in collaboration with Deloitte, EY, KPMG and

PwC. WEF employs a similar approach to the OECD and *THE* to create its network of users and co-opt them into deploying and improving its ranking agenda. As the head of the forum's 'Global Agenda' explains:

> We invite policymakers, business leaders, civil society leaders, academics, and the public at large to consult the performance of their countries in the Global Competitiveness Index and, together, identify the main challenges and barriers to growth facing their economies. We invite all stakeholders to look beyond rankings and to analyze the evolution of each indicator and each concept covered, identifying areas of improvement and areas where economies are lagging. (Samans 2017: v)

Throughout the year, WEF also convenes a host of working groups, expert panels and regional meetings, and produces dozens of reports. For example, there is an annual programme of meetings for 1,500 'premier thought leaders' in venues such as Dubai, Cape Town and Istanbul (Garsten and Söborn 2018). There is also a 6,000 strong 'Global Shapers Community', and an annual cohort of 100 'Young Global Leaders' is recruited onto a five-year programme to 'enhance their skills, broaden their world view and lead to innovative solutions' to the world's problems (WEF 2018b). Using these methods, WEF and other global organisations create networks of global opinion multipliers and epistemic policy communities. They gather under the hospitality and largesse of these organisations and promote them as promulgators of a new form of world governance.

A third feature these organisations share is their lack of any formal authority or legal and political mandate for what they do. Unlike the World Bank and International Monetary Fund (IMF), they cannot attach conditionalities to loans; unlike the World Trade Organization (WTO) they do not have an adjudications system for resolving disputes; unlike UNESCO (the UN's organisation for education, science and culture) they cannot issue declarations and conventions or require countries to submit reports demonstrating their compliance; and unlike the European Union (EU) they cannot issue directives or impose sanctions. In short, they have none of the powers and legitimate authority enjoyed by international bodies constituted through the membership of nation states. Instead, their membership is by annual subscription. For example, WEF's core funding comes from the subscriptions of 1,000 leading companies, most of which have an annual turnover in excess of US $5 billion. *THE* relies on income from its journal's subscribers and advertisers. The OECD is a membership organisation comprising 38 countries whose contribution is calculated in relation to their national income. Because these organisations rely on members continually renewing their annual subscriptions, their services and activities have to constantly energise and excite. For this reason, seduction becomes an important strategy. Davos summits are discreet and exclusive gatherings, which bestow prestige and status on those invited. Even the WEF's most vocal critics, like former US President Donald Trump, still found reasons to attend, and those attending like to be seen on the world stage in the company of global celebrities. This is testimony to the affective power and aura that the WEF cultivates and, perhaps also, to the 'fear of missing out' (FOMO) that such opulent gatherings produce.

The Operations of Soft Power: The Open Method of Coordination

The strategies deployed by the organisations cited above, are just some of the ways they exercise soft power. The EU was particularly adept at combining and honing these techniques in what has come to be known as the open method of coordination (OMC). That label was officially coined at the EU Council's meeting in Lisbon in 2000, although elements had been in development since the late 1980s. The need for the OMC arose from the fact that while successive treaties had given the EU powers to deal with economic and industrial matters, it had no legal competence to intervene in other areas of policy, including education, culture and social policy. EU politicians and policy makers therefore sought to devise informal voluntary mechanisms for Member States to achieve policy convergence. This involved bringing together experts in meetings to establish best practice and engage in consensus building and peer learning (Thedvall 2006). These meetings, in turn, produced guidelines, policy frameworks and checklists, along with timescales for follow-up meetings. Accompanying these knowledge-exchange activities, quantitative and qualitative indicators and benchmarks were developed, along with targets, milestones and periodic evaluations. The evaluations were aimed at helping Member States learn from one another and consequently improve their domestic policies. However, when rankings were accompanied by 'peer pressure' and competitive league tables, these processes had far greater influence than the terms 'coordination' and 'soft governance' imply.

The OECD developed a similar approach to the OMC. Lacking formal powers, regulatory instruments or the authority to demand compliance, the OECD needed periodically to project a vision of the future around which to mobilise its members and galvanise them into action on the issues it deemed urgent. During the 1990s there were various international debates about whether the future lay in a 'knowledge society' (also referred to as the 'information society' or 'network society') or a 'knowledge economy'. In the latter, knowledge, IT and a highly skilled workforce were seen as key raw materials that rich countries would need to maintain their global competitive advantage. The OECD gained prominence by creating a definition of the global knowledge economy, which it portrayed as an inevitable and inexorable future, and which it transformed into a measurable phenomenon. This enabled the OECD to use its statistical expertise to assess and rank each country's preparedness to meet the challenges of the advancing knowledge economy. With an enviable reputation for statistical analysis and a suite of soft-power instruments, the OECD's secretariat grew to 3,300 by 2021 (OECD 2021). Its annual budget of €386 million made it one of the world's most important policy actors.

The OECD's version of the OMC identifies trends and provides policy prescriptions, reports and guidelines. It produces indicators and scorecards that rank each country's implementation of the recommended policies and their ability to compete in the projected future. One of its key soft-power techniques is to produce success stories, guidance notes, checklists, policy briefs and action plans which are offered to governments as tools to use if they want to succeed. National politicians and civil servants are invited to contribute to OECD events and expert committees and, in turn, they invite the OECD to provide expert advice on national policy development. Member State participation is voluntary, but those who choose not to follow the recommended path to reform are courting failure. In vying with each other to act according to the OECD's standards of performance and policy prescriptions, governments gear themselves to the OECD's projected vision of the world (Wright 2020: 72).

The story of the Danish education ministry's collusive relationship with the OECD exemplifies how this works. In the 1990s, senior Danish civil servants were seconded to key units within the OECD and ministers were invited to address prestigious events. Denmark was known as an active contributor to the formation of OECD policy on university reform; and, in turn, Danish ministers and civil servants acted as a conduit to bring these policy recommendations back home. In 2003 a new University Law reformed the role, governance and management of Danish universities with the aim of driving national competitiveness in the knowledge economy. Exhausted by the protracted debates over university reform, most people in Danish higher education were expecting a period of calm to plan how to implement the new university law. Yet even as the reform was passaging through the Danish parliament, the ministry invited the OECD to conduct a 'Country Study', one of its established, soft-power methods, in order to suggest a further phase of reforms.

In preparation for the Country Study, the Danish ministry wrote a background report and an agenda that strongly steered towards a further shake up of the university system. Following standard operational procedures, the ministry organised the visit of the OECD's independent examiners to carry out the study. Again following standard operational procedures, the Danish ministry then commented on the independent examiners' draft report before it was revised and sent to the OECD. The report was published under the OECD's imprimatur as if it were an independent and neutral study. The Danish government published a memo listing the report's recommendations as if these were independent advice on the need for further reforms. Much to the disquiet of some of the examiners, the government's memo even modified the recommendations for changes in the sector to render them more radical. Despite serious reservations among university leaders, these changes were translated into policies, with the government claiming it was merely carrying out the OECD's independent expert advice (Wright 2020: 77). In short, the OECD was used as a ventriloquist for voicing the prescription for reform that the government had intended all along.

This story highlights the novel combination of soft-power techniques with 'governing at a distance' (Rose and Miller 1992: 173). The national government uses the reputation of an external and seemingly neutral international organisation to give legitimacy to its domestic policy decisions that would otherwise be highly controversial and contested. We call this 'policy laundering'; like money laundering, policy recommendations travel across borders, are surreptitiously transferred into a new 'currency', and made to appear unimpeachably legitimate. Such policy laundering was only possible because of the sustained traffic between senior Danish politicians and civil servants and the OECD's international networks and policy committees. In this way, the OECD weaves a web of influence and constructs its diffuse epistemic community based around a loosely shared ideology and reform agenda. The influence of international organisations often permeates local and national contexts because the national governments appropriate the reputation of these external organisations to pursue their own policy changes and manage dissent.

Creating Spaces of Global Governance: PISA Tests and Rankings

The OECD uses another soft-power technique to persuade governments to take its measures seriously and arouse their emotional commitment to its agendas. In the field of school education, it creates norms and publishes comparative performance indicators showing which countries have done well and which need to improve. In addition, it offers a path to redemption. Member countries accepted the OECD's argument that education was crucial to develop human capital and compete in the global knowledge economy, and they asked for more reliable international comparisons to supplement national data. In response, the OECD developed a survey in the late 1990s on international standards for schooling performance called the Programme for International Student Assessment (PISA). This extended the OECD's influence over educational governance, connecting diverse actors in a shared conceptual and normative space in what Carvalho (2014: 59) calls governing through 'mutual surveillance'.

The Evolution of PISA Testing: Comparison, Equity and Expansion

PISA has tested 15-year-old students in reading, mathematics and science every year since 2000. These tests did not compare heterogeneous national educational systems or assess students' mastery of diverse curricula. Rather, PISA developed a new comparative method focused on educational outcomes: students' capacity to apply knowledge and skills to analyse problems, reason and communicate effectively about 'real life' situations (OECD n.d.b: 7). Rather than focusing on educational inputs, the tests measured the learning capacities that students had acquired. It asked students to 'report on their own motivations to learn, their beliefs about themselves and their learning strategies' (OECD n.d.b: 7). These capacities were later framed as skills to 'improve personal outcomes, reinforce the resilience of local communities, and ultimately strengthen the social tissue of our economies' (OECD 2014: 2).

The OECD assembled a team of specialists and an international consortium of agencies to create a statistical method that policy makers would regard as scientific and free of cultural bias, prejudice and ideology (Gorur 2011: 76). Once countries had screened the questions, agencies were commissioned to administer the tests in each country. The results were decontextualised and standardised as 'detached, measurable and mobile', and made commensurable 'across time and space' (Gorur 2011: 86) in the

OECD's annual *Education at a Glance* report. Countries then use that publication 'to rate how they measure up' (Gorur 2011: 79) as the tables make visible each country's progress (or not). These international league tables become major national reputational talking points.

Whereas the original methodology produced an average for each country, it masked inequalities in educational outcomes between students from well-off and deprived backgrounds. For example, in 2000 the US mean matched the OECD mean, and while the highest achieving students were well above average, the majority were far below average. Finland, in contrast, had a much smaller range of performance. PISA designed questionnaires to investigate the social and economic background of schools in order to map associations between achievement levels and differences in social background. Australian educationalist, Barry McGaw (2008: 235) plotted these country results spanning high achievement and high equality to low achievement and low equity (Figure 4.1). Countries with high scores for equity were hailed as models of how to ameliorate social background influences on educational outcomes (McGaw 2008: 234–7, 240).

The OECD's reports have hovered between whether countries should focus on 'quality' by improving the outcomes of top achievers, or whether they can only achieve 'excellence' by pursuing educational 'equity'. Andreas Schleicher, head of the OECD's education and skills division, singled out Korea as a model country that had doubled the number of top-achieving students, but in a 2020 Ted Talk he praised those countries that were pro-

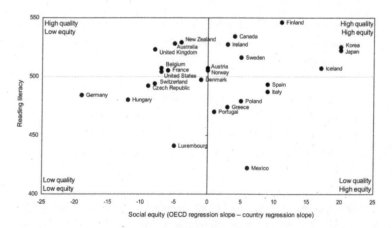

Figure 4.1   Social equity (OECD regression slope – country regression slope)
Source: McGaw (2008: 234, based on OECD data).

viding 'excellence for all'. He argued that 'you don't have to compromise equity to achieve excellence' (Schleicher in OECD 2016: 3). However, equity in PISA is less about ensuring social justice and personal development than optimising human capital and raising overall standards of competence. As Schleicher argues, 'when a large share of the population lacks basic skills, a country's long-term economic growth is severely compromised' (Schleicher in OECD 2016: 13).

The success of PISA was demonstrated by its growth. From 32 countries in 2000, it increased to 88 in 2022 (Education Research Centre 2021). Even by 2016, PISA covered 80 per cent of the world economy, although many Asian, Latin American and African countries were still not included (Schleicher and Zoido 2016: 377). Whereas PISA tests initially applied only to mathematics, reading and science, the OECD's 2012 skills strategy added non-cognitive skills important for the knowledge economy, including working collaboratively, communication and entrepreneurship. Tests were further extended in 2018 to include four dimensions of 'global competence':

> the capacity to examine local, global and intercultural issues, to understand and appreciate the perspectives and world views of others, to engage in open, appropriate and effective interactions with people from different cultures, and to act for collective well-being and sustainable development. (OECD 2018a)

A further instrument called 'PISA for Development' aimed to make its survey instruments more relevant to middle- and low-income countries. Its aims were to analyse:

> factors associated with student learning outcomes, particularly for poor and marginalised populations, for institutional capacity-building and for monitoring international educational targets in the Education 2030 framework being developed within the UN's thematic consultations. (OECD 2018b)

The OECD's expanded product range included national reports, capacity needs analysis reports, capacity-building plans, and PISA-development briefs (OECD 2018b). The OECD has established itself as a major authority and agenda-setter for global educational standards through these small yet detailed measures for translating a whole field of human activity into decontextualised and commensurable numbers and rankings.

Effectiveness of PISA and the PISA Effect

How exactly does PISA achieve its influence and effects, and get countries to use its data and success stories to reform their educational systems according to the OECD's agenda? The OECD's rationale for PISA emphasises the economic benefits of measuring and benchmarking educational standards:

> Given our global, knowledge-based economy, it has become more important than ever before to compare students not only to local or national standards, but also to the performance of the world's top-performing school systems. (OECD 2018b)

The way the OECD presents its material is a lesson in the art of persuasion or how to construct a 'problem' in a way that leaves only one meaningful 'solution' (Shore and Wright 1997a: 3; Bacchi 2009). *Education at a Glance's* colour-coded maps, graphs and overviews reveal each country's achievements in science, reading and mathematics, and in terms of gender, social background and immigrant status. The OECD also produces a vast range of general, thematic, extensive and national reports that are directed at different audiences – international agencies, national politicians, civil servants and researchers – and press releases for the media and manuals for teachers (Carvalho 2014: 66). PISA surveys are constructed as vehicles for government to drive economic growth – and for flagging the risks of not taking them seriously. For example, in 2010 the OECD calculated that if countries boosted their average PISA scores by 25 points over the next 20 years, this:

> would result in gains in the order of USD 115 trillion over the lifetime of the generation born in 2010 ... Bringing all countries up to the average performance of Finland, OECD's best performing education system in PISA, would result in gains in the order of USD 260 trillion. (OECD 2010: 6, cited in Gorur 2016: 601)

Schleicher echoes this message about future growth and calculates that if all 15-year-olds attain the PISA baseline performance, GDP would rise by

28 per cent over the next 80 years (Schleicher, in OECD 2016: 3–4). The 'lesson' from these fabulously speculative statistics is not simply that 'all countries can improve their students' performance given the right policies and will to implement them' (OECD 2016: 13), but that PISA is the oracle that will point policy makers towards fabulous riches.

PISA also gains impact through its capacity to name, shame or glorify. Much to its surprise, Finland topped the PISA rankings in 2000, 2003 and 2006, and transformed from 'a country following the examples of others to one serving as a model for others' (Välijärvi et al. 2002: 3 quoted in Grek 2009: 28). Finnish education scholars and officials received copious invitations in what became a Finnish 'PISA-tourism' boom (Grek 2009: 28; Rutkowski 2015: 684). Publishers quickly capitalised on the 'Finnish miracle of PISA' (Simola 2005), producing textbooks and 'How To' manuals based on the so-called Finnish method of teaching, including critical thinking, creativity and problem solving. The Finnish system of comprehensive schools had no national end-of-compulsory-schooling examinations. Schools and teachers had considerable autonomy and were empowered to use their own pedagogical and curricular initiatives to develop students' communication, collaboration and social skills (Grek 2009: 28).

Finland's PISA success challenged conventional wisdom about the conditions that promote educational achievement. Unlike the top-down, targeted and selectivity approaches favoured by many other countries, Finland's school system had been built from the bottom up and emphasised 'universal access to high quality childcare and early education and a strong developmental commitment to the welfare of each child in terms of health, education and care' (Darling-Hammond 2014: 10). It included highly educated, well-paid and well-regarded teachers, who were considered pedagogical experts and who exercised autonomy over choice of textbooks and teaching methods (Grek 2009). The broad curriculum included considerable time devoted to social studies, music, foreign languages, practical arts, moral or religious education and various extra-curricular activities and electives with no standardised external tests for ranking students or schools (Darling-Hammond 2014: 10). Instead, the emphasis was on flexible classroom-based assessment that allowed for a much broader definition of student achievement and 'teacher feedback to students … in narrative form, emphasising descriptions of their learning progress and areas for growth' (Darling-Hammond 2014: 10; see also Välijärvi et al. 2002).

The 'PISA Shock' Doctrine

If Finland was pleasantly surprised by its success, in Germany the first PISA round in 2000 produced a profound crisis. German policy makers and the public were completely unprepared for the low PISA results of its pupils. The results had a 'tsunami-like impact' producing what became known as the 'PISA shock', or *Bildungkatastrophe* (Gruber 2006: 195; Grek 2009). Out of 32 countries, Germany came 20th in reading, mathematics and science. It also fell in the low-quality, low-equity bracket, as there were considerable differences in educational opportunities and achievement between social groups and those of immigrant background. Highly selective gymnasium secondary schools were also not living up to their reputation for outstanding achievement (Ringarp and Rothland 2010: 424). This 'PISA shock' dominated German newspapers and television news for months (Waldow 2009: 476; Schleicher 2012) and spurred Germany to re-envision its entire educational system.

Japan experienced a similar PISA shock in 2004 following the second PISA round. Having previously been an exemplar of educational excellence, as in Germany, the results plunged Japan into serious soul searching about its education system. The national 'academic achievement crisis debate' became a moral panic over declining educational performance (Takayama 2009). In its hunt for a solution, Japanese 'journalists, scholars and government officials followed the international trend travelling to Finland in search of the secret' (Takayama 2009: 51).

Paradoxically, in attempting to emulate Finland's PISA results, German and Japanese policy makers did not follow Finland's educational practices of school and teacher autonomy and qualitative assessments rather than grades and rankings. After a long history of self-managing schools, Germany introduced mandatory standards for measuring students' competences on completing schooling, assessments of learning outcomes in core subjects, and school inspections (Grek 2009: 29; Waldow 2009: 478). Tighter controls of schools and student testing moved in the opposite direction to Finland and did not always improve the quality of school teaching (Rutkowski 2015). To enhance their rankings, Japan moved even further from Finland, the OECD's 'reference society'. They 'drew on the language of conservative critics in the United States and Britain to construct a crisis-reform melodrama and define child-centred constructivist pedagogies and leftist ideologies as "villains" which had placed their nations "at risk"' (Takayama 2009: 52). They lionised Ronald Reagan and

Margaret Thatcher's 'back to basics' reforms, with discipline, competition and standardised test-based accountability systems (2009: 52). In short, countries attempted to emulate the achievement of Finland as a PISA hero and 'reference country', but in fact implemented reforms that were the very opposite to Finland's. Instead of respecting school autonomy, teacher professionalism and narrative accountability, they introduced more, not less, centralised testing and control, and relied on numbers and rankings for accountability.

In 2009, Shanghai eclipsed Finland by leading the world with its outstanding scores for maths, science and reading to become the new 'reference society' on the global stage (Sellar and Lingard 2013; Rutkowski 2015: 684). Shanghai was a globalising city and a major Asian financial centre. In a context where testing was still deeply embedded and reinforced by parental pressure, Shanghai was gradually shifting from rote learning and persistent testing towards greater school autonomy and a curriculum more geared to 'real life problems' (Sellar and Lingard 2013: 469–70). The PISA results showed that Shanghai's schools enabled socio-economically disadvantaged students to do comparatively well (Sellar and Lingard 2013: 469) but this high equity score belied the fact that Shanghai's school system excluded most children from rural migrant families, who in 2013 constituted 11 million of Shanghai's population of 24 million (Loveless 2013).

Other 2009 top performers were Hong Kong, South Korea, Singapore and Japan. Since Western countries now saw education as one of the most powerful policy tools available to neoliberal economies, this 'rise of Asia' produced another 'PISA shock' (Sellar and Lingard 2013: 465). Each PISA cycle produces a new hero which, regardless of the contextual factors that define those different education systems, becomes the benchmark and model for other countries to follow. Despite their extremely different educational histories and current contexts, Finland, Shanghai and Singapore were each held up as 'reference societies' to be copied by lower-scoring countries. The poor performers in each PISA round reacted in different ways; Germany and Japan went into 'shock', but the UK's and US's low PISA results generated little interest among policy makers. These countries consistently lagged behind in global school rankings and their lack of equity was particularly marked, but policy makers were either indifferent towards these issues or ineffective at dealing with them (Darling-Hammond 2014; Coughlan 2016). This posed a challenge for the OECD with its strong interest in legitimising its expertise through the global uptake of its PISA rankings (Morgan and Shahjahan 2014: 192).

By-passing the State: Localising Global Governance

The OECD had to invent a new strategy to deal with countries that were indifferent to its soft-power methods. The US, as *A Nation at Risk* (Department of Education 1983), had initiated PISA in 1997, but had since ignored years of warnings about its mediocre educational standards. In 1989 President George H. Bush responded by announcing a set of national targets, which included ranking first in PISA in mathematics and science by 2000. However, in 2000 the US still only ranked 18th out of 32 OECD countries in PISA mathematics, and 14th in science (Darling-Hammond 2014: 1). In 2001, his son, President George W. Bush, introduced another major policy initiative to improve educational standards called *No Child Left Behind* (Senate and House of Representatives 2001).

The federal government had difficulty persuading schools to fall into line, a task made harder by the highly decentralised US educational system. If this was a problem for Washington policy makers, it was equally a problem for the OECD's reputation as a purveyor of authoritative data and expert statistical analyses. Between 2000 and 2012 the US's PISA rankings fell from 14th to 21st in reading, 32nd in mathematics and 23rd in science – far below many smaller countries (Darling-Hammond 2014: 2). However, calls to redress this poor achievement 'were typically met with what amounts to a national shrug and a yawn' (Rutkowski 2015: 684).

The OECD developed an ingenious soft-power strategy that by-passed government and reached out directly to schools through a PISA-Based Test for Schools. This new test was piloted in 2012 in the US, Canada and the UK, with 120 US schools participating (Rutkowski 2015: 692). Schools paid for an accredited private supplier (initially CTB/McGraw-Hill in the US, later the Northwest Evaluation Association and more recently the Australian education technology corporation Janison) to administer the test and the questionnaires on students' and the school's backgrounds. Students' performance was presented using the same six scales as in PISA tests, and the results were compared with local and national systems. Each school received a 160-page performance report and contextual data about the school, but the bulk of the report was a standard text with 17 decontextualised examples of 'best practice' from international 'reference societies' (e.g. Shanghai, Finland, Singapore), and excerpts from the OECD's education policy research, so that teachers could see what worked and seek global excellence (Lewis 2017: 284). The OECD incentivised participation by offering the trial schools a free benchmarked analysis of their students' results, which the schools could either keep confidential or, if they were good, publicise to show parents how they prepared their students for future employment. The OECD even offered to help fund the tests – approximately US $155 per pupil. The trial schools had much to gain and little to lose by this arrangement as they were able to interact directly with the policies and discourses of the OECD without the intervening presence of government (Lewis 2017: 282; Lingard and Sellar 2016: 366).

To promote uptake of its PISA-for-schools test the OECD deployed a narrative of improvement and redemption, arguing that its surveys 'empower school leaders and teachers' by providing them with 'valuable information on the learning climate within a school', an 'evidence-based analysis of their students' performance' and 'opportunities for global peer-learning' among teachers and school leaders (OECD 2018c). In these ways:

> the OECD has 'softly' created a space where they can provide 'local knowledge' that can be compared to the world, creating a commodity for local communities (in the form of indicators) that are seen as 'legitimate', normalized proof that the community has something to trade with employers. (Rutkowski 2015: 696)

In sum, through PISA, the OECD has introduced a global form of governance that extends its reach beyond national policy makers and into national schooling spaces. PISA rankings and reports not only promote the OECD's free market agenda (members and schools pay to participate in PISA and the knowledge the OECD produces is ultimately for purchase) but PISA for schools has re-scaled relations of educational governance and positioned schools within a global space of comparison (Lewis 2017: 282).

Conclusions: Standards, rankings and global governance

Like many other aspects of audit culture, PISA tests profoundly affect organisations and societies. Andreas Schleicher and the OECD insist that PISA is merely a technical and politically neutral instrument for measuring educational attainment to raise standards, yet its ideological prescriptions have brought major policy reforms and sometimes reshaped entire national education systems. As Meyer and Benavot (2013: 9) argue, 'through PISA, the OECD is poised to assume a new institutional role as arbiter of global education governance, simultaneously acting as diagnostician, judge and policy advisor to the world's school systems'. PISA clearly benefits the OECD and some professionals, including statisticians, economists and psychometricians, but its benefits for educationists or even member countries are less clear. Critics highlight PISA's numerous negative effects, particularly how its reductive and synoptic focus on output measurement narrows the purpose of education to an instrument for developing human capital and raising competitiveness in the knowledge economy (Gorur: 2016: 599).

As Sally Merry (2011) noted, numbers and indicators create an ahistorical, decontextualised and 'knowable' world, which may be useful for purposes of governance, but has personal, professional and pedagogical costs. It is questionable whether PISA's restrictive focus on testing, scoring and ranking 'outcomes' and 'student performance' in a limited range of testable (and commodifiable) literacies actually delivers long-term improvements in educational standards. It may boost short-term 'productivity', but as Gorur says: 'Many countries have imposed a series of policy changes only to see their country's scores decline ... Few nations have shown any steady increase even in the limited range of PISA's "outcome" measures' (Gorur 2016: 611).

Some educationalists argue that PISA actually damages education. In an open letter to Andreas Schleicher published in the *Guardian*, 85 leading academics and education experts from around the world wrote that 'the new PISA regime, with its continuous cycle of global testing, harms our children and impoverishes our classrooms, as it inevitably involves more and longer batteries of multiple-choice testing, more scripted "vendor"-made lessons, and less autonomy for teachers' (Andrews et al. 2014). PISA has become an instrument for enabling for-profit companies to gain financially from any deficits – real or imagined – exposed by PISA tests. Gita Steiner-Khamsi and Alexandra Draxler (2018) call this the 'scandalisation' of public education, which is used to justify interventions of direct benefit to the private sector, such as public–private partnerships (see Chapter 5). Other examples are the subcontracting of the test instruments and their administration to private external consortiums and the growth of US and UK companies operating in the emerging market of primary school provision in Africa. As Raewyn Connell (2013) and others argue, measuring, ranking and auditing systems such as PISA encourage the neoliberalisation of schools, placing teachers under performative pressures that further narrow the curriculum and increase workforce insecurity.

PISA exemplifies four features of a new international global governance. First, it propounds a narrow, instrumental definition of education as the key to human capital and economic competitiveness. By drawing ever more aspects of learning, personality and social life into its ideas of human capital, and by quantifying and comparing these domains, it opens them up to policy intervention (Lingard and Sellar 2016: 363, 365). Second, it creates a new way of 'knowing' education through its focus on outcomes assessed through a new comparative method. As Carvalho (2014: 61–2) observes, the OECD's 'imagination of a common educational model for an imagined knowledge society' has enabled it to become the creator, purveyor and legitimator of ideas which are indispensable for knowing and governing. Third, its translation of this way of knowing into methods for designing tests and developing statistical analyses helps to constitute the globe as a commensurate space of measurement (Lingard and Sellar 2016: 362). OECD results and rankings decontextualise education systems and make them legible for governing as part of a global education policy field. Fourth, like UNESCO, the World Bank and the WEF, the OECD creates an international 'epistemic community' around itself through the involvement of wide networks of experts, researchers, consultancies, think tanks, national politicians, civil servants, education administrators, teachers and the media. Their involvement in a continual flow of collaborative activities and common procedures forges a sense of membership and belonging. Through such supranational deliberation, the OECD shapes the values, norms and procedures of this global network, exercising soft power through mutual surveillance, shocking and shaming those ranked low and lionising those 'reference societies' that come out on top. These four features illustrate how indicators and rankings operate as a form of soft power and global governance, and how the organisations that produce them create markets for their own products and services.

International organisations like OECD, THE, Transparency International and the WEF have much in common: all bear testimony to the entrepreneurial skill and vision of one charismatic and strategically well-positioned cultural broker; all are built around a capillary network of actors and agencies that are assembled into relatively coherent, albeit unstable, epistemic policy communities through the activities and ingenuity of the organisations themselves. Where they are most successful is in generating new knowledge platforms (like PISA) that provide the basis for international governance through standard setting and mutual surveillance. As Carvalho says, PISA comparative data enables policy makers to:

> conduct themselves rationally; learn about the place of each educational system in the worldwide competitive space; identify their country's relative position *vis-à-vis* the 'knowledge society' ... and, consequently, to make their educational systems move to the (physical and symbolic) time of 'tomorrow's world'. (Carvahlo 2014: 62)

Policy makers also use such comparative data to broker between the national and global scales. As the Danish 'policy laundering' example shows, national governments can use the reputation of an external and seemingly neutral international organisation to make their own policy changes appear unimpeachably impartial and to manage dissent. Conversely, the OECD is increasingly enacting global governance through direct contact with the local, as the evolution of PISA testing in schools in the US shows.

While these international organisations have grown in influence to become powerful actors and global knowledge brokers, their power is ephemeral as they have no formal mandate for what they do. They therefore devote considerable time and effort to activities that will sustain their legitimacy. But herein lies another problem: their lack of any legitimate mandate also means that these organisations are immune from effective democratic control. And since they operate largely at a global level and through the mobilisation of soft-power techniques, they provide few avenues for democratic participation, even from their own stakeholders.

The interesting question is why governments so eagerly and voluntarily submit their countries to these volatile, competitive and narrowly focused ranking systems? And why do they trust that these organisations' indicators and statistics will deliver benefits when, as the PISA story highlights, there is little evidence that they improve education or produce better policy? As we have demonstrated, much of the explanation lies in the operations of discrete power; the seductive allure of belonging to a global epistemic community and of joining the glitterati on the world stage. It also lies in the ability of these organisations to generate new concepts, standards and rankings that map the competencies and performances demanded in their projected 'future world' and, beyond this, to render these things measurable and commensurable so that they can be made to count. The net effect is a form of transnational governance based on mutual surveillance through rankings and league tables, which also generates a coercive pressure to avoid being identified as the school, the government official, the minister or the country that is 'left behind'.

5

Metrics, Managerialism and Market Making: Unlocking Value in Healthcare

PPPs [public–private partnerships] originated as an accounting trick, a way round the government's own constraints on public borrowing. This remains the overwhelming attraction for governments and international institutions. Just as companies like Enron had tried to conceal their true liabilities by moving them 'off-balance-sheet', so governments ... imitate the creative accounting of some companies in the past. (Hall 2015: 7)

Introduction: Getting the Measure of Healthcare

Healthcare is one of the largest areas of government spending in most OECD (Organisation for Economic Co-operation and Development) countries. It is also one of the most audited sectors.* The global health-care industry was estimated to be worth more than US $8.45 trillion in 2018. It consumed nearly 18 per cent of GDP in the US in 2019 and 10 per cent in most other developed countries (Stasha 2022; WHO 2020). In this chapter we examine how publicly funded healthcare became entangled in the spread of audit culture and mired in projects for market making and commercialisation. Few countries better illustrate this assemblage of auditing and marketisation than the UK, where the rise of audit culture is most pronounced and where the meanings and functions of audit have changed several times with shifts in government policy since the 1980s. As we illustrate, one audit procedure can serve multiple functions in the work of professionals, management and governance in a sector. Medical audits initially involved processes to make professionally led improve-ments to medical services, but these improvements were often turned

---

* We would like to thank Safa Shahkhalili for her research assistance for this chapter.

into numerical targets for managing and controlling health services more generally, and then used by government to break up the health sector into units more amenable to privatisation and profit extraction. We examine the audit-driven processes that transformed Britain's health sector, noting how they were widely adopted by other countries and actively promoted by intergovernmental bodies including the G20 and G8 and the World Economic Forum (WEF). They have also been imposed on the Global South by making private sector involvement in public spending projects a condition for World Bank, International Finance Corporation and European Central Bank loans (Hall 2015).

We track this process in England through two parallel developments. The first was from medical audits to clinical governance, and the second was from New Public Management (NPM) to market making and financialisation of public health services. Medical audits started in the 1980s when doctors and health professionals began to develop ways to improve patient outcomes and strengthen the professionalism of medical staff and their workplace interactions. Health professionals initially invited managers into the process in a support role, but a new cadre of centralised managers soon took over these audit initiatives and progressively transformed them into a form of 'clinical governance'. This still involved medical professionals conducting qualitative reviews, but managers used them to judge outcomes against specific external standards of clinical performance and to drive quality improvement and achieve efficiencies. In the second development, starting in the 1990s, government pursued the NPM philosophy of creating pseudo-markets in the public sector by dividing health services into those that 'provided' services and those that 'purchased' them. Audit now took on different meanings and a new role, which was to facilitate the functioning of the internal market by acting as an instrument for measuring and ranking the performance of providers – whether these be hospital units, doctors, or other healthcare professionals. Using new IT systems, hospitals were audited annually and given a Michelin-style rating from 1 to 3 stars based on level of achievements from 9 key targets and 36 indicators across three focus areas – clinical, patient and logistics (Levtzion-Korach and Israeli 2005). Poor providers were named and shamed while successfully performing 'three-star' hospitals were allowed, from 2003, to become 'foundation hospitals', which earned them some 'autonomy' and a reduced audit burden, often called 'light-touch' auditing (Bevan and Hood 2006: 419).

This second development took a further turn in the 1990s with the development of Public Finance Initiatives (PFIs) in health. PFIs, a UK model of PPP, involved private companies financing and building new hospitals and health centres (along with other public infrastructure projects including schools, roads and prisons). The hospital trust then leased the facility for 25–40 years and the private company was not only paid to maintain the facility, but often also to run the service (NAO 2018b: 4). At the end of the contract, the private company owned the facility, and often the public land on which it was built. Initiated by the Conservative government in 1992, PFIs increased massively under New Labour governments from 1997 to 2010. Their attraction was that governments could engage in building or renewing public infrastructure using debt raised by the private sector. Even though the taxpayer ultimately repaid the debt through monthly payments and leasing arrangements, these were treated for accounting purposes as revenue items, not capital expenditure. As they were not counted as public sector debt, borrowing for renewal of public services could be achieved without threatening the nation's credit rating (NAO 2018b: 11, 44). This 'off balance-sheet' way of funding new hospitals gave the government the appearance of fiscal responsibility and avoided the immediate burden of providing capital for these projects, but the costs to the public over the longer term were exorbitant. PFIs opened the door for private corporations to make risk-free profits at taxpayers' expense, a problem that continues to haunt public sector finances across a range of services.

Tracing the development from medical audit to clinical governance, and from NPM to market making and financialisation, we show how audit acquired two very different yet parallel meanings. The first emphasised medical judgement and professional outcomes. The second, based on a proliferation of metrics to meet performance targets and drive down costs, shifted the meaning of audit away from a focus on professional care and towards value-for-money accounting. In the most recent developments, the private capture of publicly funded healthcare has seen this assemblage of metrics, managerialism and market making take an increasingly international turn. Even though the UK's PFI model was widely discredited and eventually abandoned in 2018, it has re-emerged in the form of PPPs and the companies that engage in them operate on an increasingly global scale.

Against this historical background we ask, how have indicators and rankings been mobilised to reshape the health sector and open it up for corporate gain? How has audit been used to hollow out the public sector,

and what effects have PFIs/PPPs had on public health service provision
and governance? We conclude by examining how audit processes drive
privatisation initiatives and dismantle political accountability. In what
follows, we trace the processes by which different auditing systems have
been developed, and the effects this layering of audit technologies has had
on England's National Health Service (NHS).

From Medical Audit to Clinical Governance

Health professionals and clinicians themselves initially pioneered medical
audits with the aim of achieving better quality of care through improved
professional practice. Medical audit was a 'confidential peer-review
process with professional ownership and control of audit' (Buxton 1994:
31–2) – or, as one former director of public health described it, an audit
conducted 'between consenting adults and for medical professionals only'
(personal communication). Initially it was based on doctors reviewing
their case notes, but gradually it was crafted into a nine-step cyclical
process to check if improvements in clinical practice identified in one
round had been acted upon, and whether they had been successful in
making a difference to patient outcomes and care (Buxton 1994: 32).
Doctors soon realised the reviews needed to include the perspectives of
nurses and others to improve patient care and develop a shared language
for collaboration (Humphris and Littlejohns 1995: 221). Medical audits
became more systematic, quantified and formal than traditional ward
rounds and case presentations, with recommendations circulated to all
staff. Later reviews made recommendations to managers about changes
in the organisation of services that would enable improvements to clinical
policy and practice (Shaw and Costain 1989). These medical audits were
typically conducted by enthusiasts on a voluntary basis, although, as they
became more elaborate, even enthusiasts found it harder to sustain the
full cyclical process. Until the end of the 1980s, medical audits – bar a few
top-down national initiatives such as confidential enquiries into maternal
death – were the preserve of the innovators and early adopters.

The government's 1989 white paper *Working for Patients* (Secretaries of State for Health ... 1989) made medical audit the principal means
of assuring the quality of NHS medical care. While ministers, managers
and professional bodies agreed that medical audit should be implemented throughout the UK, they could not agree on who should define
its purpose. The white paper defined audit as 'systematic, critical analysis

of the quality of medical care, including the procedures used for diagnosis and treatment, the use of resources and the resulting outcome for the patient' (Secretaries of State for Health ... 1989). This definition included both medical and managerial considerations, whereas Charles Shaw and David Costain (1989) noted that the main purpose of medical audit was 'clinical, not managerial'. Russell and Wilson (1992: 52) agreed: audit was a rigorous scientific process conducted by senior clinicians to enhance clinical decisions and the quality of care, and they specifically stated that it was not designed for making decisions on resource allocation. However, this 'medical model' of audit was in competition with a more managerial approach and consumer interest groups were also trying to claim a more effective role (Pollitt 1993a).

By the early 1990s, regular audits, as the pathway to best practice, had become not only the new common sense but also compulsory and all doctors were required to engage, including 'laggards'. A medical audit committee was established in each health district to oversee the development of audit in all units within their geographical locality (Humphris and Littlejohns 1995: 210). Making audit universal and compulsory offered managers an opportunity to constrain the behaviour of hospital doctors (Pollitt 1993a). As Berger (1998) noted, audit was used by clinicians against managerialism and by managers against politicians. Some clinical audits remained local and focused on patient care and professional practice, but when audits were managerially commissioned in response to political pressure to 'do something', their values and concerns became very different from those of clinicians.

With this change of status, audits were increasingly called 'clinical audits' rather than 'medical audits', which was the professional enthusiasts' original term. By 1998 the promised harmonious cycle of improvements in health service practice had evidently failed to materialise. An 'Action on Clinical Audit' by the NHS Executive found that management boards gave low priority to clinical audits and they had failed to produce improvements in the activities of those health services under scrutiny (Dixon 1996). As Abi Berger, associate editor of the *British Medical Journal*, noted (1998: 876), this failure crushed two core assumptions: first, 'that good audit always leads to better quality of patient care, and, secondly, that clinicians and managers work well together'. Despite the government's enthusiasm for evidence-based medicine, these inconvenient facts were typically ignored as it absorbed clinical audits into its idea of 'clinical governance'.

According to Bruce Charlton (2001), the term 'clinical governance' derived from corporate governance, particularly arguments outlined in the 1992 Cadbury Report to address the problem of loss of investor confidence resulting from the corporate scandals of the late 1980s. As a form of regulation, clinical governance entailed a shift from outcomes to processes. That is, rather than seeking to exercise quality control over 'outputs', which was the traditional approach to regulation, the focus now became systems and processes. This had the effect of 'liberating "quality enhancement" initiatives from the need to define desirable outcomes and best practice' (Charlton 2001: 2). Managers could now stop worrying about whether they were measuring real-world quality or the vexed debates over what constitutes reliable outcome measures. Instead of developing incremental improvements to professional practice, as in 'medical audit', guidelines on best practice were now turned into written standards and became criteria against which to judge audits (Humphris and Littlejohns 1995: 215). Criticism that guidelines were inadequate ways to synthesise the complexity of clinical practice and the provision of health cut little ice (McKee et al. 2011). All efforts were to focus on obtaining adherence to a standard system of practice for clinical quality assurance 'in which all essential elements can be planned, documented and monitored' (Charlton 2001: 2). While this had the benefit of making managers more aware of clinical issues, and medical audit continued to improve processes and practices aimed at raising standards, the new system also rendered the NHS more amenable to external audit through decontextualised standards and managerial control at a distance. The appeal of clinical governance as a new form of quality assurance was that it offered managers – and government – a powerful mechanism for external control over clinical practice in the NHS. This move towards regulating *systems* rather than outcomes, as Charlton noted, made possible the vast expansion of the kind of at-a-distance auditing that Michael Power (1997) famously captured in his book *The Audit Society*.

Market Making in the NHS

The shift from medical to clinical governance developed in parallel with ideas for creating a healthcare market. These two projects later came together when the national clinical audit programme took on new and greater roles in the construction of a 'managed-market' system. Measures to create a healthcare market and instil an 'enterprise culture' within the public sector started in the 1990s. The NHS and Community Care Act created a spilt between purchasers and providers of health care in an attempt to foster a competitive internal market that would achieve cost-effectiveness and managerial efficiency (House of Commons 1990). Quality would be assured by purchasers restricting contracts to only those providers whose services were shown to be clinically effective (Humphris and Littlejohns 1995: 207).

The Thatcher government began to create internal markets throughout the public sector. The evolution of a managed market in healthcare can be traced to 1988, when nurses in Britain's NHS took unprecedented industrial action to demand more money, not just for themselves but also for the underfunded NHS. Their demands were mostly ignored, but their action brought the state of nursing and the NHS to the attention of the media and the nation (Hayward and Fee 1992). An open letter to the prime minister by the presidents of three of the Royal Colleges of Medicine declared that the NHS was in crisis. Mrs Thatcher responded by setting up a secret committee whose solution was to adopt a proposal by US management consultant Alain Enthoven to create a purchaser–provider split (Leys 2001: 170). The internal market was quickly introduced 'without any formal public debate or, indeed any electoral mandate' (Leys 2001: 171). In fact, it was not a market but a 'shadow market' of seemingly decentralised units tightly controlled from the centre by directives to the health authorities and a stream of so-called 'guidelines'.

Whereas district health authorities (DHAs) had previously held the budget for healthcare and managed hospital and community health services in an integrated system, the 1990 NHS and Community Care Act required DHAs to become 'purchasers' of services for the population they served from 'providers'. Larger practices of family doctors (GPs) could also become purchasers (called 'GP fundholders') and choose which hospital services to purchase for their patients, and how to spend their budget on practice expenses and patients' medication. The 'providers' were to compete for contracts from the DHAs and GP fundholders (Ham 2009: 39–41). Hospitals and other providers could become self-governing 'NHS trusts', which assumed responsibility for the ownership and running of facilities previously managed by the health authorities. They would be self-financing and generate revenue by competing for patients and gaining contracts from purchasers, selling hospital services to private patients, offering faster access, more comfortable and better-staffed rooms, and providing better food than that given to 'ordinary' patients. They could also sell property, borrow funds from the public or private sectors and employ staff on their own terms (Clatworthy et al. 2003: 1402).

NHS trusts were officially classified as 'public corporations' or 'market units controlled by government' (Price et al. 2011: 465). They were called 'quasi-corporate' and 'self-governing' because their appointed boards of directors were responsible for determining the trust's strategic direction, execution of policies, effective financial control and value for money (Clatworthy et al. 2003) – although this devolution of responsibility was constrained by central guidance from the Department of Health (Ham 2009: 43). In England and Wales the conversion of hospitals into trusts increased from 51 in 1991 to 459 by 1997 (Ham 2009: 43) and GP fundholders grew in number from 306 in 1991 to 1,200 in 1996 (Ham 2009: 41). The government pushed through this major NHS reorganisation with such speed that health policy experts warned of 'gaps in the government's thinking' and claimed the proposals lacked coherence (Ham 2009: 42). DHA managers, NHS trusts and GP fundholders were left to negotiate locally 'on the hoof' over the meaning and implementation of purchaser and provider relations. As a result, 'the internal market became a *managed* market in which competition and planning went hand in hand' (Ham 2009: 43). An analysis of the impact of the reforms on the quality of care showed that hospitals in competitive areas had poorer outcomes than those in areas with little or no competition, and a systematic review of the reforms in terms of efficiency, equity, quality, choice, responsiveness and accountability could detect little change – either positive or negative (Ham 2009: 44–5).

The purchaser–provider model was adjusted in a stream of further NHS reorganisations under Conservative governments. New Labour had opposed this model in opposition but once in office in 1997, it embraced the separation between 'planning and provision' (Secretary of State for Health 1997: 12). It also combined the devolution of responsibilities with centralised measures for monitoring and accountability against national frameworks and performance standards (Ham 2009: 52–3). The reforms to the NHS continued, with a 2001 white paper called *Shifting the Balance of Power*. This sought to empower frontline staff to develop 'a more patient-centred service' (NHS 2001: 3), however, it failed to redress the power imbalance between purchasers and providers. Multiple purchasers responsible for small populations had neither the power nor skills to exert influence over providers. GPs fundholders had evolved into 481 primary care groups (PCGs) in 1999. Now all doctors and community nurses were to belong to primary care trusts (PCTs) so that staff with the closest contact with patients could commission the provision of services for the population they served (Ham 2009: 61). They were to control over 75 per cent of the NHS budget. NHS trusts continued to run hospitals, mental health and other services, and to provide services specified in agreements with the PCTs. Initially, the highest-rated NHS trusts – and gradually all of them – were expected to become NHS foundation trusts. Parliament established them as a special type of competing, non-profit, 'public benefit corporation' independent of government (Price et al. 2011: 463). No longer controlled by the Department of Health, they were intended to involve local communities, staff and other stakeholders in the management of services – even though there was no requirement for members to be representative of the local population or accountable to them (Pollock 2004: 72).

Prioritising patient choice through a plurality of provision was elaborated further in *Delivering the NHS Plan* (Secretary of State for Health 2002). Through a system of paying hospitals by results, money was to follow patients to providers (Ham 2009: 63–4). Market competition was moderated by major increases to the health budget, using fixed tariffs to allocate payments, and creating a new Commission of Healthcare Audit and Inspection to monitor the quality of performance through a framework of national standards. NHS foundation trusts were moved closer to a marketised system. They were public benefit corporations, to be run as non-profit, but nevertheless commercial concerns. Their assets ceased to belong to the state. They were free to set their own pay scales, retain operating surpluses, borrow on private markets, enter into contracts with private providers, and establish private companies and joint ventures (Ham 2009: 212; Pollock 2004: 71). They could not charge fees to NHS patients or increase the proportion of their income from private fees. But as Pollock notes, their 'freedom to enter into contracts with private sector companies means that all the things they are themselves prohibited from doing may be done with these joint ventures' (Pollock 2004: 72). A joint venture could charge fees, make profits, and distribute them to shareholders. It could also finance private loans out of NHS revenues and the sale of any assets would boost the balance sheets of the foundation trust and not

go back to the NHS (Pollock 2004: 72). The first NHS foundation trusts
were established in 2004 and there were 115 by 2009.

Private Finance Initiatives: Refashioning Hospitals for the Market

Running alongside the development of hospital trusts and NHS foundation
trusts, PFIs were a radical new way to finance hospital building projects
using private capital. The UK was one of the first countries to develop PFIs
and, from the late 1990s, the New Labour government expanded them
across all areas of public spending, including education, roads, prisons and
the military. NHS hospitals were the most publicised examples (Pollock
2004: 53). A PFI is a contract between a government body and a private
company to 'Design, Build, Finance and Operate' a public service which
is then paid for over several years either directly by leasing the building
to the public body or through charges to users (HM Treasury 2019). This
joint venture model was introduced to deliver public sector projects more
quickly, efficiently and to achieve better value for money. Importantly, the
idea was that public and private partners would share risk, and private
sector capital and expertise would relieve pressure on public finances,
which were often constrained by neoliberal fiscal limits on government
borrowing. Accounting rules allowed PFIs to be treated as private borrowing, not government borrowing and therefore be kept off the balance
sheet. This gave the impression of prudent financial management, but it
also collapsed the boundaries between public and market provision.

The PFI was developed in the 1990s and appealed to the Conservative
government as it offered yet another form of privatisation that allowed
companies to profit from public expenditure while public services were
required to provide profitable market opportunities. As David Hall (2015:
8) wrote, '[f]or the private companies involved – the banks, the builders
and the service companies – PFIs represent an extremely attractive opportunity. A single contract gives them a flow of income for 25 years or more
– usually underwritten to a great extent by the government itself.'

Under the PFI, a Special Purpose Vehicle (SPV) – usually a consortium of construction firms, companies managing the facilities, banks and
investment firms – is set up to build a new hospital and then operate it.
The SPV is a subsidiary of the parent companies designed to 'securitize
debt so that investors can be assured of repayment' (Hayes 2021). At the
same time, it is created as a separate company with its own balance sheet
so as to isolate the parent companies from risks and negative financial

impacts of failure. The consortium raises money to build a hospital by borrowing and issuing bonds and shares and then leases it to the hospital trust and receives a service fee for running it for the next 25–40 years. The Labour government in 1997 vastly increased the number of PFI projects. Its reasons for doing so were primarily because Tony Blair, eager to convince the City of London and sceptical voters that Labour could be trusted with the public purse, had promised to keep within the spending plans of the outgoing Conservative government for at least two years. Public buildings had been allowed to deteriorate through years of Conservative government cutbacks, yet the Treasury was prohibited from borrowing to rebuild hospitals and other public infrastructure because this would add to the public debt which, in turn, risked the UK's credit rating and market confidence in the pound.

To keep capital spending off the balance sheet (a policy also shaped by Chancellor Gordon Brown's strategy of shadowing the European Union's (EU) Maastricht Treaty's 'euro convergence criteria', which required strict limits on public debt and spending), the government made PFI a compulsory element of capital investment. As the House of Commons' Public Accounts Committee (PAC) later noted, under New Labour, PFI became 'the only game in town' (House of Commons 2011a: 7). The theory was that PFI would transfer the risk of capital investment and building procurement to the private sector, but these claims about risk transfer were greatly exaggerated. Ironically, when consortia raise money for PFI projects the credit rating agencies award them 'AAA ratings' because their long-term contract – paid from (and guaranteed by) public taxes – is correctly judged to incur very low risk. The public sector had been heavily criticised by Conservative politicians and the media for its alleged inability to deliver large-scale projects on time and within budget. Bringing in private sector management expertise, they claimed, would also provide better value for money. Trusts were therefore obliged to put hospital projects out to tender. Initially, PFIs were also attractive to hospital trusts because they had been required to pay 6 per cent per annum on their capital assets as part of a government-enforced efficiency drive to ensure the NHS used its capital assets wisely (Pollock 2004: 55). The advantage to the trust was that they would not start paying this 6 per cent to the government until the building was complete; only then would they pay an annual charge to the SPV to cover its borrowing costs, and for leasing the building and running the facility. However, the first wave of PFIs found these annual payments to be two to three times higher than the previous 6 per cent capital charge.

Moreover, at the end of the 25- or 40-year contract, it was the SPV not the hospital trust who owned the building. As Pollock summed it up;

> the public would still be paying for the hospitals, but payment would be deferred, like hire purchase (but minus the purchase, since when a PFI hospital contract comes to an end the land and building will in most cases still belong to the private owners, not the NHS). (Pollock 2004: 53)

Although New Labour's manifesto had pledged to 'end the internal market', its policies for creating GP primary health care trusts, foundation hospitals and PFIs actually intensified the growth of the market state and PFIs played a key role in this process.

Britain's First PFI Hospital: The Norfolk and Norwich Hospital Trust Saga

The Norfolk and Norwich University Hospital in eastern England was the earliest and most important of the NHS PFI projects. The appointment of an ambitious DHA chief executive, combined with a national policy to promote uptake of PFIs and a Labour government eager for new public infrastructural projects that would be off the official balance sheet meant that this became a 'flagship' project. The DHA was instructed to facilitate the policy and, in 1998, the newly created Norfolk and Norwich University NHS Trust drew up a PFI contract with a private sector consortium called Octagon. Under this contract, Octagon was to build the hospital and maintain and manage it for 30 years (House of Commons 2006: 8). The new hospital was built speedily and leased back to the NHS trust in 2001. However, negotiations over the terms of the PFI were confined to a small 'policy implementation network' consisting of senior trust managers, a Treasury civil servant, national civil servants from the Department of Health, and the private sector. There was no input from the local health community. Just two years after the hospital opened, Octagon refinanced the project, increased its borrowings by 53 per cent and accelerated the financial repayments to its investors. Of the £116 million refinancing gain, Octagon kept £82 million, trebling its internal rate of return from the original contracted 19 per cent to 60 per cent (House of Commons 2006: 13; Greenaway et al. 2007: 717). Octagon was able to reap such enormous profits because the trust had made no provisions to ensure it received a fair share of any refinancing gain. It received just £34 million (29 per cent) of the refinancing gains, paid over the life of the contract rather than upfront, as with Octagon. Accepting the terms of the refinancing deal exposed the trust to new risks and costs while Octagon substantially reduced its risk. Octagon also extended the PFI contract from 34 to 39 years, guaranteeing it five more years of income, while the trust accepted that liabilities for early termination of the contract could increase by up to £257 million.

In its assessment of this 'flagship' PFI project in 2006, the House of Commons PAC gave a damning indictment of the trust for allowing Octagon to exploit the public. 'The opportunity for large refinancing gains on this early PFI deal does not seem to have been seriously considered as part of the original deal negotiations', it wrote, adding:

> Yet, through simply borrowing more, the benefits to Octagon's investors have soared on refinancing to levels which are unacceptable even for an early PFI deal. The Trust further contributed to the inappropriate outcome by accepting that, should it wish to end this contract early, its liabilities could now include all the additional borrowings Octagon used to boost its investors' returns. We would not expect to see another Accounting Officer appearing before this Committee defending what we believe to be the unacceptable face of capitalism in the consortium's dealings with the public sector. (House of Commons 2006: 4)

The PAC held the NHS trust solely responsible for this debacle, yet as George Monbiot (2006) showed, it was government ministers and the Department of Health that had forced the trust to accept the refinancing terms in order to retain private sector interest. Even the National Audit Office (NAO) concluded that the trust could have brokered a better deal had it not been constrained by governmental pressure 'to close a pathfinder deal which had already been assessed as value for money' (NAO 2005: 4).

Consultancy fees added to the NHS trust's expenses. Testimony from Richard Abadie from PwC to the UK parliament's Treasury Select Committee suggests PwC charged US $312,550–$500,000 in advisory fees for a school PFI project and US $625,000–$1,000,000 per hospital (Benjamin and Jones 2017: 3). Despite criticisms that PFIs cost more than using public finance and undermined public services, government continued to promote them. As Hellowell and Pollock (2009) illustrate, capital investment through PFIs may have been 'off balance-sheet' and outside the Public Sector Borrowing Requirement rules, but it still created large public sector cash liabilities. Furthermore, the test of whether PFIs delivered value for money was heavily skewed. The NHS was obliged to construct a theoretical alternative to the use of the PFI (a 'public sector comparator') but in practice, this test usually found that the private sector represented good value for money. Jeremy Colman, former deputy general of the NAO, confirmed flaws in the value-for-money tests, telling parliament's Select Committee on Health that many PFI appraisals suffer from 'spurious precision' while others are 'utter rubbish' and based on 'pseudo-scientific mumbo-jumbo' (Hinchliffe 2002).

By 2011 there were about 920 PPP and PFI projects in the UK with a capital value of £72.3 billion (Whitfield 2011: 9). These had accounted for 10–15 per cent of public sector capital investment since 1996. In the health sector alone, 102 PFI projects with a capital value of £11.5 billion constituted 91.6 per cent of major capital investment in the NHS between 1997 and 2008 (Whitfield 2011: 10). However, after 2009 the number of new PFIs declined, partly because banks had introduced tighter regulations following the 2008 global financial crisis, but mainly because PFIs were generating a massive problem of hidden public debt (Booth 2018). Even the existing PFIs continued to cause concerns. In 2015, the health minister himself acknowledged in parliament that his 'greatest concern is that many of the UK's hospitals now facing huge deficits are seeing their situation made infinitely worse by PFI debt' (J. Hunt 2015). Despite this, there were still 719 operational public sector private finance deals with a capital value of £60 billion in 2018 (Syal 2018). In 2018 the NAO investigated 700 of these projects and found that the cost of privately financed public projects was 40 per cent higher than relying solely on government money. The annual charge for these 719 deals was £10.3 billion in 2016–17 and, as Syal (2018) calculated, 'even if no new deals were entered into, future charges that continue until the 2040s amount to £199 billion ... equivalent to NHS funding for 20 months'. The average profit for health sector PFIs in the period 2003–9 was 66.7 per cent, which far exceeded average profits for all other PFIs (at 50.6 per cent) (Whitfield 2011: 4). An independent report later concluded that while the PFI brought £13 billion of private equity into the NHS, the 'cost to the health service will ultimately total almost £80 billion and, over 20 years since the first of these contracts was signed, the NHS still has payments of £55 billion outstanding' (Thomas 2019: 9). The private consortia's profits came not only from the hospital trusts' payments to manage the hospital, but also from sales of equity in PFI companies, which rose rapidly between 2003 and 2013, largely unaffected by the global financial crisis.

PFIs also failed in their prime purpose of raising the quality of care while achieving efficiencies. The hospital trusts had to find the repayment fees from their operating budgets and were forced to make savings. The only way they could do this was by making the new hospitals smaller, regardless of the health needs of the population they served. As Pollock (2004: 56) observed, the first PFI hospitals had '30% fewer beds than the hospitals they replaced, and budgets and numbers of clinical staff were cut by up to 25%'. As plans for each PFI were driven by financial considerations, this fragmentation seriously undermined the ability of health authorities to plan for the health needs of their area. Critics observed at the time that PFI hospitals had resulted in 'major reductions in the clinical workforce, and service capacity – in direct contradiction of government policy' (Pollock et al. 1999: 179). The once-outstanding effectiveness of the NHS was sacrificed to parsimony and market dogma as bed shortages became more acute, waiting times lengthened and staff turnover increased. Britain began to lag behind comparable countries in survival rates for heart disease, cancer and even infant mortality (Pollock 2004: 54–5). Government responded by reinforcing its national performance targets, pushing hospitals to further direct their scarce resources to whatever that year's targets were.

The Proliferation of Audit: From Accountability to Fragmentation and Privatisation

The point of this convoluted story of continuous reform is that both Conservative and Labour governments tried to work with markets and devolve responsibility for health to local-level providers and private interests while maintaining centralised accountability and regulation over an erstwhile 'national' health service. The result was a proliferation of new agencies and systems designed to measure, monitor, rank and manage the different components in an increasingly fragmented landscape.

The NHS was fractured into 100 or so health authorities, 400 hospital trusts and increasing numbers of 'fundholding' GP practices. These increased from 55 per cent of GPs in 1997 to all GPs in 2002 (Pollock 2004: 44, 138). New auditing mechanisms were needed to reassure professionals and the public that standards would be maintained and costs controlled. From 1993/4, the Department of Health funded the development of 'clinical multi-professional audits', which were to be included in providers' contracts (Humphris and Littlejohns 1995: 211). The 1990 NHS and Community Care Act extended the Audit Commission's remit beyond auditing local government to include NHS trusts. To oversee these, the Audit Commission sometimes appointed its own arm's-length audit agency, the District Audit Service, but by1999/2000 the (then) Big Five audit firms, and notably KPMG and PwC, accounted for about 29 per cent of all NHS trust external audits and their market share was rising (Basioudis and Ellwoodan 2005: 221). A proliferation of agencies with different roles in external auditing and monitoring health services ensued. Sometimes the NAO conducted value-for-money studies on the same topics as the Audit Commission while the NHS Executive set standards for compulsory performance monitoring.

In its 1999 'Modernising Government' initiative, the Labour government created the National Institute for Clinical Excellence (NICE) to define good and cost-effective clinical practice across the NHS and established the Centre for Health Improvement (CHI) to enforce NICE recommendations. In 1999–2000 the NHS National Performance Framework compared local performance against national standards and there was also an Annual Survey of Patient and User Experience of the NHS. By 2000, the line between clinical audits based on professional judgements and external managerial audits had been formally breached: chief executives were given statutory responsibility for the quality of clinical care – and control over clinical resources (Ham 2009: 115). All NHS hospitals and health authorities were subject to measurement against 47 performance indicators ranging from hospital treatment outcomes, to prescribing patterns, cancer registration and dental care (Bowerman et al. 2000: 80). To promote these clinical quality, market-efficiency and value-for-money goals still further, in 2002 the government created a single new body called the Commission for Health Audit and Inspection (CHAI). This took over the work previously done on the NHS by the Audit Commission. The following year the government created an independent regulator to license foundation trusts. Henceforth, this regulator would decide what each trust provided, but would be free from any obligation to provide equal comprehensive health services for all and would not be answerable to the Secretary of State (Ham 2009: 77).

Besides these national systems, a range of local service, accountability and performance agreements (set against various standards, objectives, targets and indicators) were drawn up between the health authorities, primary care groups, NHS trusts and the NHS Executive. Public sector organisations also began to pursue external quality accreditation through schemes inspired by the private sector, such as Charter Marks, Investors in People, ISO 9000/14000, and the European Quality Foundation (EQF)'s 'Business Excellence Model'. Similarly, the Labour government rewarded services that consistently met key performance targets with the award of 'Beacon' status. As Bowerman et al. observed:

> Thus, in an NHS hospital trust ... it is possible to find audits being conducted by the NAO, Audit Commission, internal audit, the Department of Health, quality auditors/certifiers (e.g. such as BSI, ISO and the Health Quality Service in association with the Kings Fund, other internal quality audit teams and clinical/medical audit groups). (Bowerman et al. 2000: 88)*

These systems were all underpinned by self-assessment practices that required staff to engage in continuous monitoring, reviewing and improving performance against external quality standards – all under the banner of clinical governance and in readiness for external audits and inspections. This heavy burden of audit and performance measurement still failed to prevent scandalous malpractice. For example, Dr Stephen Bolsin, an anaesthetist and whistleblower at the Bristol Royal Infirmary, struggled for years to get his hospital trust, the NHS, the Department of Health and the Royal Colleges to investigate failings in paediatric cardiac surgery services. The unit had a dismal record of death and brain damage after surgery since 1991 and a 2001 inquiry found that deaths of 30–35 children under one year of age would probably have been avoided in other NHS units (Kennedy 2001: 4). The inquiry attributed this to organisational confusion, staff shortages, inadequate facilities, poor leadership, lack of accountability, and failures in teamwork, but also found that critical clinical audits had been brushed aside by the clinicians concerned (Kennedy 2001; Bowerman et al. 2000: 84).

This proliferation of auditing was not only ineffective but also expensive. The Audit Commission's annual report for 1998 found that the cost of auditing the NHS and local government over seven months was £50 million, while the value of improvements identified was just £44 million

---

* BSI – British Standards Institution; ISO – International Standards Organization.

(Bowerman et al. 2000: 92). Over the six previous years, audits had identified savings of £520 million, of which £236 million had been realised.
The NAO said the cost of NHS clinical audit between 1989 and 1995 was
£279 million, but neither report explains how these costs and benefits
were calculated (Bowerman et al. 2000: 93). Hood et al. (1999: 30) found
that, over 20 years, the cost of audit, inspection and regulatory activities
had risen three to six times faster than the growth in public expenditure
and had become a £1 billion business employing 20,000 people. Eric
Pickles, the Conservative Secretary of State for Communities and Local
Government, focused on the cost of the Audit Commission and suddenly
announced it would be abolished in 2012 and its audit functions would be
moved to the private audit firms – a move critics described as 'jumping off
a cliff' without saving money (Eaton 2010).

PFIs were extolled as a cost-effective way to improve health services
but, for the ten years when the number of PFIs was growing fastest, there
were no effective checks on their costs to the public. In 2011 the House of
Commons' PAC carried out a major review of the UK's experience of PFIs.
In his evidence to that committee, David Metter, chair of the PPP Forum
and CEO of Innisfree, a PFI company, explained the funding model. The
PFI programme, he noted, then cost £130 billion: £65 billion from the
long-term financial contracts that had been entered into 'by parties acting
in good faith on both sides'; the other £65 billion was service charges and,
he said, there were lots of opportunities for companies to make savings
by changing and re-gearing those contracts (Metter, cited in House
of Commons 2011b: Evidence 8). As Metter explained: 'We look at the
returns that come out of these projects when we are asked to bid for them,
and we have a certain return range that we look for, because we know we
can raise funds to invest on that basis. Currently we need to get about 8%
to 10% … That is the negotiation: that is how PFI developed' (Metter,
cited in House of Commons 2011b: Evidence 9).

Responding to this, PAC member Austin Mitchell summed up the
situation:

> You have got a pretty good racket here, have you not? Here you are with
> contracts and a guaranteed return over 25–30 years, in which you are
> providing services, again, with a guaranteed charging rate. At a time
> when government is examining every public service through a micro-
> scope to see what they can cut and who they can fire, your return rolls
> on, and your money comes in whatever you do: it is guaranteed. You

have purchased that and you are not prepared to share it with anyone else retrospectively. This is an insane situation, isn't it? Here we have manufacturing, which is looking to make a return of base rate plus a couple of percent, not much; you are on a return of base rate plus six to eight percent – quite a high return. Every public service has been examined for cuts, you are not. The efficiency savings you make and any savings from scale you make, go into your back pocket, not into the public purse. That is a pretty good racket. (Mitchell in House of Commons 2011b: Evidence 10)

How was this situation made possible? The NAO only conducted its first serious investigation in 2011, thirteen years after the first hospital PFI. This identified key weaknesses in the way PFIs were negotiated and managed, and a lack of contract management skills and commercial awareness among government negotiators. The Department of Health was criticised for lacking central oversight, failing to optimise its buying power to benefit the public sector, and not obtaining further efficiencies during contract periods of 30 years or more (NAO 2011: 6–9). The PAC also concluded that the Treasury should develop tests on value for money and incentives to ensure buildings are maintained to a high standard over the life of PFI contracts. Perversely, despite the government's fixation with developing systems of audit to deliver value for money and transform the NHS, it had developed no system for assessing the value for money of PFI schemes themselves.

Weakening Accountability and Democracy

Analysts argue that the use of audit to manage healthcare markets was 'messy' and changed the meaning of audit itself, while weakening accountability. Audit traditionally meant independent, external verifications of accounts but was now more like performance measurement – although the Audit Commission had tried to combine audit with inspection to provide more coherent oversight of public services. Bowerman et al. (2000: 96) summed up the situation: 'auditing, inspection and performance monitoring are well entrenched but appear to be muddled, uncoordinated and lacking clear purpose'. The emphasis on clinical audit or self-assessment was also contrary to the traditional independent monitoring function of audit and meant that the Audit Commission's auditors reviewed data collection systems rather than verifying the data itself (Bowerman 1995: 179). As Power put it:

> instead of regulation seeking to penetrate organisational culture from the outside, the image proffered is more of a form of self-control embodied in the quality assurance system extending its visibility beyond the organisation. The externalisation of internal control and the internalisation of external controls are no longer clearly distinguishable. (Power 1997: 62)

Audit's external independence was originally aimed at enhancing public accountability. But the proliferation of disconnected audit bodies now makes it unclear who is the audit client and who is being held accountable. In the private sector, the purpose of audit is to inform the owner or shareholders (the principal) about the probity and efficiency of their agents. But the managed market of the health sector lacks a clear principal–agent relationship (Clatworthy et al. 2003: 1404–5). In the public sector context, is the principal the electorate, the patients, or central government ministers and politicians? To whom does the auditor owe a duty of care? Whose performance do the indicators reflect, and who should be held accountable for any shortcomings? The Audit Commission does not distinguish which indicators applied to managers, councillors, contractors, or central government. Audits were sometimes even conducted under the control of those to be held accountable. For example, the NHS Executive was responsible for gathering data, regulating the audit process, and coordinating performance monitoring and clinical audits:

> Such a degree of involvement questions the independence of public audits as so many are being conducted under the close watch and control of those who are supposedly, ultimately responsible (and accountable) for the use of public funds ... such a structural arrangement gives funding bodies the clear opportunity to play a type of 'buffer' role, wherein they can deny publicity to audit findings or pass the blame for poor standards of public services down the managerial hierarchy. (Bowerman et al. 2000: 88)

The spread of audit also eroded the distinction between politics and management. Replacing political debate with technical managerialism weakened the accountability of politicians and meant that consumers and citizens could only receive audit information, not act to hold anyone to account (Bowerman 1995:189). The Audit Commission's role was initially to use audit as a tool for changing management culture, but when performance targets became part of managers' incentive structure, managers focused on reporting acceptable performance rather than changing substantive activity in their organisation. Objectives and reported performance may be distorted as this also 'encourages managers to manipulate information systems and to redefine organisational politics' (Gray and Jenkins 1993). The government's instruments of choice for driving the managed market – performance targets, league tables and star ratings – were open to gaming and, as the Audit Commission found, chief executives were manipulating the figures (Ham 2009: 117).

Profiting from Failure: The International Spread of PFIs and PPPs

The companies involved in PFIs began to operate on a global scale. Investors from other parts of the world sought to invest in the UK, as the frontrunner, and Europe. For example, the Ramsay Group, Australia's largest private hospital operator, established in 1964, began expanding into the UK and France in 2010. It bought Capio UK's portfolio of hospitals and in France, acquired Proclif, a leading private hospital operator (8 hospitals, 1,000 beds) and Générale de santé, France's largest private hospital group (Lethbridge 2015: 18). Other investors in the UK hospitals and health services came from Africa (Netcare), Singapore (Parkway Holdings) and Eastern Europe (Medicover, Euromedic International) (Lethbridge 2015: 16). In April 2022, US private equity group KKR offered to buy Ramsay Health Care for US $14.9 billion (£11.8 billion) (Fernyhough 2022).

One of the largest PFI projects was the £1.45 billion investment in 2010 to build the Nya Karolinska Solna (NKS) hospital in Sweden. This was to be one of the world's most advanced and specialised hospitals with a 'patient-centred' focus on quality and clinical outcomes. Instead, it became known as the most expensive hospital ever built. The Swedish government, on the recommendation of professional accountancy firms PwC and Ernst & Young, adopted the UK's NHS PFI model. They were guided by the belief that this would bring three potential benefits: 'certainty of costs, certainty to deliver, and better value' (Eurodad 2018: 17). Despite high initial interest, the tender was awarded without any competition to the only bidder; a consortium consisting of a big Swedish construction company and a UK investment firm called Swedish Hospital

Partners (SHP), which already managed the PFI for Barts Trust's Royal London Hospital.

The new hospital was supposed to open in December 2015, but a series of technical, financial and logistical problems meant that by 2018 it was still not fully operational. The project's spiralling costs were only fully exposed in 2015 by journalists at the *Svenska Dagbladet* newspaper. These stood at Kr 22.8 billion (£1.91 billion) in 2018, and by 2040 it is estimated that it will have cost Swedish taxpayers a staggering Kr 61.4 billion (£4.96 billion) (Paterlini 2018). The NKS was criticised for its controversial 'patient first' model, which focuses on patient groups arranged by themes and coordinated by a 'patient flow manager'. It became mired in scandal after appointing Paolo Macchiarini, the charismatic thoracic surgeon whose novel transplant procedures using synthetic windpipes resulted in a police investigation for manslaughter and a protracted enquiry into breaches of professional ethics (*Nature* 2016: 137). Sweden's national media have reported other major issues with the project, including an extraordinarily large bill of Kr 257 million (£20.8 million) over six years from US management consulting company Boston Consulting Group (BCG). There have also been allegations of collusion between the executive board of the hospital and BCG. In April 2018, the New Karolinska board members resigned their seats (Paterlini 2018). Meanwhile the private consortium has made a significant profit. As with UK PFIs, the reasons for the failures are difficult to discern: a European Commission report noted that 'no contract details are available or published' because this information is classified as 'commercially sensitive' (Eurodad 2018: 17).

Significantly, the largest profits from PFIs came not from building or running a hospital but from selling the PFI's SPV on the international financial markets. This financialisation of health services took off in the period from 2000 to 2004. Compared to average operating profits in construction companies of 1.5 per cent between 2003 and 2009, the average profit from the sale of equity and secondary funds in PFIs was 50.6 per cent (Whitfield 2011: 4). Health was the sector with the highest average profits at a staggering 66.7 per cent (2011: 16). In his analysis of the wider PPP landscape, Dexter Whitfield traced 240 PPP sales of equity and secondary funds between 1998 and 2010, involving 1,229 PPP projects whose transactions had an estimated value of £10.0 billion (2011: 14). This included 166 health projects covering hospitals and health centres (2011: 11). For example, through four equity transactions, the HSBC bank's infrastructure fund raised its stake in Barnet Hospital from 30 per cent to 100 per cent. As with 91 other PPP projects, this HSBC infrastructure fund was registered in an offshore tax haven (Whitfield 2011: 12). In the city of Newcastle, equity in seven large PPPs was sold from 2006 to 2011, and in three cases the equity was owned by infrastructure funds registered in tax havens. These companies not only made huge profits from their investments in the UK public sector, they also avoided paying taxes that might have funded public services. Government did not quantify this loss of public funding because, as Whitfield's database of PFI/PPP equity transactions showed, 'the sale of [PPP] equity is significantly higher than the sales identified in HM Treasury PFI equity database and estimated by the National Audit Office' (2011: 4).

Despite these large profits from financialising the health sector, there are numerous cases where governments have tried to make PFI/PPPs more attractive to the private investors by subsidising their operational costs. Governments have also had to buy out failed PFIs and return hospitals and other services to the public sector. In 2012, the Department of Health provided a £1.5 billion bailout fund to NHS trusts with large PFI projects because, according to the NAO, their plans were unviable without central support (Whitfield 2017a: 5). Whitfield estimated that NHS trusts were likely to require a further £1.5 billion in additional support for PFI projects by 2037. Over 20 years from the late 1990s, 74 PFI/PPP projects in the UK – one-third of contracts by capital value – were terminated, bought out, or experienced major problems. This was a much higher failure rate than World Bank-funded PFI projects in developing countries (Whitfield 2017a: 7, 23). However, in the UK there is a lack of transparency over the public costs of failure as the Treasury and the Scottish government eliminate data about bought-out and terminated PFI projects from their statistics. Sixteen failed PFI/PPP projects had cost £114.3 million, and Whitfield estimated that over 20 years, the public cost of buyouts, bailouts, terminations and major problem contracts was £27.9 billion (Whitfield 2017a: 5–7, 25).

A notorious example of the consequences of PFI/PPP failure for public finances comes from a town in Valencia, in Spain which has given its name to the 'Alzira model'. The regional government created a company (Ribera Salud) to bid for the contract to design, build, finance, operate and manage a new hospital, which opened in 1999. Ribera Salud was owned by two regional banks and other consortium members included the insurance company Adeslas and two building firms (Sevillana et al. 2012). As Acerete et al. (2012) show, politicians dominate the governing boards of Spanish regional banks, and this ensured favourable terms for Ribera

Salud. The banks provided 25 per cent of the equity capital, whereas the usual rate is 1–5 per cent, and provided debt at preferential rates to the private sector partner. Even with such favourable treatment, the contract was still unviable. This led to a government bailout, compensation for lost profits, and a new 15-year contract in 2003, under which the private contractor received a larger fixed annual sum per local inhabitant (capitation) from the regional government. The new contract extended the PPP's scope to include the primary care of the surrounding area, giving Ribera Salud control of patient referrals and demand on services. The new model was deemed significantly more successful and financially viable because, in PwC's words, it 'enabled the private partner to better manage costs through service integration, better referrals and strategies to manage the upstream health of the population' (PwC 2018: 40). However, following the 2008 global financial crisis, Ribera Salud's profits fell, leaving the Valencian government again at risk of having to bail out the company. The collapse of the two regional banks in 2011 meant Ribera Salud had to put itself up for sale. In April 2018, when the administrative concession was expected to be renewed, Valencia's health authority, led by a new regional administration, decided to terminate the concession and revert to direct public provision (Comendeiro-Maaløe et al. 2019: 408). As Acerete et al. argue (2012), instead of the PPP transferring risk from the public to the private sectors, political interests were locked in to the viability of the regional savings banks and making the model a success. They conclude, 'the political implications should not be overlooked as the political risks of being unable to let the contract fail has [sic] meant additional cost to government' (Acerete et al. 2012: 314).

As these examples show, these PFI and PPP models signally failed to deliver their promise of certainty of costs, effective delivery, and better value for taxpayers. They did, however, generate large profits for some consortia, external consultants, and the advisory arms of the Big Four. Notwithstanding the lack of clarity regarding their benefits and costs, PFIs/PPPs have been promoted globally as models for funding public projects and increasing the efficiency and quality of healthcare services.

Going Global: PPPs in the Developing World

Led by the World Bank and supported by European banks and the International Monetary Fund (IMF), the 1990s saw the development of a remarkable network of international organisations, corporations, national government and philanthropies advocating for PPPs on a global scale. These used forums like the G20, G8 and WEF to promote their uptake. As Hall (2015: 13) notes, 'this promotion takes two forms: a marketing and propaganda campaign on a global scale; and the use of public money to subsidise the private borrowing of PPPs'. Governments and the EU also created special units to provide subsidised loans and guarantees to support PPPs. For example, David Cameron's Conservative government established a permanent centre to promote PFI projects around the world, staffed mainly by private sector executives, inside the Treasury itself. The UK government claimed that 'through partnership with the private sector, PPPs enable the delivery of efficient, cost-effective and measurable public services within modern facilities whilst minimising the financial risk' (UK Government 2013). A steady stream of publications from legal firms and external consultants, including McKinsey and PwC, provided further legitimacy and impetus. As a result of this enthusiastic proselytising, the PFI model has been adopted by several countries in the Global South.

The push for PPPs in public health was led by the World Bank, which approved 78 health facilities between 2004 and 2016 (Lister 2018: 272). This dominance was achieved by displacing the World Health Organization's (WHO) 'horizontal', holistic and coordinated sector-wide approach to the health of a population focused on distributive justice and the socioeconomic determinants of health inequalities. By contrast, the World Bank promoted a vertical, 'results-based financial management' approach (Lethbridge 2015: 4) and advanced public–private partnerships. By the late 1990s, the WHO had aligned itself with the World Bank's agenda and, from 1998, 10 new global health partnerships were established annually, with 100 in operation by the mid-2000s. These involved businesses concerned with health infrastructure and delivery systems, drug companies and philanthropic organisations. For example, by 2007 spending by the Bill and Melinda Gates Foundation roughly matched that of the WHO (Ruckert and Labonté 2014: 1601).

Many of these PPPs adopted a vertical approach to intervention that was effective within its narrow focus but was not sustainable or coordinated with other donors or local health providers. For example, 75 per cent of PPP funding targeted specific infectious diseases that yield auditable results, even though these are not major causes of ill health in most of the world. The major killers, like childhood diarrhoea, are the outcome of poverty and other less auditable social factors (Ruckert and Labonté

2014: 1604). PPPs had some positive effects, including the development of 50 vaccines and 25 drugs for diseases affecting impoverished populations (2014: 1602). However, many involved partnerships, for example between Coca-Cola and the Bill and Melissa Gates Foundation, Coca-Cola and Save the Children, Cadbury and UNICEF (the UN Children's Fund), and Hershey and the American Cancer Society (Ruckert and Labonté 2014: 1606). This has given private corporations whose products are linked to the rapid increase worldwide in obesity and diabetes, an opportunity to 'white-coat' their activities in ways reminiscent of the tobacco industry.

The Big Four also played a key role in encouraging the private health care providers in North America and Europe to expand their PPP operations. As a report by Deloitte argued, the global healthcare market was projected to exceed US $8.5 trillion by 2020. 'Global healthcare spending outside the US is expected to grow at more than twice the rate of the US – 8.7 percent by 2022 compared to only 4 percent within the US' (Deloitte 2020). PwC made similar predictions that global spending on health would increase by 65 per cent from 2010 to 2020, and that a growing number of middle- to lower-income countries would be seeking healthcare PPP projects (PwC 2018: 7, 10). To take advantage of these emerging markets, the international accountancy firms offered their services to help North American and European operators create strategic partnerships and adapt their business models to local healthcare markets in Asia, Africa and South America. PwC identified three models of healthcare PPPs: (1) an infrastructure-based model (similar to the UK's PFI) for building hospitals and other healthcare facilities; (2) a discrete clinical services model, which focuses on a specific healthcare service (like dialysis); and (3) an integrated PPP model which provides a comprehensive package to finance, design, construct, manage and deliver health services to a whole area (PwC 2018: 12). They note that such integrated PPPs require governmental capacity to create and monitor complex agreements with private consortium partners, yet they do not discuss how feasible this is for developing countries (PwC 2018: 30).

Regardless of the problems with PPPs in the Global North, they have been extolled by PwC and others as success stories to be copied by developing countries (PwC 2010: 20). Lesotho is the most cited example of a country that has adopted the integrated PPP model. It also serves as a warning about the dangers and costs of PPPs (Hall 2015; Lister 2018). The Queen Mamohato Memorial Hospital was built to replace Lesotho's old main public hospital under an integrated PPP, the first of its kind in a low-income country. It is the country's main teaching hospital for both doctors and nurses. It is owned by the private South African healthcare company Netcare, which employs over 21,000 staff and in 2006 bought a controlling stake in General Healthcare Group, the UK's largest private hospital group with 54 hospitals across the UK. This PPP covered the hospital's building and running, its clinical services and three filter clinics in the surrounding area. Even though the World Bank questioned the proposal's cost-effectiveness and alternative public financing options were available, the International Finance Corporation (IFC) advised the Lesotho government to adopt the PPP and gave a US $6.25 million grant for the project. Opened in 2011, the hospital encountered major financial problems from its first year of operation. For its first annual charge, the Losotho government had to pay US $32.6 million, almost double the annual budget of the old hospital. Persistently understaffed, the hospital failed to recruit enough doctors and has paid its staff less than their former salaries. 'The level of services was deliberately reduced, including the exclusion of some services, as well as a cut in the number of beds, and limits on the number of patients' (Hall 2015: 24). In addition, the Lesotho Ministry of Health had to pay for patient referrals to Netcare's South African hospitals, which increased by 61 per cent from 2007 to 2012 (Lister 2018: 277). While services declined and costs increased, shareholders expected the PPP to generate a 25 per cent rate of return on equity and a total projected cash income 7.6 times higher than their original investment (Marriott 2014: 2).

The Queen Mamohato hospital PPP was meant to be the IFC's flagship model to be replicated across the continent. Instead, as an Oxfam study concluded:

> the Ministry of Health in one of the poorest and most unequal countries in the world is locked into an 18-year contract that is already using more than half of its health budget (51 per cent), while providing high returns (25 per cent) to the private partner. This is a dangerous diversion of scarce public funds from primary healthcare services in rural areas, where three-quarters of the population live. (Marriott 2014: 1)

That 'dangerous diversion' continues as the hospital serves only 16 per cent of the Lesotho population but consumes more than half the government's annual health budget (Lister 2018: 278). It is costing so much that the government believes it will be more cost-effective to build a brand-new district hospital in the capital to cater for excess patients rather than pay the private partner to treat them (Marriott 2014: 2). In contrast to the waste and exploitation caused by the global spread of PPPs, Oxfam International's (2014) research highlighted the powerful role that free, universal and equitable public health services can play in reducing inequality in rich and poor countries alike.

Conclusions: The Shift from Audit to Privatisation and its Implications

This chapter asked: how has audit been used to reshape the health sector, and how have indicators and rankings been mobilised to marketise a public service for corporate gain? We traced the metamorphosis of audit from locally embedded processes by health professionals to improve their own practices and patient outcomes to a set of external, disembedded, managerial techniques for controlling professionals and health institutions. From here, audit became a device to help lay the ground for transferring public services to the private sector through systems of measurement, ranking, star ratings, quantification, league tables and discourses of quality assurance, excellence, efficiency, best practice and value for money. The next step was to use these instruments to facilitate the ingress of private money and interests into the public sector, and the PFIs and PPPs, with their Special Purpose Vehicles, provided the perfect tool for achieving these goals. Selling these SPVs in the international financial markets massively increased the profit margins from PPPs.

Although little evidence was offered to show that PFIs/PPPs provided better services at lower costs, the momentum and enthusiasm created by their advocates – an increasingly self-sustaining and collusive network of politicians, consultants, and finance industry experts – resulted in the export of PPPs to other European countries and to the Global South.

Documents produced by the leading proponents of PPPs convey the excitement of unlocking healthcare spending for private sector capture. As a 2020 Deloitte report proclaims, 'Healthcare is big business – really big – and it touches every human life, often in very profound ways … There has never been a better time to look beyond the US border for opportunities.' PwC echoes this evangelical tone. Its 2010 report – subtitled 'the (r)evolutions in healthcare' – advises prospective clients not to invest in building infrastructure (which accounts for only 5 per cent of government spending), but to venture across the new frontier into health service provision, which they estimate would account for 95 per cent of government spending and over US \$68.1 trillion by 2020 (PwC

2010: 5). While donors claim that PPPs are a way of 'leveraging' private finance into supporting public projects, the greatest flows are exactly the other way around. Private companies and private equity funds use a small amount of their own capital as equity and manage to leverage extra equity investment from international public donors and financial institutions, as well as raising debt that is either guaranteed by the public sector, or even provided directly as a loan by government (Hall 2015: 22). Thus, contrary to claims about a legitimate dividend for shouldering risk, many of these private investors are not even risking their own capital.

If the subject of audit is less evident or visible in the latter phases of our account, it is because PFIs/PPPs themselves have eluded public scrutiny and audit. Even PwC acknowledges this:

> Across healthcare PPPs little work has been done to identify or establish clear metrics to measure clinical performance and impact. Additionally, few projects include formal project evaluation as part of the contract. The challenge of evaluating healthcare PPP projects is further compounded by a general lack of published data on past PPP projects. (PwC 2018: 43)

PwC goes on to lament the limited number of baseline studies, and the lack of data collection and accessible benchmark data. However, this data deficit is no accident or oversight but rather the result of politically convenient myopia and the deliberate exclusion of failed PPP projects from national statistics. Pollock illustrates this in her book *NHS PLC*. The management consultancy named 'Dr Foster', in a contract with the Department of Health, produced a *Good Hospital Guide* with league tables for hospital performance and mortality (or 'death charts'). These were shown to be based on statistically invalid data and contained spurious measures but were nevertheless used to promote privatisation (Pollock 2004: 117, 202).

This lack of transparency and misuse of evidence undermines accountability and democracy. As noted earlier, even if citizens do see the results of audits of public healthcare bodies, it is seldom clear who is responsible for failures. This makes it difficult to hold anyone to account. Public sector audits are meant to generate accountability but in reality, they have the opposite effect. The lack of auditing of PPPs and private companies creates further opacity. When the original parties to a PPP sell their equity or SPV to international financiers, many of whom operate from offshore tax havens, ownership and accountability become even more obscure. With each international transaction the chain of accountability is extended and weakened. The sale of equity, as Whitfield observes:

> is not subject to democratic accountability and public bodies have no control over which PPP assets are sold, when or who acquires them. The scale of profiteering invalidates the original value for money assessment. Most PPP projects would not have proceeded had this been taken into account. (Whitfield 2017b: 8)

In this account of healthcare reform, audit changed from providing measures of service quality to efficiency, then privatisation and financialisation. In the process, what constitutes 'value' shifted from the concerns of highly skilled medical professionals to the pecuniary interests of investors, consultancies and the international agencies who brokered these PPPs.

6

Reforming Higher Education: The Kafkaesque Pursuit of 'World-class' Status

'I see you've misunderstood me', said the supervisor who was already at the door. 'It's true that you're under arrest, but that shouldn't stop you from carrying out your job. And there shouldn't be anything to stop you carrying on with your usual life.' (Kafka, *The Trial*, 2009: 11)

The previous chapters examined the new ways that indicators and rankings are used in the governance and reform of public sector organisations and the new normative order of economic efficiency and financial calculation that these are based upon. We showed how one instrument – a clinical audit or a PISA score – can be used to generate competition, reorganise an entire sector, become a tool for internal management and control, and re-frame what 'counts' in professional practice and individual behaviour. While a calculative technology can work across multiple scales to bring individuals and organisations into alignment with the logic of the market and neoliberal governance, it can also produce perverse effects. This chapter explores another site – higher education – where the rationality of accounting and the spread of audit culture has both transformed an entire sector and produced effects contrary to its very purpose. Since the 1980s, universities have been subjected to a seemingly continuous process of reform designed to make them more economic, efficient and effective, according to yardsticks defined by governments and university managers. The pursuit of 'excellence', 'international standing' and 'world-class' status have become key drivers in the world of academia and are fuelling what Hazelkorn (2008) terms a 'rankings arms race'. These competitive rankings are profoundly changing the mission and meaning of the public university, and the culture of academia itself. These trends can be best analysed and understood as a product of audit culture and the Kafkaesque worlds it often creates. Drawing on ethnographic examples especially from the UK, we ask: How are higher education institutions being reconfigured by these new disciplinary regimes of audit? How are indicators of 'world-class' ranking and performance changing institutional behaviour and transforming academic subjectivities?

The Kafkaesque World of the UK University

In 2014, Dame Marina Warner (DBE, FRSL, FBA), professor of English and celebrated novelist, suddenly left her post at Essex University. Writing in the *London Review of Books*, she recounted the events leading to her resignation, starting with a meeting chaired by the vice chancellor, Anthony Forster:

> The Senate had just approved new criteria for promotion. Most of the candidates under review had written their submissions before the new criteria were drawn up, yet these were invoked as reasons for rejection. As in Kafka's famous fable, the rules were being (re-)made just for you and me. I had been led to think we were convened to discuss cases for promotion, but it seemed to me we were being asked to restructure by the back door. Why these particular individuals should be for the chop wasn't clear from their records. Cuts, no doubt, were the underlying cause, though they weren't discussed as such. At one point Forster remarked aloud but to nobody in particular: 'These REF stars – they don't earn their keep.' (Warner 2014)

At that stage UK universities were still obsessively focused on meeting the demands of the government's latest Research Assessment Exercise (RAE), the 'Research Excellence Framework' (REF), a five or six-yearly research evaluation exercise which determines a large part of universities' budgets. Little did academics know that the criteria for funding had suddenly changed:

> Everyone in academia had come to learn that the REF is the currency of value. A scholar whose works are left out of the tally is marked for assisted dying. So I thought Forster's remark odd at the time, but let it go. It is now widely known – but I did not know it then – that the rankings of research, even if much improved, will bring universities less money this time round than last. So the tactics to bring in money are changing. Students, especially foreign students who pay higher

fees, offer a glittering solution. Suddenly the watchword was 'Teaching, Teaching, Teaching'. (Warner 2014)

Warner had just been invited to chair the Man Booker International Prize for 2015. Her dean had encouraged her to accept – and promised to cover her teaching duties – and the vice chancellor had written a letter of congratulation, enthusiastic about the prestige this would bring – and evidence of her research 'impact' – a key criterion for the REF. However, a few months later the university's priorities had shifted. The executive dean for humanities now presented Warner with the university's 'Tariff of Expectations' consisting of 17 targets, and she was told her success in meeting them would be assessed twice a year. Suddenly, the promises of adjusting her workload to meet her public commitments evaporated and her 'workload allocation' became impossible to reconcile with the commitments she had been urged to accept. If she could not teach while chairing the Man Booker Prize committee, the university asked her to take a year's unpaid leave: in that way they would save her salary, yet her research would still count towards the next REF and earn the university future income. 'I felt that would set a bad precedent', wrote Warner: 'other colleagues, younger than me, with more financial responsibilities, could not possibly supervise PhD students, do research, write books, convene conferences, speak in public, accept positions on trusts or professional associations, and all for no pay.' So she resigned.

Marina Warner's story highlights several significant features of the shifting – and often obtuse – higher education policy regimes and their anxiety-inducing and subjectifying effects. Warner likens her situation to that of Kafka's protagonist, Joseph K., who is permanently wrong-footed by the ever-changing and inscrutable rules of the administration. In her case, what had changed were the key policy drivers of the university funding system. Teaching had always yielded the central and relatively stable funding of departments, whereas research funding depended on the fluctuating outcomes of the REF assessments. In 2010 the government suddenly removed direct funding for teaching and transferred the resources into loans that students could take out to pay higher fees – but with the likelihood that these loans would never be fully recouped (McGettigan 2013, 2021).*

---

* In 2022, the total annual expenditure on student loans was £20 billion, and the value of outstanding loans was £182 billion and predicted to rise to £460 billion by the mid-2040s (Bolton 2022: 4).

The new basis for departments' and institutions' financial viability lay in attracting ever-increasing numbers of students paying high fees, and to this end staff resources were concentrated on achieving high 'student satisfaction' scores for teaching. Alongside the goals of pursuing 'research excellence' and achieving 'world-class' status, UK universities were also subject to an annual National Student Survey to measure student satisfaction with their degrees and a Teaching Excellence Framework (TEF) that the government hoped could be used to link student intake numbers to an institution's reputation for quality teaching (more on this below). As Warner's case illustrates, these shifting and cumulative workload priorities created incompatible demands on the individual academic's time and energy. In what follows, we examine the features of this higher education regime and its implications for academia. We ask: How are these disciplinary regimes of performance measurement and rankings changing institutional behaviour and transforming academic subjectivities, and at what cost? What kind of governance regime is produced by the proliferation of 'audit culture' in higher education?

Context: Universities and the Rise of Audit Culture

Warner's allusion to Kafka is both fitting, yet problematic. The term 'Kafkaesque' describes those contexts where individuals are confronted with a bizarre and impersonal bureaucracy, they feel powerless to control or understand (Edwards 1991). Kafkaesque situations usually have a nightmarishly complex, uncanny, confusing and illogical quality. While the goalposts for university funding and reputation management keep changing, unlike in Kafka's castle there is a fathomable rationale behind these shifting priorities that relates to changes in the political economy of higher education. As Slaughter and Rhoades (2004: 17) put it, universities provide the two 'raw materials' of the global knowledge economy; the knowledge and graduates that can be converted into innovative products. However, whereas in the past universities were called upon to support their governments' attempts to make their countries more globally competitive, now they are regarded as economic players themselves and integral drivers of that economy. In English-speaking countries in particular, the market for high fee-paying international students, often termed 'export education', has become a major industry. For example, in 2019, international education earned Australia £20.8 billion and was the country's fourth largest export industry (Brumby 2021). For the UK, the figure is even larger. The total benefit to the UK economy from the 2018/19 cohort of international students was £25.9 billion over the entire period of their studies (London Economics 2021: 1).

In a world composed of competing states, each struggling to increase its share of capital and footloose assets in an increasingly mobile, insecure and risk-averse global knowledge economy, the role of national governments is now often depicted as one of finding and galvanising into productivity the under-productive, under-utilised and dormant resources in the sector as a whole – including the unharnessed potential of each individual. Various government reports on higher education reform have termed this 'realising our potential' (UK Cabinet Office 1993) or harnessing the sector's 'untapped capacities'. This explains the plethora of attempts to render universities more accountable through ever more elaborate and calculative systems of measurement and auditing. In turn, the ranked results of these competitive audit systems are linked to differential funding. Within this punitive system winners are rewarded with funding and prestige, while losers are named, shamed, and have their resources withdrawn and reallocated to more successful competitors, thereby placing them in further jeopardy – what Warner aptly terms 'assisted dying'. According to the rationales of neoliberal governments, this system of economic rewards incentivises institutions and individuals to mobilise all their resources so that they become more efficient and productive. In the eyes of many government ministers and those higher education reformers who believe that outsourcing and commercialisation are the solution to current funding shortages, academics are basically 'lazy' and 'inward looking' and prone to teaching from dusty old lecture notes, while leaving their more valuable ideas languishing in the bottom drawer of their desks. The role of the 'competition state' is to incentivise academics and university managers to activate these dormant resources and untapped human capital by putting them to work for the benefit of the economy.

The mobilisation of these supposedly under-exploited resources requires a new set of disciplinary technologies for steering institutions, reorganising work and incentivising desired changes in academic behaviour. The introduction of these new management systems – which include leadership frameworks, benchmarks, barometers, output targets, workload allocations, performance appraisals, and various measures of quality and productivity – does far more than simply incentivise behavioural changes: they have a transformative effect on social relations and academic subjectivities (see Shore and Wright 1999, 2015b). They alter the way individuals see their work, their institution and themselves. While some policy makers contend that standardised measures create better opportunities for personal and professional advancement – because they make performance expectations more explicit and transparent – others experience them as a source of deep anxiety and insecurity. As Bovbjerg's (2011) research shows, opening oneself up to an institutional gaze where one is unable to predict or control the way supposedly objective information will be used is inherently stress inducing. However, these mechanisms of measurement and audit are extremely effective in raising productivity and enabling managers to govern 'at a distance', as many senior university leaders have discovered. This emphasis on 'governing by numbers' and the utility of calculative practices is a central feature of the continuing advance or 'roll out' of neoliberal governmentality (Peck and Tickell 2002).

How best to theorise these developments? Among the most notable concepts and frameworks that have been advanced to help explain these trends are 'academic capitalism' (Slaughter and Leslie's 1999) and the 'entrepreneurial university' (Marginson and Considine 2000). Other authors have deployed suggestive epithets to capture the transformation of the sector, ranging from *The Fall of the Faculty* (Ginsberg 2011) and *Wannabe U* (Tuchman 2011), to *University, Inc.* (Washburn 2005), *College for Sale* (Shumar 1997), *The Exchange University* (Chan and Fisher 2008) and *University in Chains* (Giroux 2007). What all these books share is an analysis and critique of the way higher education has become progressively more marketised and commoditised. As an addition to the analyses advanced by these texts, we suggest that the concept of audit culture offers a further useful theoretical framework for understanding the transformation of universities today. Audit culture highlights the way that whole areas of academic work have been refashioned – and colonised – by the logic of financial accounting and the way this brings together the 'twinned precepts of economic efficiency and ethical practice' (Strathern 2000c: 2), all in the name of enhancing accountability, transparency and value for money.

The growth of audit has been accompanied by the rise of new actors and industries geared to producing indicators, inventing systems for measuring outputs against targets, and generating rankings in order to raise performance and productivity. Like the world described in Kafka's books *The Trial* and *The Castle*, this new bureaucracy produces a frustrating and arbitrary controlling system with which academics, like K's fellow villagers, try to comply even though they often realise auditing in pursuit of 'excellence' and 'world-class' status is a futile chase after an unfathomable and unobtainable goal. Auditing is effectively a new form of knowledge/power (i.e. a new configuration of what Foucault termed disciplinary power), with new sets of professionals creating new kinds of proprietorial knowledge and also new commercial operators (such as providers of 'edtech', student management software, and online conferencing systems), who find new ways to extract profit. In this respect, audit culture is both cause and effect of itself: not only do its regimes of accountability recreate organisations by rendering them auditable, they also create the raw material that feeds the expansion of the auditing and accounting industries. In the context of higher education, these technologies often have an authoritarian character: the 'tyranny of transparency' (Strathern 1998) – or 'coercive commensurability' (Brenneis et al. 2005) – is one of the key reasons why universities have lost the ability to run themselves or act as self-governing institutions.

Measurement and Quantification of Everything

Universities – and education systems more generally – have long been sites where the testing, marking and grading of individuals have been instruments of ranking and discipline (see Chapter 1), and in many countries such assessments continue to serve as vehicles for the reproduction of elites. In recent decades, however, this process has been extended. No longer are pupils and students the only ones subject to regular performance assessments; now whole institutions, including their professionals, administrators and leadership teams, must contend with the demand to continually improve performance.

The imperative to perform is cogently exemplified in Espeland and Sauder's (2007) analysis of the ranking of US law schools. Even though many law-school deans view these rankings as absurd, calling them an 'idiot poll', 'Mickey Mouse', 'plain wacky' and 'totally bonkers' (Sauder and Espeland 2009: 68), every decision they take is now made with a view to its effects on their college's rankings. The rankings have become 'omnipresent' and impossible to avoid. Any drop in a law school's position has immediate repercussions on student recruitment and hence on income, with cuts, redundancies, and loss of reputation as inevitable consequences. The rankings they take most seriously are those published by U.S. News & World Report, an American media company founded in 1948 by conservative newspaperman David Lawrence. At the time of Lawrence's death in 1973, this magazine had reached a circulation of over 2 million and subsequently became a major competitor to *Time* and *Newsweek*. However, in 2010 it changed to an online-only format and switched its business to ranking services. The company now produces rankings across a vast swathe of areas, from 'Best Doctors and Medicare Plans' and 'Best Pensions', to 'Best Cars', 'Best Vacations', 'Best Hotels', 'Best Real Estate Agents', 'Best Financial Advisors', and 'Top-Performing Funds' (U.S. News & World Report 2016). It also publishes an annual 'Best College Guide' that ranks all types of colleges, and this has become the most important source of information for prospective students when deciding which programmes to choose. Indeed, even when it was still a magazine, the spike in sales for its annual *Best College Guide* was so high that this became popularly known as their 'swimsuit edition'. However, the methodologies used to construct these league tables are questionable and far from scientifically robust (Wright 2012). As Gladwell (2011) points out, 20 per cent of the overall grade comes from 'Faculty Resources', which is calculated from a weighted combination of class size, faculty salary, percentage of professors with highest degree, student–faculty ratio, and percentage of full-time faculty. These measures are bad proxies for education and do not capture in any way how a college informs, inspires and challenges students. Another category – 'Undergraduate academic reputation' (22.5 per cent of the mark) – is based on a survey of presidents, provosts and administrative deans who are asked to grade 261 national universities. '[W]hen a president is asked to assess the relative merits of dozens of institutions he [sic] knows nothing about, he relies on *their* ranking' (Gladwell 2011, our emphasis). In short, reputation and ranking become a mutually constitutive circuit. The rankings induce involuntary 'reactivity' and their unwilling endorsement by the deans 'makes these shaky measures pervasive and generative of the organisation itself' (Sauder and Espeland 2009: 68). These rankings and guides are just some of ways that information is provided to students as 'consumers' so that they can make more informed, rational choices when selecting their courses. In England, evaluations of education quality were traditionally uncoupled from issues of funding as university teaching used to be covered by a block grant from government. However, since 2004 the economic survival of universities has increasingly come to depend on their reputation and rankings and ability to attract fee-paying students. This began with the introduction of a market in fees that year by the New Labour Government but was massively amplified after 2010 when the coalition Liberal Democrat and Conservative government took the highly controversial decision to triple university fees and withdraw funding for all teaching except for the STEM (science, technology, engineering and mathematics) subjects. This was done despite a strong public pre-election pledge by the Liberal Democrat Party leader, Nick Clegg, that, if elected, his party would not raise student fees. Currently, one of the main sources of information for students (and parents) choosing university courses is rankings – notably the QS World University Rankings or *Times Higher Education*'s World University Rankings – yet none of these metrics actually measures education or teaching. The other main source of information about universities, the National Student Survey, has been run annually since 2005 by the national student union. It is based on an online questionnaire administered to final year students with 22 'attitude' questions about the 'learning experience', with measures for teaching, assessment, personal development, academic support, learning resources, organisation and management, and overall satisfaction. As in the United States, university managers take enormous pride in positive results and use these in profiling and promoting their institutions to prospective students. However, a critical report by Ipsos MORI found major flaws in the reliability of these data (Jump 2014). This was attributed in part to students filling out their questionnaire as quickly as possible and ticking 'yes' to everything (the average time was five and a half minutes, but 20 per cent completed it in under two minutes), but also to the fact that students have a 'vested interest' in the 'over-zealous promotion' of their institutions (Havergal 2015a). This report concluded that since the NSS scores are 'likely to benefit both students and institutions themselves' there may 'be some incentive on the part of both to encourage or give positive ratings' (Havergal 2015a).* UK universities are not alone in mobilising students to enhance their ratings: the University of Auckland in one of its advertising poster slogans proclaimed: 'Let our reputation build yours!'

A key problem for governments is that there are few reliable metrics for evaluating education or teaching. In response to this, in 2017 the UK government introduced the 'Teaching Excellence Framework' (TEF) to help students 'drive' the system and allow the top-tiered universities to increase their fees. The hunt for a suitable concept and method to evaluate

---

* Despite this claim, student unions at 25 universities (out of 164) followed a National Union of Students' call to boycott the NSS in opposition to government proposals to link NSS results to increasing fee levels (Grove 2017).

teaching has led some to look at the US Collegial Learning Assessment system, which aims to test and measure student 'learning gain' over the period of their study. The problem is that while these tests purport to be a neutral measure of generic skills (e.g. problem solving, interpersonal communication, use of digital information, and dealing with complex situations), 'the contents of a test will be far more closely related to some subjects ... than others' (Wolf, cited in Havergal 2015b: 21). The UK government also decided to include 'employability' as a metric to evaluate teaching excellence. They use the Destinations of Learners in Higher Education (DLHE) survey to measure the proportion of students who are in highly skilled employment or further study six months after graduation (Blyth and Cleminson 2016).* At one point the Office for Students (OfS) even proposed calculating graduates' employability using data from Her Majesty's Revenue and Customs office (OfS 2018: 4, 17). The capacity of universities to embed 'employability' and the ability of students to gain meaningful employment was therefore to be measured by financial earnings and tax returns, reinforcing the neoliberal assumption that the value of a university degree must be financialised and measured in terms of value for money and return on investment.

Auditing Research Excellence: The Managerial Uses of Pseudo-scientific Measures

> These managers worry me. Too many are modest achievers, retired from their own studies, intoxicated with jargon, delusional about corporate status and forever banging the metrics gong. Crucially, they don't lead by example. (Bignell, cited in Colquhoun 2012a)

University research is another area that has been subjected to repeated attempts to measure the quality of academic work. Since the 1980s, there has been an explosion of national research evaluation exercises aimed at improving performance, output and competitiveness among individual researchers, their departments, their institutions and even entire countries. The UK's RAE was one of the first of such exercises, introduced in 1984 as part of a package of neoliberal reforms developed by the Con-

---

* This is in fact a measure of employment (for which universities cannot be held responsible) rather than an assessment of whether universities have embedded the attributes of employability into courses and students' experiences.

servative Thatcher government. The RAE (subsequently rebranded as the 'Research Excellence Framework' or REF) is an intensive research evaluation exercise conducted every four to six years that measures and competitively ranks the research outputs of university departments across the UK. While the evaluations are based on peer review, the academic community has no influence over the resulting allocation of resources, which are in the hands of the government.

There are four points of significance about this process. First, the number of academics on teaching and research contracts in any given department or unit determines the number of outputs required for the REF submission. Each of these academics has to contribute at least one major piece of new work to the submission. Those without 'REFable outputs' are placed in a vulnerable position regarding their continuing employment and are often transferred to teaching-only contracts. Second, evaluations are based on panels of experts in each field who are expected to read the books, articles and scholarly publications or creative works submitted. The guidelines for the 2021 REF stated explicitly that 'No sub-panel will use journal impact factors or any hierarchy of journals in their assessment of outputs. No output will be privileged or disadvantaged on the basis of the publisher, where it is published or the medium of its publication' (REF 2021: 40 §207). Third, these research assessment exercises have been used to stratify the higher education sector. Successive exercises have been used to concentrate research funding in ever fewer institutions and departments. This strongly incentivises university leaders to maximise their REF scores by making 'strategic decisions' about where to invest and which subject areas or departments to close. It also incentivises academics to publish at any cost and everyone in the university therefore learns what 'counts' and is pressed to reorientate their energies accordingly in a process that has been termed the 'RAE-fication' of academia (Loftus 2006: Shore 2008: 290–91; Lucas 2017: 216). This pressure has led to some extraordinary levels of 'productivity'. For example, psychologist Mark Griffiths, director of the 'International Gaming Research Unit' at Nottingham Trent University, is reported to have published one academic paper every two days in 2020 with his stable of PhD students and 898 co-authors (Grove 2020). Fourth, and unsurprisingly, national reviews have revealed massive gaming as academics and managers seek to play the research assessment system (Lucas 2006; Wright 2009).

Universities have developed strategic plans to climb up the ranking ladder that involve ever greater expectations about the output of each individual academic. For example, Queen Mary University of London was ranked 48 in the RAE 2001 and made an astounding leap to 13th place in RAE 2008. The leadership then devised a strategy to elevate the university into the top five UK universities by RAE 2015. In 2012, the university produced a table of its expectations for academic performance over four criteria: the quantity of papers published; the quality of journals where papers are published (proxy measure is journal impact factor); total research income; and research income as 'principal investigator'. Furthermore, these criteria were applied *retrospectively* to assess the performance of academics over the period 2008 to 2011. To keep their jobs, academics at Queen Mary had to meet the minimum threshold in three out of four categories. For a lecturer, that included five papers, one 'quality journal' paper, £200,000 in research income and at least half of that as the principal investigator. For a professor, the expectations were eleven papers, two in top journals, £400,000 in research income of which at least half was as principal investigator.

As well as being unattainable for many academics, Queen Mary's yardsticks were condemned as 'utterly brainless' (Colquhoun 2012a). As Sir David Colquhoun (a professor of pharmacology, member of the Royal Society, and honorary director of the Wellcome Trust) noted, mass producing articles is discouraged because it either results in publishing data in multiple fragments, or in appending a senior researcher's name to somebody else's work, often without properly reading or checking the data. 'Such numbers can be reached only by unethical behaviour' and 'the rules provide an active encouragement to dishonesty' (Colquhoun 2012a). There are many Nobel Prize winners (including Andrew Huxley, Bernard Katz, Bert Sakmann and Peter Higgs) who published very few papers in their lifetime and who would have doubtless been fired on these grounds.

The university's criteria defined high-quality journals as those that have an impact factor greater than 7. However, as Colquhoun notes, for some disciplines the highest ranked journals have impact factors of only 4 or 5, while in others, the top journals only publish review papers not original research. Moreover, the number of citations that a paper receives bears no relation to the impact factor of the journal (Seglen 1997). Colquhoun (2012a) quotes an analysis of the journal *Nature* that found the mean number of citations for a paper was 114 but whereas one paper had 2,364 citations, 35 other papers had 10 or fewer. Similarly, a study in 2001 of the citations accrued by the 858 papers published in *Nature* in 1999 found 80 of them

(16 per cent) accounted for half of all the citations (Colquhoun 2012a). In addition to these faulty yardsticks, every academic at Queen Mary had to produce at least one PhD student in the assessment period. Given the state of the employment market and lack of jobs for such graduates, the ethics of expanding research by increasing numbers of doctorates simply to increase a university's league table standing is highly questionable.

The use of such spurious metrics to evaluate scientists was criticised publicly by several scholars, including two from Queen Mary University itself. In a letter published in the *Lancet*, two biologists, John Allen and Fanis Missirlis, criticised the way the criteria had been applied to the School of Medicine and Dentistry (where 29 academics were facing dismissal for not meeting the performance criteria). They made four important points. First, these targets often hit the wrong people because the head of school and human resources relied on cold, abstracted metrics rather than an understanding of the quality of an individual's research or potential. Second, this disciplining was conducted through a punitive procedure. Targeted victims had to justify their 'retrospective crimes' in an audience with the head of school and human resources in a manner reminiscent of the Spanish Inquisition or, to continue our Kafka analogy, like those court officials who explained neither the procedures nor the offence that the condemned Joseph K. had been accused of. Third, the criteria failed to address the quality of science itself; as Allen and Missirlis (2012) noted, 'there are no boxes to tick for advances in knowledge and understanding – no metrics for science itself ... [this] slaughter of the talented relies entirely on a carefully designed set of retrospective counts of the uncountable'. Finally, these performance criteria were rarely applied to the 'Grand Inquisitors' themselves who, as the authors noted, would have conspicuously failed by their own criteria, 'yet to question them is heresy'. That last statement proved prophetic as the authors of the *Lancet* letter were subsequently charged with misconduct and then sacked. Their department was the second chosen for this treatment, having under-performed in the 2008 RAE, and Missirlis was dismissed for not having met the criteria. Allen – a highly respected and productive professor who did meet the criteria – was initially sanctioned by having all of his specialist teaching taken away and being required to teach service courses instead. When he indicated his unwillingness to accept this punishment he was sacked for 'refusing to obey a reasonable management instruction' (Jump 2015b). He subsequently moved to University College London, but without a lab.

What is interesting in this and many other cases where performance measures are turned into managerialist tools for ranking, disciplining and firing staff is the pseudo-scientific language that is typically used to justify such decisions. In response to Colquhoun's criticisms the Vice Chancellor of Queen Mary University of London (QM), Professor Simon Gaskell, wrote a letter to *The Times* arguing that as QM was ranked in the top dozen research universities in the UK, these actions were necessary to address areas where 'performance does not match expectations' so as 'to ensure that our students receive the finest research-led education' and 'to safeguard QM's financial stability'. Management had 'applied objective criteria to the assessment of individual academic performance based on generally recognised academic expectations' and now he would invest to rebuild those areas where staff had been fired (Gaskell 2012). This discourse combines several threads: the imperative to 'safeguard' the university's financial future by raising its rankings; an ethical obligation to defend its students' interests; and the application of strictly 'objective' and impartial criteria based on 'recognised' and commonly accepted expectations of academic performance.

In fact, none of these claims were true, as Colquhoun (2012b) noted in his rejoinder. The number of publications demanded of QM academics was far beyond what the REF required and staff who produced large numbers of publications were unlikely to have the time or inclination to teach students as well. To improve its standing in the REF, QM's leadership deployed methods that had been explicitly ruled inadmissible in the REF guidelines. When evaluating the research output of individuals, management assumed that research was the primary activity of an academic, whereas Missirlis was shouldering high teaching loads. As in Marina Warner's case, this highlights the Kafkaesque way in which the orientation of an institution changes, jibbing and tacking to follow the changing winds and directions of government funding. This creates a volatile environment in which, when teaching funding is stable, managers focus primarily on pursuing variable funding from research, but when teaching funding follows students, the focus suddenly becomes 'teaching, teaching, teaching'.

Effects of Indicators and Rankings on Academia

The question posed at the outset was: How should we theorise these trends in higher education, and what effects does this quest for world-class status through a proliferation of performance targets, indicators and rankings have on academics and on universities? Do they actually deliver the better outcomes and organisational transparency that they proclaim? As the examples above illustrate, the REF system has perverse effects on the public university and corrodes its civic mission. Peter Scott (2013), professor of higher education and former editor of *Times Higher Education* (*THE*) likens the REF to a monster; 'a Minotaur that must be appeased by bloody sacrifices'. Like the Minotaur, it too occupies a place that is labyrinthine in its complexity and that has consumed the professional lives of many of its victims. At QM, the fate of Missirlis and Allen can be conceptualised as sacrificial offerings to the new regime of academic accountability; they were effectively 'collateral damage' in a system where institutions and individuals believed they had no real choice but to play this high-stakes game. Yet the overall result was a corruption of the university's main purpose so that pursuing better REF grades rather than producing good science and scholarship becomes the ordering principle. As Scott (2013) puts it, 'research is reduced to what counts for the REF' – and those aspects of academia that cannot be counted or rendered commensurable on numerical score sheets, by definition, do not "count"'. Reflecting on Warner's experience, Meranze (2014) similarly concludes 'the demands for scholarship were increasingly irrelevant for the funding of the university or for the allocation of resources within the university'. Rendering certain aspects of university life visible – and therefore more calculable and governable by senior managers and administrators – is a logical counterpart to the systematic downgrading or invisibilising of other areas of academic life (like scholarship for its own sake, critical research, unconventional yet inspirational teaching) that are inconsistent with the neoliberal and managerial vision of the competitive 'world-class' university.

However, it would be misleading to conclude that the effects of these indicators and rankings are simply repressive or perverse: they are also performative and productive and, for senior administrators and managers at least, often extremely empowering. Indeed, one of the most important effects of this avalanche of indicators and rankings has been to reinforce a series of developments already under way as a result of the neoliberal reforms of higher education. The first of these was to recast universities as transnational business corporations operating in a competitive global market. This development has been particularly evident since the 1980s in the UK, the US, Australia, Canada and New Zealand, but also increasingly in many European countries. A second development was the withdrawal of public funding across the sector and universities being encouraged to pursue alternative revenue streams, particularly from the private sector. Managers have financialised and marketised the university throughout its operations as it has increasingly come to resemble a for-profit organisation (Lewis et al. 2022; Komljenovic and Robertson 2016). A third development is the shift in power from academics towards senior administrators and managers, who increasingly arrogate to themselves the role of decision making, steering the enterprise and deciding on its policy priorities – even to the extent of claiming ownership of the university and referring to *themselves* as 'the university' (Shore and Taitz 2012; Ørberg 2007).

Indicators and rankings have thus helped to establish a new regime of governance and authority, one that equates the role of a vice chancellor with that of a private company's CEO, with corresponding executive salaries and privileges. They have also reinforced the new hierarchies and cleavages that have come to characterise the neoliberal university, particularly the division between a new class of professional administrators (the 'administariat') and the burgeoning ranks of increasingly de-professionalised and casualised academic workforce (the 'precariat'). One of the paradoxical effects of these changes is that while universities have been given greater institutional autonomy and 'freedom' to manage their own financial affairs and risks, they have also become increasingly dependent on and vulnerable to market pressures and servile to government political agendas. Many university management teams, like that at QM, impose minimum expectations for research performance in their efforts to improve their institution's standing in the next RAE. In some instances, these performance targets have been pitched at such a high level that they are unachievable. At Newcastle University in 2013, for example, under the terms of a new management initiative called 'Raising the Bar', professors, readers and senior lecturers in the humanities and social sciences were expected to bring in at least £6,000 to £12,000 a year in external grant revenue (for lecturers the required amount was £3,000 to £6,000 a year), as well as producing at least four three-star research outputs in the period before the next REF (Grove 2015). Even more unrealistic was the expectation that each academic should graduate one PhD student per year, as this target would have required Newcastle University to capture the entire supply of publicly funded PhDs in the UK (BBlaze, 2015).

Academics rightly fear that these new targets could be used to make individuals redundant on capability grounds – which is undoubtedly part of the rationale behind the initiative and a logical consequence of failure to meet the targets. In 2019 there was a dispute at Liverpool University after the administration informed junior academics that they would not pass probation unless they published a paper that was 'judged to be internationally excellent' every 18 months. This level of output was far in excess of what the REF demanded and was accompanied by a new timetable policy which, staff claimed, cut research time, thus making these targets even more difficult to reach (Grove 2019). Similarly, at the University of Exeter, the probationary period for new lecturers in the social sciences was increased to five years, during which time they were expected to have raised £100,000 in external grants (personal communication). A 2015 survey found that one in six universities in the UK had introduced individual performance targets for obtaining research grant money (Jump 2015a). As Grove (2015) notes, such funding income targets also represent a threat to academic freedom 'as they would effectively govern the way academics approach their subject', leading them to forgo 'blue skies' research and pursue smaller, short-term 'normal science' projects to meet income targets (Wright 2009). In some universities this process has been taken further, with senior managers and research commercialisation units now deciding on academic appointments based on their own calculations of research areas that promise the greatest commercial or financial returns to the university in the future (Lewis and Shore 2017).

Conclusion: The Costs of Being 'World Class'

Global ranking and the pursuit of 'world-class' status are clearly having a transformative effect on universities. They have also been catalysts in reshaping academic behaviour and recasting academics as atomised individuals operating in a competitive higher education market; a de-professionalised workforce of researchers and teachers whose work must be incentivised, monitored and measured by management. Academics must also constantly measure their own performance in a labyrinthine system whose logic is often lost or meaningless for those on the front line of academic teaching and research. The university arms race for 'world-class' status is conducted through auditing procedures which have departed from a search for probity and trust and deviated into calculations, proxy measures and rankings driven largely by financial bottom lines. As in the bureaucracy emanating from Kafka's castle, the system is riddled with contradictory logics and perverse effects: it claims to be founded on economic rationality yet its consequences are profoundly irrational; it fetishises innovation and entrepreneurship and yet produces conformity, conservatism and risk-aversion; it lionises competition, individualism and choice yet most of academia works through cooperation; and it now claims to put 'the student experience' first yet the level of debt and stress it produces seems to have created an epidemic of anxiety and mental health problems both among students (Richardson et al. 2017) and academics (Morrish 2019).

As Kafka's protagonist Joseph K. found, it is difficult to locate the author or agent behind the processes that created this system and futile to ask who (or what) is leading the incessant drive towards ever more coercive and calculative forms of measurement and control. The process has gone feral and increasingly runs according to its own logic, feeding on the metricised and performative world it creates. It has also become so normalised that it is now part of the fabric of contemporary university life. Despite its evident flaws and shortcomings, the use of metricised performance targets, indicators and rankings appear to many as both unstoppable and impossible to oppose. However, like any regime of truth, they are in fact assemblages of diverse and contingent threads, held together in arbitrary webs of power which, when examined more closely, turn out to have little substance, although they have powerful effects. In this case, what these calculative practices and financialised targets are producing is a new kind of university regime, one increasingly orientated around neoliberal policy agendas, financial markets, and the priorities of a new class of senior administrators and managers.

How then are these disciplinary regimes of ranking and performance indicators changing institutional behaviour and transforming academic subjectivities, and at what cost? As our examples show, university management's increasing reliance on instrumental and calculative performance measurement creates its own dynamic, one that further institutionalises the spread of audit culture. These performance indicators and targets are instrumental in producing calculable, accountable, 'responsibilised' and self-disciplined subjects: that is, the qualities of the 'ideal' academic in the new managerially led and neoliberalised university (Dean 1999; Lund 2012). Yet this ideal is itself far from fixed or stable, always shifting according to the latest changes in priority or new calculations of what pays, and therefore what 'counts'. The net result of these proliferating systems of performance measurement is a regime of governance structured around out-of-reach or impossible targets that can then be used to discipline and punish dissenters and laggards. For academics, these measuring and ranking systems generate a sense of permanent insecurity and the feeling that one can never quite do enough. Sociologist Vik Loveday captures this perfectly when reflecting on her own university's attempt to introduce 'change management':

> in universities, staff anxieties have long been framed as a problem of the individual rather than the product of structural conditions: staff are incited by employers to take personal responsibility for their own anxieties even when stress is exacerbated by toxic work environments, employment uncertainty, endless metrics and league tables, and increasing competition between 'providers' for students and funding. Yet while anxiety is a symptom of this wider context ... it has become an intrinsic part of a dysfunctional HE [higher education] sector: a 'stick' that drives competition by exploiting our vulnerabilities. We are told we should be working harder, bringing in more money, getting better evaluations, publishing more – we are never quite 'excellent' enough; meanwhile, we must negotiate risks, take personal responsibility for failure, and develop greater resilience. The 'neurotic academic' (myself included) is governed *through* anxiety, not in spite of it. (Loveday 2021)

Structurally produced anxiety is not only highly instrumental in promoting increased centralisation, reducing academic freedom, and intensifying academic workloads, it also induces problems of health and wellbeing, including stress, depression, isolation and burnout.

Throughout this chapter we have likened the regime of metricised performance management in universities to the alienating and surreal world of Kafka's castle, but how useful or appropriate is this analogy? Kafka's novels typically depict nightmarish settings in which characters are crushed by blind authorities or systems that are incomprehensible and inscrutable. Their sense of reality begins to fall apart as they struggle to grasp their changed circumstances. Kafka's best-known fiction *The Trial*, for example, portrays a world gone mad. As Ivana Edwards explains, the book:

> is about Joseph K., who, although in hot pursuit of the truth, is executed for an unnamed crime. Time and space are rearranged so they can work

either for or against the protagonist; the horror of that world is that he never knows what is happening, or when. (Edwards 1991: 12)

Many academics would no doubt recognise these elements of the Kafkaesque in their own workplaces. However, according to Edwards: 'You don't give up, you don't lie down and die. What you do is struggle against this with all of your equipment, with whatever you have. But of course you don't stand a chance. That's Kafkaesque' (Edwards 1991: 12). In fact, *The Trial* ends with Joseph K. voluntarily submitting to his accusers and being led away to his execution. But this need not be the outcome. In Marina Warner's case, she managed to find a path that led her away from the castle. She gained a new position as professor of English and Creative Writing at Birkbeck, University of London and became a fellow of All Souls College in Oxford. In 2017 she was elected as the first ever woman president of the Royal Society of Literature. A high-profile resignation, it would seem, can have a resounding impact and is not necessarily the death of an academic career, even in the Kafkaesque university. However, as Warner herself acknowledged, few academics have the prestige or the financial wherewithal to navigate a successful relocation in this way.

7

The New Subjects of Audit: Performance Management and Quantified Selves

> Google demonstrated that the same predictive knowledge derived from behavioral surplus that has made the surveillance capitalists wealthy could also help candidates win elections. (Zuboff 2019: 122)

What counts as evidence of good performance, behaviour or character and what are the politics behind projects to measure or construct good citizens and workers? And how do organisations and governments seek to instil the norms and values of desired ethical conduct? Previous chapters explored the ways that metrics have been used to govern organisations, manage professionals and steer workforces towards what 'counts' according to ministers and managers. This chapter focuses on the rise of other forms of audit – scorecards, self-tracking, and social credit systems. It explores their effects by examining, first, how governance systems and organisational management initiatives have been used to shape individuals into trusted, predictable and auditable subjects; and, second, how metrics and self-management have become increasingly entangled with new forms of surveillance and capitalism.

New Public Management (NPM) used numerical indicators both to provide evidence of individual and collective performance and to stimulate economy, efficiency and effectiveness in organisations. Employees and managers saw which numerical scores acted as 'proxies' for quality or excellence and therefore knew it was sensible (if not in keeping with their personal or professional values) to focus on what 'counts'. Commercial companies have long used loyalty cards and credit checks as a strategy to elicit more predictable and appropriate behaviour in customers. Workplaces not only measured workers' productivity, but developed a range of techniques, like scorecards and dashboards, to align workers' efforts with the company's values. Even before the 2020–21 Covid-19 pandemic forced many white-collar staff to work from home, new technologies calculated the time people were *actually* working and adjusted salary payments accordingly. For example, 'WorkSmart' software provided automated tracking of time spent clicking on a computer – but did not count meetings, telephone calls, reading or thinking (Kantor and Sundaram 2022; Leonhardt 2022). To overcome the problem of defining what constituted productivity, one business software company simply measured the time spent moving a mouse or using a computer keyboard. It logged employees' work in 10-minute chunks, during which time a camera took a snapshot of their face and screen to verify they were actually working; no other activity counted. Staff had to accumulate 10-minute timecards of computer action as a basis for their salary. One finance executive found that she had to work 60 hours per week in order to be paid for 40 hours' work (Kantor and Sundaran 2022).

This reliance on remote surveillance and panopticon-like time-tracking aims to instil an unrelenting work ethic among employees. Some platforms that provide on-demand labour, such as Deliveroo, measure every move that a worker makes, including the amount of time taken at every stage of a delivery (Warin and McCann 2018: 10). Automated systems of measurement have increasingly replaced trust and professional judgement, yet these measures of input have often borne little relationship to the actual work done, let alone levels of efficiency and productivity. For example, the employer of hospice chaplains, whose job was to help patients wrestle with deep-searching questions as they approached death, required them to predict each morning how many 'productivity points' they would earn that day. A visit to the dying was one point, participation in a funeral was one-and-three-quarter points and a visit to grieving relatives was one-quarter point.

> Every evening software would calculate whether they had met their goals. But dying defied planning. Patients broke down, cancelled appointments, drew final breaths. These left the clergy scrambling and in a perpetual dilemma. 'Do I see the patients who earn the points, or do I see the patients who really need to be seen?' (Kantor and Sundaram 2022)

As the former vice president for workplace intelligence at Microsoft admitted, 'We're in this era of measurement but we don't know what we should be measuring' (Kantor and Sundaram 2022). It perhaps comes as little surprise that the designer who created the WorkSmart remote tracking software left the company after the tool was applied to his own work performance. He became awash with anxiety and concluded that the technology was 'powerful but dangerous' (Kantor and Sundaram 2022). Paradoxically, many of these surveillance systems are promoted on grounds of 'monitoring for training purposes' or protecting workers' wellbeing.

Technologies of tracking and metricised self-management have fuelled new forms of capitalism. Social media and computer technologies offer individuals opportunities to engage in populist projects of self-scrutiny and self-management on, for example, daily exercise and fitness, heart rates, stress levels, sleep patterns and menstrual cycles. Often these projects are presented as ways for people to take more control over their own health and lives. People often think of themselves as consumers of a free service but do not realise that their personal and intimate data is a product that they give voluntarily or unknowingly, through apps and gadgets, to commercial companies and governments. Shoshana Zuboff (2019), in *The Age of Surveillance Capitalism*, explains how companies collect and analyse people's personal and private data opaquely, without their knowledge or consent. Google, Facebook and Microsoft generate stupendous profits by harvesting these data and creating detailed personal profiles of millions of individuals that can be used in personally pinpointed advertising to shape consumer, social and even political behaviour. While surveillance capitalism in the West goes largely unnoticed, China's social credit system has attracted far more attention and opprobrium. As we detail below, each citizen is allocated a numerical score according to their financial, civic and social trustworthiness. The workings of this system appear much more transparent and publicly understood in China. Rewards of better or privileged services entice people to volunteer information about themselves. The gamification of this project invites individuals to publish their personal 'ratings' and compete with friends for status points. Whether in the West or China, the uses of metrics and audit reflect an expansion of what Foucault (1998) called 'biopower': the simultaneous disciplining of individuals and whole populations to perform according to new state and commercial norms about the reliable/conforming 'good' citizen, worker or consumer. Not only are governments and private companies using these data to discipline and manage individuals; individuals actively make themselves into objects and subjects of surveillance and exercise self-governance. These novel governing techniques combine corporatism and populism in new assemblages of power/knowledge.

This chapter is set out in three sections. First, we trace how, since the 1990s, a new range of performance indicators aimed at fostering workers' self-management was developed in the military and transferred to private companies and the public sector. Those technologies typically entailed objectifying persons and fragmenting them into specific competencies and capacities that can be measured against an organisation's objectives. Second, we examine the shift, exemplified in the 'Quantified Self' (QS) movement, in which individuals use hi-tech wearable gadgets to gain 'self-knowledge through numbers', take responsibility for their health and medication, and monitor the performance of their own lifestyle. We note how individuals are producing data about themselves that both states and private companies are using, not only to measure and manage populations, but also to generate huge profits. Finally, we examine the emergence of China's social credit system. Often portrayed in the Western media as an Orwellian bogey man, we suggest that China shows what is already happening in the West. We ask, what kinds of 'auditable selves' are these technologies creating? Are these technologies laying the ground for totalitarianism or can individuals use them creatively to exercise autonomy and agency?

From Military Technologies to Self-managed Workers

As Chapter 1 illustrated, many of the techniques for enhancing individual self-management were pioneered by the military then taken up by private companies and subsequently adopted by public organisations. This transfer from the military to business is exemplified by the transnational consultancy firm McKinney Rogers, which, its website proclaims, 'applies military philosophy and real-world experience to equip business teams with the tools and capability to deliver high-performance'. Its founder, Damian McKinney, was a British Royal Marine who served for 18 years as an operations commando before becoming a businessman. He discovered that 'the Royal Marines' Mission Command approach to talent management, business process redesign, and project planning and execution was directly relatable and transferable to the business world' (McKinney Rogers 2016). The company's oft-quoted 'Mission Leadership Dashboard' technique involves each individual understanding their role in an organisation – what is termed 'empowerment through transparency'.

This clarity drives alignment, instils a sense of personal accountability, and promotes the independent thought and agility necessary to deliver mission-critical results despite obstacles faced. (McKinney Rogers 2016)

The 'Mission Dashboard' enables people at all levels to keep track of their contribution to a company's strategic objectives. Like in a car, the 'dashboard' installed on their computer screens gives them a one-page overview of the company's business targets and sets a target for each individual, the indicators used to measure them, and the progress of their performance against the plan (Syrett 2007). This method builds on initiatives during the 1990s to develop comprehensive, long-term strategies that would align individual behaviour with company missions and targets. In 1993, Kaplan and Norton's influential article in *Harvard Business Review* explained how the engineering and construction company, Rockwater, had developed a 'balanced scorecard' to drive performance (Figure 7.1). Instead of just focusing on financial indicators, they added three other dimensions deemed crucial to the company's long-term success: customer perspective, internal management processes, and employees' innovation and learning. Each required its own 'scorecard measures', and work teams throughout the organisation were expected to translate these into their own 'critical success factors' and measures by which performance would be assessed (Kaplan and Norton 2004: 7–10). Ultimately, these measures were turned into individual scorecards, which would fold up and fit into a (presumably male) employee's shirt pocket or wallet (Figure 7.2). This scorecard 'gives managers a way of ensuring that all levels of the organization understand the long-term strategy and that both departmental and individual objectives are aligned with it' (Kaplan and Norton 2004: 38).

In the early 2000s, BT, the UK-based global telecommunications company, developed an instrument for driving what it called 'end-to-end process management', which aligned employee performance with the company's vision and strategic imperatives. After the 2001 'dot-com' collapse, and faced with a broadband revolution, they wanted to deliver 'transformational change' through 'distributed leadership', 'higher employee engagement' and 'enhanced organisational capability' (Syrett 2007: 71). In their BT People Strategy, they first defined the company's five 'core values' – Trustworthy, Helpful, Inspiring, Straightforward and Heart (Dennison 2008) – and the ideal 'capabilities' through which each employee would embody and 'live' those values. Four times a year, each team member had

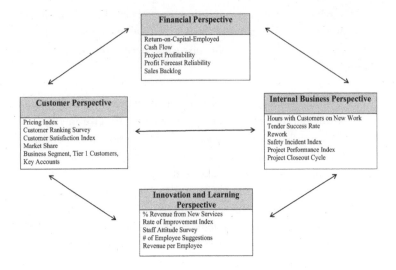

Figure 7.1   Diagram of Rockwater's Balanced Scorecard
Source: Based on Kaplan and Norton (1993: 7).

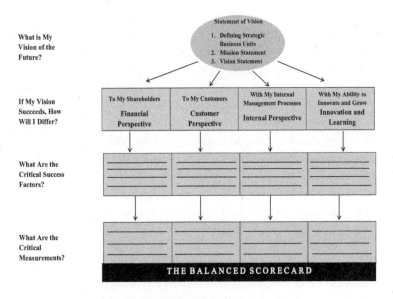

Figure 7.2   Diagram of Rockwater's Individual Scorecard
Source: Based on Kaplan and Norton (1993: 10).

to assess their behaviour under each category. The results were aggregated in an end-of-year Development Performance Review (DPR). Individuals with high scores would be eligible for a bonus payment, but only if their team score was also high. Individual scores were also 'levelled' against their peers, officially for fairness (BT 2010: 17) but, as one employee told us, scores tended to be 'levelled down' below the bonus-earning threshold if the company's finances could not support all the bonuses for which employees were eligible. BT's top management seems to have been exempt from such links between the company's financial performance and their own pay.* As a study by the High Pay Commission (2011: 8) found, 'excessive high pay bears little relation to company success and is rewarding failure'.

Many bowdlerised versions of these performance management techniques have been transferred to the public sector. Universities have given a particularly novel gloss to these experiments in aligning employee capabilities with strategic goals. The work of Australian 'change management' expert Geoff Scott echoes BT's focus on metricised 'capabilities' and 'distributed leadership' and has been taken up by several Australasian universities (Scott et al. 2008; Fullan and Scott 2009). Scott's model was adopted by the University of Auckland in its 2013 'Leadership Framework' programme. Where BT's model had five key 'values', Auckland University's model has five 'leadership dimensions': Personal Leadership, Setting Direction, Enabling People, Innovating and Engaging, and Achieving Results – each of which is also given a Māori name (Figure 7.3).

These leadership dimensions each require particular 'capabilities' (13 in total). Each 'capability' is then described in detail. For example, 'Setting Direction' ('Mana Tohu' in Māori – represented by the five stars of the Southern Cross), is defined as 'Establishing and committing to plans and activities that will deliver the University's strategy', while 'Exhibiting personal leadership' (Rangatiratanga – symbolised by a silver fern) is someone who 'displays integrity and professionalism', 'adapts to change' and 'demonstrates University citizenship' (University of Auckland 2013: 7). To become a senior academic leader one must also have entrepreneurial skills and be someone who:

---

* For example, BT's Chief Executive Office Sir Peter Bonfield received a remuneration package of £3.1 million when he left the company in 2003, topping *The Independent*'s (2003) 'Fat Cat List'. This remuneration package came despite the company having to carry out a £6 billion rescue rights issue in 2001 following a string of bad investments under Bonfield's leadership.

Figure 7.3   The Leadership Framework
Source: University of Auckland (2013: 6).

Demonstrates an understanding of the competitive global environment and key market drivers and ... uses this understanding to create and seize opportunities, expand into new markets and deliver programmes ... The behaviours of a leader who demonstrates global and commercial acumen are:

- Develops in-depth understanding of the University and tertiary sector
- Pursues discipline/market/professional skill-set information and maintains global awareness
- Recognises impact and opportunity of national and global trends
- Leads and inspires innovation
- Pursues ambitious ventures
     (University of Auckland 2013: 8; see Amsler and Shore 2017)

The Leadership Framework's philosophy is that everyone in the organisation must take responsibility for leading and aligning their behaviour with the strategic goals set by senior management. While distributed lead-

ership recalls the tradition of university autonomy where academics relied
on their own sense of professionalism to set their direction in teaching
and research, this model is top-down, authoritarian and skewed towards
an idea of the university as a business corporation. However, unlike
BT's 'end-to-end performance management', the values and capabilities expected of academics were not converted into precise performance
measures. Instead, Auckland University developed a separate policy
detailing quantified criteria for promotion. For example, candidates for
promotion to professor in the social sciences, must have published over
50 articles in leading peer-reviewed journals; supervised at least 8 MA and
8 PhD students; generated three 'major' external research grants (where
'major' meant in excess of NZ $100,000); and demonstrated 'outstand-
ing leadership' consistent with the Leadership Framework' (University of
Auckland 2016).

Denmark's IT University further adapted these ideas in a model that
quantified performance expectations and individual output targets under
a single currency. Academic performance was calculated in a 'performance
points' (PP) system, which aimed to raise the IT University's performance
to that of the average Danish university (IT University 2014). The performance of a professor or associate professor was calculated at 100 PPs per
year. For teaching, 1 PP was equal to 14.5 European Credit and Transfer
System (ECTS) points, and a professor had to earn 50 points over two
years. For research, professors were required to earn 40 PPs over two
years, where 25 PPs were allocated per 2.55 points in the national biblio-
metric research indicator (BFI). Professors also had to earn at least 10 PPs
each year on 'spending external funding', where 25 PPs were allocated per
1,114,540 DKK (roughly US $167,000). To raise and spend US $167,000
each year was probably impossible for most humanities or social science
professors. Even postdoctoral students were expected to produce 55 PPs
per year. Should anyone under-perform, then other colleagues had to
ensure that their unit would meet its members' combined target. Like the
BT model, this relied not just on individual self-management, but compelled colleagues to monitor each other's performance. Those who fail to
meet their target were warned that 'yes, firing may take place' (personal
communication).

What connects these stories about 'mission dashboards', 'balanced
scorecards', 'values and capabilities', and 'distributed leadership' is that
they all highlight attempts to enhance workers' performance by mobilising
metrics in twin processes of 'disciplining' and 'catalysing'. This is typically

justified by the popular maxim – wrongly attributed the management guru Peter Drucker (Zak 2013) – 'if you can't measure it, you can't improve it'. Auditing performance is thus impelled by an ethic of improvement, both of the organisation and the individuals within it. What we see here is the confluence of two different rationalities. First, a neoliberal emphasis on producing autonomous, self-disciplined individuals whose behaviour is tailored to programmes of continuous self-monitoring and improvement, or what Mitchell Dean (1999: 147) termed neoliberal 'reflexive projects of the self'. Second, a calculative and instrumental conception of employees as assets whose capacities must be harnessed and continually expanded by managers so that they become go-getting, risk-taking entrepreneurs. This figure represents modern management's vision of ideal workers: proactive, unbounded, self-driven, forever expanding their capacities, willing to take on any challenge, with a seemingly inexhaustible capacity for work (Bovbjerg 2011; Shore 2008: 285; Wright and Ørberg 2017: 84). According to Emily Martin (1997), such qualities are similar to those of people with Attention Deficit Disorder. Constructing ideal workers in terms of the virtues of being positive, enthusiastic and entrepreneurially proactive, renders it unacceptable for a 'good employee' to resist or say 'no' to new challenges (Bovbjerg 2011). This begs the question: when is self-auditing a form of managerial oppression and when is it a genuine expression of personal autonomy and selfhood?

Quantifying and Rating Oneself: Surveillance or Empowerment?

Whether self-auditing is oppressive, or liberating is a question that lies at the heart of the 'Quantified Self' (QS) movement. This movement, whose slogan is 'self-knowledge through numbers', began in California in 2007 but has gone global. Quantified Selfers audit their daily activities by wearing sensors and using computing technology to monitor their heart rate, mood, stress levels, calorie intake, activity levels, alcohol consumption and sleep patterns. The movement was started in San Francisco by Gary Wolf, author and editor of *Wired* magazine and co-founder of the 'Quantified Self' blog. Its membership is an eclectic mix of 'early adopters, fitness freaks, technology evangelists, personal-development junkies, hackers and patients suffering from a wide variety of health problems' (*The Economist* 2012a). From the start, regular meeting groups were formed and, within five years, they had spread to over 50 cities. Accounts of QS meetings highlight the way participants share stories about the positive effects of metricising their everyday lives. The technologies allow individuals not only to observe and improve their own performance, but to share data with friends and compare or compete with others. This reflects what Whitson (2013) calls the 'gamification' of everyday life, a process that, in his view, turns surveillance into something that is also highly pleasurable.

There is a growing market for these self-monitoring technologies. Fitbit initially led the field in 'wearable technology' with sales topping 4.4 million gadgets in 2015 (Gil 2015). By 2021, Apple dominated the market with 38.25 million sales (or 30.1 per cent of the market), followed by the South Korean brand Samsung (10.2 per cent or 13 million smartwatch devices) and Chinese company Huawei (7.7 per cent or 9.8 million smartwatches) in 2021 (Sharma 2022). Worldwide sales of smartwatches totalled 127 million gadgets in 2021 and a year later, sales had jumped to 270 million gadgets (Laricchia 2023). The Covid-19 pandemic fuelled the surge in sales as smartwatches were able to monitor important health dimensions, including blood pressure, electrical signals from the heart (ECG) and blood oxygen saturation (SPO2).

The data that individuals collect on their head, chest and wrist-band gadgets is transmitted onto personal computers and then to the manufacturers of these devices. For example, data on personal sleep patterns are transmitted to the Zeo website, which now boasts the world's largest database on sleep stages. Wolf (2010) called this combination of micro and macro data gathering technology a 'macroscope' – bringing together the best of both a microscope and a telescope by combining systems for gathering small observations in nature with computing technologies that store and analyse these data. Wolf also predicted that, in future, measurement devices that people currently wear (belts, wristbands) may be put inside their bodies, leading him to ask, 'So what is the macroscope doing to us?' (Wolf 2011). Wolf addressed that question in a TED talk in Amsterdam in 2011. The macroscope, he declared, is both a window to collect data for 'systematic improvement' and an inward-looking 'mirror' for 'self-improvement, self-discovery, self-awareness and self-knowledge' (Wolf 2011). For Wolf, the 'self' is 'our operation centre, our consciousness and our moral compass. If we want to act more effectively in the world, we have to get to know ourselves better' (Wolf 2011).

Does QS therefore empower people, or subordinate them to a new normative order of panoptical control? According to Reyes (2014: 372), the quantified self is 'an algorithm of an individual's social networks, interactions, activities, purchases and whereabouts'. Self-quantifiers offer up this data to the life science, health technology and pharmaceutical industries and who owns the data is not always clear. This combination of epidemiological and personal data is also important for the development of individualised medicine and the future of the pharmaceutical industry. Significantly, many of the QS conferences are organised or sponsored by major corporations such as Intel, Vodafone and Philips – the latter has even produced its own QS promotional video (Philips 2015).

Others take a more optimistic view of the advance of quantified selves. Based on their ethnographic work, Nafus and Sherman (2014) propose that QS participants exercise a form of 'soft resistance'. They argue that because QSers assume multiple roles – 'as project designers, data collectors and critical sense makers' – and 'are constantly shifting their priorities', the data sets become fragmented, and participants escape the categories created by the biopolitics of the health technology industry. However, their ethnography also shows that QS-ers do *not* 'keep track of what [they] are tracking' (2014: 1788). They conclude that the QS 'movement does not escape the wider biopolitics of late capitalism that rely on radical individualism to drive consumption as a dominant mode of expression and to elide structural inequalities by framing all actions in terms of personal "choice"' (2014: 1788).

There seems little concern among the general public that there are no effective constraints on companies that own private data on an individual's health and welfare entering into commercial partnerships with insurance companies to determine people's premiums (Al-Saggaf 2015). Data-owning companies can also combine with mega data brokers like the US corporation Acxiom, which tracks people's online purchases to build psychological profiles for advertisers and marketers to sell bespoke products to targeted individuals. Google was the company that pioneered many of the personal data-mining activities that underpinned the rise of surveillance capitalism. The company created automated methods to analyse 'data exhaust' from people's searches, internet purchases and other online interactions. They used these to create psychological profiles to predict the needs of individuals for targeted advertising (Zuboff 2019: 68). This 'raw material', harvested from people's online preferences and behaviours, was the 'product' that Google sold to third parties. Other data-capturing techniques involved mapping streets, videoing building interiors and tracking individuals' locations throughout the day. Google's ways of appropriating data from different domains have been layered upon each other and expanded by a plethora of other companies including Facebook, Microsoft and Amazon. Google aims to 'co-pilot' individuals through life, not only by reflecting their needs but by 'influenc[ing] actual behaviour as it occurs in the real spaces of everyday life' (Zuboff 2019: 153).

Google's activities were given a massive boost following the 9/11 2001 terrorist attack by Al Qaeda. The CIA 'scrambled' to identify and track security threats by 'mak[ing] sense of the unstructured data floating around in the internet and elsewhere' (Zuboff 2019: 116). This led to an 'elective affinity' between the CIA and Google, which by this point had learned how to use 'behavioural surplus' from computer interactions and develop algorithms for handling massive quantities of data exhaust. The US intelligence community institutionalised a strategy for 'information dominance' and 'surveillance exceptionalism'. As Zuboff (2019: 115–18) details, the National Security Agency's 'Total Information Awareness' project assigned $64 million in 2002 to the Pentagon for research on 'novel intelligence from massive data', and $2.07 million in 2003 to Google to outfit the agency with technology 'capable of searching 15 million documents in 24 languages'. That same year, Google began customising its search engine under a special contract with the CIA to 'oversee top secret, secret and sensitive but unclassified intranets' for intelligence community agencies. The following year, Google acquired 'Keyhole', a satellite mapping company backed by a venture firm created by the CIA. This satellite mapping became the backbone for Google Earth, Google Maps and Google's Street View project. In 2009, Google joined with the CIA's venture firm to fund a start-up company that monitors every aspect of the web in real time in order to predict future events (Zuboff 2019: 115–17).

Secrecy was key to the above work, and Google's data capture and use more generally. In 2000 the US Federal Trade Commission outlined legislation to protect consumers which:

> demanded 'clear and conspicuous' notice of information practices; consumer choice over how personal information is used; access to all personal information, including rights to correct or delete; and enhanced security of personal information. (Zuboff 2019: 113)

However, following 9/11, everything changed, and surveillance exceptionalism led to the defeat of this attempt to protect the security of personal information (Zuboff 2019: 113). Instead, the strategy of Google – later emulated by Facebook, Microsoft and other Silicon Valley firms – was to operate opaquely and make increasingly audacious incursions into personal and public spaces and claim ownership of ever-greater spheres of private data. Zuboff quotes a paper as early as 2013 that:

> Facebook 'likes' could 'automatically and accurately estimate a wide range of personal attributes that people would typically assume to be private,' including sexual orientation, ethnicity, religious and political views, personality traits, intelligence, happiness, use of addictive substances, parental separation, age, and gender. (Zuboff 2019: 273)

Any public outcry or resistance, or attempts at regulation, were skilfully diffused. Facebook and Google would first respond with elaborate public relations gambits deflecting attention from the company's appropriation and use of data. They also made statements that were simply misleading about their predatory practices and engaged in lengthy legal combat. These ploys were designed to buy time so that people would become habituated to outrageous acts – what Zuboff (2019: 137) calls a 'cycle of dispossession' leading to 'psychic numbing' – until eventually their practices became normalised.

A rare instance of public outrage at the appropriation of personal data without people's knowledge or consent in order to steer their voting behaviour erupted in 2016 over Cambridge Analytica's use of Facebook data (Cadwalladr 2017). Cambridge Analytica was a data analysis firm, part of the SCL Group, a private British behavioural research and strategic communications company. It specialised in 'psychological operations' (psyops) for military actions and elections, defined as 'changing people's minds not through persuasion but through "information dominance", a set of techniques that includes rumour, disinformation and fake news' (Cadwalladr 2018). With some 200 experiences of 'cyberwarfare for elections' in underdeveloped democracies, in the 2000s, SCL turned its attention to US elections and the UK's Brexit referendum about whether to stay in the European Union (EU). In 2014, SCL contracted with Global Science Research, a company owned by Cambridge University researcher, Aleksandr Kogan, to harvest and process Facebook data so it could be matched to personality traits and voter rolls (Cadwalladr 2018). Kogan used a method developed by colleagues at Cambridge University's Psychometrics Centre. Through Amazon's crowdsourcing marketplace, 'Mechanical Turk' he offered to pay each volunteer $1 to engage in a personality quiz. This scored them in relation to five personality traits – openness, conscientiousness, extraversion, agreeableness and neuroticism. Some 320,000 people participated, each consenting to Kogan's accessing their Facebook profiles and those of their friends, none of whom knew their data had been harvested (Cadwalladr 2018). By summer 2014, Kogan's business partner boasted that Global Science Research had developed detailed characteristic and trait profiles on 40 million+ people in the US (Davies 2015). Cambridge Analytica later said they had psychological profiles of 230 million Americans. In the 2016 US presidential election and in the UK Brexit referendum, bespoke advertisements were targeted to voters in strategically important constituencies according to their psychological profile. Rather than engaging with voters in political debates, each advert was designed to trigger an emotional response (especially anger) that would spur them to vote for Trump or for Brexit, respectively. This chimed with the philosophy of Steve Bannon, then editor-in-chief of Breitbart and vice president of Cambridge Analytica, that 'politics is downstream from culture', so to change politics you need to find an inflection point that will change cultural perceptions (Cadwalladr 2018).

People continue to volunteer information about themselves that can be used against them. In October 2015, an app called 'Peeple' was about to be launched through the Apple App store. Described by its creators as a 'positivity app for positive people', it let users rate their friends, family members, neighbours, baristas, bosses and other social contacts – but without their consent. Use of the app would be free provided a person was 21 and had an established Facebook account and registered their mobile phone number (which would be stored on the company's database). Scoring would involve assigning people one to five stars, like the Michelin restaurant guide or a TripAdvisor hotel rating. According to its promoters, the Peeple app 'allows us to better choose who we hire, do business with, date, become our neighbours, roommates, landlords/tenants, and teach our children ... there are endless reasons why we would want this reference check for the people around us' (Hunt 2015). In her pitch to private shareholders and Silicon Valley venture capitalists, Julia Cordray, the app's co-founder and CEO, argued that 'people do so much research when they buy a car or make those kinds of decisions. Why not do the same kind of research on other aspects of your life?' At the time of its launch in October 2015 the company's shares were valued at US $7.6 million (Dewey 2015). However, following criticism that it would invite cyberbullying and stalkers, 7,000 people signed a petition organised by the campaign group 38 Degrees to have the app removed. Concerns were raised about its privacy policy, terms of service and plans for monetising.

The company withdrew the app but tried to re-launch it five months later with minor modifications, attracting 15,000 users in the first two weeks. In this modified version, individuals would be able to opt-in and approve comments about themselves before they were posted online and hide negative comments on their character. However, the company announced plans to launch an additional 'truth licence', which would allow fee-paying customers to review *all* comments somebody had received or written about others – including unpublished ones (Monticello Kievlan n.d.). As CEO Julia Cordray told a CCTV interviewer in 2016: 'whether people like it or not, the world is headed toward a place where people will find it valuable to manage their online reputation' (CCTV America 2016). It was Peeple's own tarnished reputation and declining share value that ultimately brought about the app's quiet withdrawal.

As each of these examples illustrates, digital technologies of measurement and self-tracking are creating new kinds of auditable selves, consumers and citizen-subjects. The way companies are using personal data, whether gifted by consumers or appropriated without their knowledge, is making possible new forms of biopolitics and new ways of governing people's behaviour, consumer preferences and political choices. Surveillance capitalism builds on and extends the key elements of monitoring, measuring, calculating and comparing that are fundamental to audit culture, and has found new ways of making profits from the data generated by these technologies.

Measuring Performance in China: Citizenship and Social Credit

So far our examples of how subjects are shaped through big data, rankings and performance metrics have come from Western societies, suggesting that such individualising and totalising techniques of governance are particular to market economies. However, interesting variations on these trends can be seen in contemporary China. A major problem for China's leaders has been how to ensure effective legal and regulatory compliance across a range of fields, from environmental protection and food safety to the enforcement of civil judgments and academic honesty. In 2014, China's State Council released a blueprint, 'Guidelines of Social Credit System Construction (2014–2020)' setting out its goal to build a national social credit system (SCS) in six years (Liu 2019: 22; Reilly et al. 2021). As Rogier Creemers explains, this initiative had complex historical and intellectual roots as, in China, law is not seen as an autonomous sphere but as 'a tool to cultivate subjects' moral sentiments and transform their worldview, in order to achieve social and cosmic harmony' (Creemers 2018: 6). In China, government agencies had a tradition of administering disciplinary punishments through 'discredited subject blacklists' and rewards based on 'redlists' recording acts of conspicuous merit (Creemers 2018: 13; Liu 2019: 24). As China opened its economy, it found that it lacked a system for assessing financial creditworthiness of the kind well developed in the West and established another type of SCS that allocated scores to companies and individuals. (Liu 2019: 23). Jiangsu's provincial government extended this further by using its own available data to create an experimental 'mass credit programme'. Each individual was allocated 1,000 credit points, which could then be deducted for infringements of legal, administrative or moral norms such as drink-driving, having a child without family planning permission or non-payment of loans. Citizens were ranked from A to D according to their scores. Although the Jiangsu system was criticised, most provinces and virtually every city in China developed its own SCS (Liu 2019: 24, 26). These diverse credit systems each sought to promote socio-ethical behaviour and trustworthiness among citizens using a variety of techniques like naming and shaming, sanctions against rule-breakers, and credit mechanisms that were extended beyond a market context (Creemers 2018: 10).

In 2015, the People's Bank of China authorised eight Chinese companies to commence work on state-approved pilot projects with the aim of developing one national SCS capable of scoring and ranking the character and 'trustworthiness' of each citizen. Numerical scoring systems were based on an individual's repayments, purchase history and personal characteristics in what was an extension of China's recently introduced financial credit rating system. The most well known of the eight pilot schemes was 'Sesame Credit', an internet-based scoring system built and run by Ant Financial, a subsidiary of Alibaba, the Chinese e-commerce giant. With over 900 million active users (Ma 2022), Alibaba is China's largest online shopping platform, and has more transactions than Amazon and eBay combined. When first listed on the New York Stock Exchange in 2014, its market value was a staggering US $231.4 billion. Together with the IT company Tencent, Alibaba runs the Chinese equivalent of all social networks (Falkvinge, 2015). The Sesame SCS allocated each person a score between 350 and 950 based on factors such as their financial, purchasing and spending history. The higher a person's score, the greater the rewards. For example, 600 points would allow an individual the privilege of taking out an instant loan up to US $800 when shopping online. Someone with a score of 650 could rent a car from the Chinese companies eHai.com and Car Inc. without leaving a deposit, or get a faster hotel check out (Hodson 2015). Someone with 700 points would earn a reduction in the time taken to obtain a travel permit for Singapore, while 750 points enabled fast-track treatment in processing a Pan-European Schengen visa. Spending through Alibaba's payment app (Alipay) or conducting transactions that recruited friends to Sesame Credit also raised a person's score, as did personal hobbies, interactions with friends, lifestyle and consumer purchases. For example, someone who buys work shoes, local produce or nappies (responsible purchases), receives more points than someone who buys online videogames (irresponsible). Promoters stimulated take-up of this system by presenting it as a game. A mobile phone app designed by Sesame Credit invited users to guess whether their social credit scores were higher or lower than their friends' and encouraged people to share their ratings. Zheping Huang, a Hong Kong-based journalist, chronicled his own experience with the game in October 2015 saying, 'in the past few weeks I began to notice a mysterious new trend. Numbers were popping up on my social media feeds as my friends and strangers on Weibo and WeChat began to share their 芝麻信用分, or "Sesame Credit scores"' (Huang 2015). China's largest matchmaking service, Baihe, also combined with Sesame to promote clients with good credit scores, giving them prominent spots on the company's website (Hatton 2015). Users were encouraged to flaunt their good credit scores to friends and potential marriage partners.

According to Huang (2015), Sesame Credit operated independently of government and 'works more like a loyalty program than a credit rating system'. However, others saw a more political agenda at work. In an interview with the business journal *Quartz*, Creemers warned that the programme was far more than just a credit-tracking method: 'The government wants to build a platform that leverages things like big data, mobile internet, and cloud computing to measure and evaluate different levels of people's lives in order to create a gamified nudging for people to behave better' (cited in Huang 2015). Acknowledging this, China's State Council explained that social credit would 'forge a public opinion environment that trust-keeping is glorious', but also warned that the 'new system will reward those who report acts of breach of trust' (Creemer, cited in Hatton 2015). Sesame Credit was open about its government links, candidly conceding that it worked closely with the Ministry of Public Security, the

Supreme People's Court, the Ministry of Education and the State Administration for Industry and Commerce. However, in a letter to the *Financial Times*, Sesame's general manager, Hu Tao, later denied that the company shared its data with the government (Tao 2017).

What was striking about the Chinese government's attempts to shape and control its citizenry is that it sought to harness all of the elements of performance and governance identified earlier: that is, state control and private companies combined with big data and popular social media to steer individuals towards a constant monitoring and disciplining of their own behaviour, and a performative marketing of their 'good character'. As Clover (2016) says:

> China's Internet is fast becoming a laboratory where the march of technology combined with profit-driven private companies, authoritarian politics and weak civil liberties is creating a toxic cocktail. If unchecked, the 'social credit' system … could be used to assign citizenship scores to everyone based on 'patriotic' criteria such as whether they buy imported products, or the content of their postings on social media. (Clover 2016)

No such totalising system is yet in place. Sesame's SCS remains voluntary and, while the Chinese government had declared that it wanted it to become mandatory from 2020 (Osborne 2015), this did not happen. The licences allocated to the eight companies were not renewed, although each subsequently received a stake in a unified national credit-scoring platform called 'Baihang', in which the People's Bank of China held significant control (Donnelly 2023). The reason the licences were not renewed was not to do with freedom or privacy but because the government feared that the credit companies would become too independent. It decided to rein in risky financial behaviours, particularly the 'systemic risks from the purchase of overseas assets with money raised through high-interest financing products' (Hornby 2017). Concern about the growing power of giant digital conglomerates like Alibaba and Tencent was another factor. Indeed, after Jack Ma, the business magnate and billionaire co-founder of Alibaba and Ant Group, publicly criticised the banks and tech industry regulators, there was a crackdown on his businesses, and he mysteriously disappeared from public life (Sweney 2022). In 2023 Ma announced he would cede control of his companies and the Chinese government subsequently took 'special management shares' in Alibaba and Tencent, giving them special rights over business decisions (Sweney 2023). While the government has tightened its control over China's private fintech industry, its plan for a unified national 'record for people, businesses, and government, which can be monitored in real-time' (Donnelly 2023: 3) has not materialised.

The 2020 deadline for creating a unified SCS may have passed, but the comprehensive roadmap set out in the 2014 planning document continued to be implemented through a range of technical, bureaucratic, legal and financial measures. To date, the 'corporate' aspects of the SCS are more advanced than those addressed to government or individuals. A recent study showed that between 2003 and 2020, '73.3 percent of mentions in official documents identified "companies" as the targets of social credit, compared to just 10.3 percent for individuals' (Reilly et al. 2021). Miscreants are punished by being blocked from particular activities, like receiving government subsidies, entering the civil service, the Communist Party and the military, or purchasing real estate. Companies and individual citizens can be barred from travelling on high-speed trains or on civil aircraft. According to Creemers, they are also not allowed:

> to visit star-rated hotels or luxury restaurants, resorts, nightclubs and golf courses, to go on foreign holidays, to send their children to fee-paying schools, to purchase particular kinds of high-value insurance products, to buy or renovate their homes, or purchase cars. (Creemers 2018: 15)

At the time of writing, China's multiple social credit systems remain fragmented and share only common aspirations and language. They are nevertheless evolving and could become more unified. The Central Committee of the Chinese Communist Party (CCP) has issued a 'new roadmap to 2025 for the "construction of a rule of law society" in which the social credit system is set to play a major role' (Reilly et al. 2021).

Western media and politicians have heavily criticised China's social credit systems, describing them as 'terrifying', 'totalitarian' and an attempt to 'turn obedience to the state into a game' (Osborne 2015). The American Civil Liberties Union (ACLU) called Sesame Credit an 'Orwellian nightmare' and 'a warning for Americans' (Storm 2015). Others claimed its scores could be shaped by a person's political opinions so that posting comments on Chinese dissidents, Tiananmen Square, Tibet, or the Shanghai stock market collapse would lower one's scores, as would political posts on these events by friends (Falkvinge, 2015). Even the usually more sober *Financial Times* headlined it as 'China: When Big Data Meets Big Brother' (Clover 2016). However, China's use of big data as a technology of citizenship reflects trends also occurring in Western countries, as the Edward Snowden and Wikileaks disclosures revealed. Even the *New Scientist* conceded that, as in China, 'people who live in the West are being tracked and ranked all the time. For now, though, this is serving commercial interests rather than those of the state' (Hodson 2015). If China's attempts to develop social credit systems are an egregious invasion of privacy and encroachment into civil rights, they are no less intrusive – and certainly not as covert – as the activities of Google, Facebook, Microsoft and other surveillance capitalist firms. Moreover, the way that major companies in Silicon Valley have developed their technologies in intimate collaboration with the military and security services puts into perspective Western concerns about the possibility of the Chinese government using big data to impose tighter political control over its citizens.

Conclusions

We began by asking 'What counts as evidence of good performance, behaviour and character?' and 'What are the politics behind projects to measure or construct good citizens and subjects?' We have illustrated several key trends in the way that performance indicators and personal data are being used – by companies, by the state and by individuals themselves. But what is the larger story that these examples tell? In developing his work on governmentality, Foucault (1991) observed how state authorities made absolutely explicit why the subject of power was being disciplined, what the norms were behind these disciplinary regimes, and how individuals could use redemptive therapies to align themselves with the normative order. This is particularly evident in the models used by BT, McKinney Rogers and Auckland University, and these organisations even coach staff in how to improve their performance and themselves. But in the Quantified Self example, individuals do not have to comply with the values and measures of an employer's framework; instead they set their own targets and engage with measurement technologies following an ethics of self-empowerment. At the same time, they give away to third parties valuable data about themselves, their conduct and their performance with no knowledge or control over how this data will be used. The popularisation of self-tracking devices places individuals under even greater pressure to monitor and audit themselves, inside as well as outside the workplace, and creates the possibility for even more individualising and totalising systems of governance. Whether presented as techniques to enhance production and improve quality, a game, or a vehicle of empowerment, these examples all illustrate ways in which performance metrics are being mobilised as disciplinary instruments to create auditable selves and governable subjects (Cruikshank 1999). While there are obvious continuities with the type of governmentality that Foucault analysed in the second half of the twentieth century, projects like those of Google and Cambridge Analytica have opened up a new terrain for the art of government. They have provided political rulers and private corporations with immense scope – and chilling possibilities – for employing covert instruments to shape the way individuals construct and conduct themselves, while also generating enormous profits for surveillance capitalism.

8

Conclusion: Repurposing Audit – Restoring Trust, Accountability and Democracy

[A] politics of possibility … cannot simply be put 'out there' in the world with the hope that it will flourish. It needs to be sustained by the continual work of making and remaking a space for it to exist in the face of what threatens to undermine and destroy it. (Gibson-Graham 2006: xxvii)

The Problems with Audit

This book traced how the calculative practices and technologies of audit and accountancy have travelled, the ways they have been used to reshape contemporary societies, and how auditing relates to wider processes of disciplining, managing and governing individuals and populations. As we have shown, the meaning of audit changed as it migrated from its origins in checking accounts and ensuring financial probity. In the private sector, this entailed a fundamental shift from accountancy activities geared to bookkeeping and certifying the accuracy of financial reports to a vast array of advisory services that included taxation, risk management, financial planning, IT systems, human resources and organisational restructuring. With the post-1990s advance of New Public Management and neoliberal reforms, audit, like policy, became an instrument of choice for introducing economy and efficiency into public services (Klein 2008: 50) and for 'reinventing government'. This has spawned a whole new way of managing and governing based on performance indicators, proxy measures for quality, competitive league tables, and best practice, as defined by its calculative rationalities. Yet as we have demonstrated, these instruments are often dysfunctional and have perverse effects. The questions we asked were:

• How should we theorise audit culture?

- What is fuelling its expansion, and what implications does this have for individuals, organisations and society?
- Who are the auditors and rankers today and how are their activities promoting the spread of audit culture? What role do international accountancy firms play in shaping the audit society?
- Why do governments, policy makers and managers continue to use audit and accountancy practices despite evidence of their flaws and deleterious effects?

One of the factors that legitimates the use of audit is its capacity to reshape entire sectors such as the automobile and other industries, education, health and wellbeing on both national and international scales. If governments find audit a useful technology for holding organisations and whole sectors to account, within organisations, managers use audit as an instrument for enhancing performance and productivity. It is also an important device for controlling the workforce. It sets the measures and expectations by which individuals are to conduct themselves as 'good' employees, blaming, shaming and punishing those whose performance falls below standard. When internalised by subjects, the calculative practices of audit construct individuals as 'accountable' and 'free' agents who succeed by mobilising their personal resources to optimise 'what counts'.

Our analysis highlighted three key perverse features of audit. First, while audit culture has proliferated and radically transformed organisations in the public, private and non-government sectors, the quality and effectiveness of accounting-industry audits has declined. For major audit firms, their income now comes mainly from management consulting and tax advisory work and financial audit has almost become a loss-leader. Financial regulation through audit in the private sector has also become riddled with failure. Second, we highlighted the runaway and 'domaining' effects of audit, and the way it produces spirals of surveillance, inspection, paper trails and other data whose comparisons and rankings create the need for even more audits. Audits acquire a life of their own that outlives and transcends the intentions of their inventors. They place continuous and relentless demands upon individuals and organisations to improve themselves and modify their behaviour according to the logic and templates of what is being measured. Third, performance measures for public service organisations are often inconsistent with the values and priorities of professionals and undermine their capacity to exercise informed judgement. There is an increasing distance and detachment between those who deliver services and create value in organisations – the auditees – and those who audit and inspect them – the new managerial 'auditocracy'. A new class of technocrats (data analysts, finance officers, risk and compliance experts, customer satisfaction analysts, human resources officers, and executive leaders), has formed around the spread of audit and its systems of accountability, performance measurement and management consultancy. These actors have become part of a wider social configuration or assemblage that draws together across multiple sites and scales the individuals, institutions, industries, agencies and ideas that have formed around the principles and practices of auditing. This configuration is a central aspect of what we term 'audit culture'. One might even call this the 'world' of audit.

However, while audit culture can be seen as an organising principle that structures that configuration, this does not imply some kind of cultural determinism. Audit does have tangible social, political and material effects, but these must be understood in terms of the wider political economy that underpins it and creates the conditions for its existence. This raises important questions about the role of audit in new forms of capitalism and the regulatory role of the state. The rise of audit, particularly in Western societies, is symptomatic of a particular type of economy that has emerged out of four decades of neoliberal and New Public Management reforms of the state. If audit was a key instrument in the neoliberalisation of economy and society, it has developed into a form of capitalism itself, as exemplified by the power of the Big Four and other international institutions that shape the global economy. The features of audit capitalism are as pervasive, distinctive and dominating as finance capitalism, surveillance capitalism, vulture capitalism and other varieties of contemporary capitalism. All of these involve the capture and privatisation of public and personal assets to generate profits for a privileged few. However, unlike these other forms, audit capitalism is predicated on a state-guaranteed market for its services and advances on the pretext that it serves the public good by promoting accountability and transparency. It camouflages its actions under the cloak of narratives about improving quality, raising standards, ensuring value for money and enhancing the effectiveness of services.

Reclaiming Accountability and Trust

This concluding chapter asks: Is the expansion of audit culture unstoppable and inevitable, and where is this trajectory leading? What alternatives are there? How can professionals and citizens reclaim the autonomy and trust that audit practices have stripped from their organisations and from society? We argue that audit culture is not inevitable: some professionals and citizens are finding ways to create spaces to reclaim control and enact visions for a more accountable and democratic society. To illustrate this, we explore initiatives that are taking place on four different scales. The first concerns the way individuals find room for manoeuvre within their own organisations to pursue activities that accord with their own professional values, to ameliorate or subvert externally imposed measures, and redefine what 'counts'. We use a case study from higher education in the UK to highlight this. The second focuses on the reform of a whole sector of public services, in this case, through the concerted efforts of professionals and researchers in the field of child protection. The third concerns initiatives by national governments to reform the accounting industry, implement measures to end the spate of audit failures and fraud scandals, and restore trust in the probity of financial audit. The fourth highlights efforts to rethink the very concepts of accountability and audit in ways that promote public trust and rescue democracy from audit capitalism, drawing on inspiration from the work of critical accountants, social scientists and philosophers.

Mobilising the Agency of Individuals: Scale 1

One reason for the expansion of audit was a crisis of trust in the professions fuelled by neoliberal reforms from the 1980s onwards. In the UK, the market-making agenda required radically changing the practice of professionals in the institutions of the welfare state. Lawyers, doctors, academics, teachers and other public professionals were accused of being 'supply-oriented', cosseted, out of touch with the 'customers' they were supposed to serve, and irredeemably self-serving. This meant that it was no longer legitimate for public sector professionals themselves to define what services they would provide for the sector. To make them 'demand-oriented', auditing standards, benchmarks and targets were used to shape their priorities and performance and meet what government, policy makers or managers deemed to be the needs of customers. If Conservative Party ideology sought to discredit and demonise the autonomy of professionals, a series of high-profile scandals assisted in rocking public confidence in public servants. Revelations included the systematic abuse of children by those responsible for care homes in England and Wales;

decades of paedophilia by priests in the Catholic Church that had been known about yet covered up; the unnecessary deaths of 35 children undergoing heart surgery because of the reported 'club culture' of doctors at the Bristol Royal Infirmary; and the discovery that the kindly family doctor, Harold Shipman, turned out to be the greatest mass murderer in British history. Many politicians drew the conclusion that professionals could not be trusted to govern themselves and saw audit as the answer to improving professional practice and restoring public trust. Yet auditing does not promote trust and, in many instances, creates spirals of mistrust (Power 1997; O'Neill 2002). When the penalty for performing poorly in a centralised and competitive system is loss of status or withdrawal of resources, individuals are incentivised to 'perform' to the target and game the system in ways that maximise the appearance of success. External conformity, rule bending, and a culture of compliance are inevitable outcomes – as the notorious examples of fabricated factory production reports in the former Soviet Union remind us.

Although bureaucratic conformity and managerial compliance are key aims of audit, some professionals have nonetheless found ways to create the space to develop practices in accordance with their own professional values and challenge those of audit culture. Examples of this can be seen in initiatives by individual academics in higher education. In the UK, the marketisation of higher education entailed recasting students as customers of the university. Degree programmes are now commodities regulated according to consumer rights legislation and the Competition and Markets Authority (CMA). The assumption was that academics only pursued their own research interests in their ivory towers, and that marketisation would make them, and their universities, more consumer oriented and responsive to the demands of students, parents and employers. However, some lecturers have been able to work the cracks in the system and respond to students as learners rather than consumers. For example, Anke Schwittay, a professor of international development and anthropology at Sussex University in the UK, has developed a critical pedagogy in her book, *Creative Universities* (2021). She highlights the action she was able to take within her own immediate orbit. However, she also indicates the seeming impossibility for such bottom-up initiatives to transform the top-down audited, and managerialist university. This is just one example of how academics inhabit what Harney and Moten (2013) call the 'undercommons', where they generate enlightened ideas but these have little effect on what 'goes on upstairs' (2013: 26).

Schwittay saw how the relentless critique of existing approaches to development left students feeling disillusioned and unable to see how they could make a positive change in the world. In response, she developed a pedagogy that not only critiqued the present but also fostered students' creative capacities to imagine and build alternative futures. She did this in three steps. First, by reflexively considering her goals; second, by critically analysing the contestable key words in educational discourses – 'creativity', 'future', 'alternatives' – so as to be clear about what she meant by them; and, third, by turning her meanings into a set of educational practices. For example, 'creativity' is a keyword in discourses about the knowledge economy, corporate growth and national competitiveness. Translated into higher education, it meant teaching students how to maximise and adapt their capacities to meet the demands of rapidly changing workplaces. In contrast, Schwittay's idea of critical-creative pedagogy entailed a search for radical alternative futures *outside* mainstream capitalist growth agendas (2021: 12–13).

Schwittay notes that academics have little time to reflect on the aims of their teaching or do the research and thinking necessary to rebuild their pedagogy 'when teaching loads are increasing, when core modules with mandatory content need to be taught, when fixed learning outcomes ask for conformity and when conventional modes of assessment are the norm' (2021: 5). She was able to find space for manoeuvre within a three-year research project that gave her the time to properly research bodies of literature on creative methods from design and the arts, experiential learning, educational practices, open-ended and iterative enquiry, and critical hope, and work out how to integrate these ideas in what she called a critical-creative pedagogy (2021: 4). She radically transformed the two modules she convened. Being head of department, she was able to engage colleagues in wider discussions about the curriculum and pedagogy of the degree programmes. With other lecturers, she also participated in a university-wide Active Learning Network that created a supportive environment for nurturing reflexive pedagogy. These were the 'cracks in the system' where she found room to manoeuvre in an increasingly constrained university environment.

To create such spaces for individual agency requires the following moves:

1. Develop a 'politically reflexive practice' (Wright 2004) that examines how an organisation is positioning the individual as a worker, subject, auditee or professional academic.

2. Interrogate the key terms used to define individuals and their work in order to de-naturalise these narratives and think about how things could be done differently.

3. Reflect deliberatively on one's own values to ask, 'what am I trying to achieve?'

4. Look for places within the institution where the individual can act in accordance with their own values, otherwise known as 'institutional capture' or 'steering from below'.

5. Create a community of practice to engage a wider range of colleagues and students in discussions about educational aims and practices (Lave and Wenger 1991; Willett 2013).

6. Constantly question and seek new ways to act within a system that is continually changing.

7. Encourage students to adopt this politically reflexive practice and take it into the world.

Schwittay's example also illustrates the limits of individual action. Although she successfully transformed the education practice of her own courses and engaged with colleagues in their own community of practice, her bottom-up initiative had little influence over the institution's top-down strategy to transform the university's education. While the pro-vice chancellor's 'Pedagogical Revolution' invited academics to initiate change, Schwittay's ideas of creative pedagogy were dismissed as potentially off-putting to some students and staff (Schwittay 2021: 11). The distances that reforms have created between university managers, academics and students limit the ability of creative ideas from below to travel within, or transform, the organisation.

Child Protection: Whole-system Changes in Scale 2

Reclaiming an organisation from the grip of audit and transforming an entire sector through the collective efforts of professionals and researchers is difficult but not impossible, as our next example shows. The whole social work sector in the UK, particularly child protection, is undergoing a systematic change in recognition of the damaging effects of audit. Changes have been introduced to restore the professionalism of frontline workers and build a system of management and data collection around them that will enhance the learning of individuals, institutions and the system as a whole. One major difference between higher education and social work, at least in the UK, is that the latter is a 'regulated profession'. This means that to become a qualified professional social worker one must have completed a degree approved by a specialist regulator body, Social Work England, which is answerable to both the Department for Education and the Department of Health. Beyond this, government sets standards and guidelines for the practice of social work which are, in turn, audited by Ofsted (the Office for Standards in Education, Children's Services and Skills). This regulation means that, in contrast to higher education, the whole sector can be reformed in response to professional initiatives. Previous reforms had introduced highly regulated and computerised auditing systems, but more recent, national-level changes have drawn on isolated child protection initiatives in a few local authorities and built up a system-wide reform aligned with these bottom-up developments and social workers' professional values.

Child protection is an issue of major concern for social-work professionals. In 2010, at any moment in the UK, some 62,000 children were looked after by the state and there were 'protection plans' for an additional 34,100 children because they were suffering neglect or abuse (Munro 2010a). Each occurrence of the tragic death of a child under local authority care has precipitated a national commission to review the child protection service. Eileen Munro, Emeritus professor of social policy at the London School of Economics, conducted a comprehensive study of these national reviews between 1973 and 1994. Her analysis revealed that mistakes in social work reasoning were happening repeatedly. Each report produced recommendations about how to tighten regulations to prevent those mistakes, yet the same mistakes kept recurring. Munro concluded that the problems needed looking at in a different way.

For over two decades, these reviews had recommended an ever-tighter system of bureaucratic control and compliance. The government established a computerised 'Integrated Children System' and accompanying assessment frameworks and policy documents, with the idea that computerisation would reduce the scope for human error. However, Munro argued that these systems could not eradicate the 'complexity and associated uncertainty of child protection work' (Munro 2011: 6 §2). As a philosopher interested in social work reasoning, Munro asked, does this system make it easier for social workers to do the right thing, or harder for them to do the wrong thing? She concluded it did neither. The mandatory use of the Integrated Children System was counter-productive as the way it collected and presented data did not make it easy for social workers to reason about families and children's safety – should a child be removed from their family, or can the family be worked with to make a good home and life for the child? Instead, the software produced 40 pages of boxes of data but no useful narrative about what was happening to the child.

In June 2010, Michael Gove, Secretary of State for Education commissioned Munro to conduct a national review of child protection. Her 'systems approach' (2005, 2010b) regarded social workers' agency as shaped by the system around them. Whereas previous reviews blamed mistakes on individual social workers, she presented a more complicated picture of causality.

> The human operator is only one factor; the final outcome is a product of the interaction of the individual with the rest of the system. It has been found that human errors are not usually random but can be understood and predicted by seeing them in this wider context. (Munroe 2005: 534)

The key question she posed was what form of human interaction with technical systems 'helps professionals make the best judgements they can to protect a vulnerable child?' (Munro 2011: 6 §1). To achieve this, social workers needed the knowledge, confidence and support to use their professional judgement as best they can. Munro also emphasised that government and the public needed to accept that, even when social work practice is optimal, it cannot 'ensure' the safety of children as tragedies will happen.

Her first report criticised 'the undue importance given to performance indicators and targets which ... have skewed attention to process over the quality and effectiveness of help given' (Munro 2010b). She depicted 'a defensive system that puts so much emphasis on procedures and recording that insufficient attention is given to developing and supporting the expertise to work effectively with children, young people and families' (Munro 2011: 6 §3). Practitioners and managers told the review that:

> statutory guidance, targets and local rules have become so extensive that they limit their ability to stay child-centred. The demands of bureaucracy have reduced their capacity to work directly with children, young people and families. Services have become so standardised that they do not provide the required range of responses to the variety of need that is presented. This review recommends a radical reduction in the amount of central prescription to help professionals move from a com-

pliance culture to a learning culture, where they have more freedom
to use their expertise in assessing need and providing the right help.
(Munro 2011: 6–7 §5)

These comments echo situations found in other professions that have
been turned inside-out by audit culture, including education, nursing,
policing and local government. Munro's final report proposed 'moving
from a system that has become over-bureaucratised and focused on compliance to one that values and develops professional expertise and is focused
on the safety and welfare of children and young people' (Munro 2011: 6
§1). This involved overhauling all the elements in the sector, starting with
ways to educate social workers and develop their professional knowledge
and judgement, and consider ways to support them and generate reflective practice. Second, she emphasised the importance of social workers
being able to convey to managers the effects of institutional arrangements on their social work practice, and for managers to take up these
suggestions to create a learning organisation. Third, she recommended
government revise statutory guidance to remove prescriptions that are
unnecessary and distort good practice. Instead, regulations should focus
only on essential rules and principles that underpin good social work
and facilitate multi-agency collaboration (Munro 2011: 7 §6). Fourth, the
review worked closely with the national auditing and inspection service,
Ofsted, to look at how inspection could focus on and measure what *really
matters*; that is, whether children have been helped. She pointed out that
'Inspection is a key influence on priorities in frontline practice so needs
to support the change from a compliance to a learning culture' (Munro
2011: 7 §7). The review recommended that Ofsted change its auditing by
putting the experiences of children, young people and their families at the
heart of the inspection system and examining the efficacy of inter-agency
working between social work, health, education, police, probation and the
justice system.

As studies in the anthropology of policy show (Shore and Wright 1997b,
2011), new policies often come from local initiatives; policies do not
always start in government and trickle down. Some local authority social
work departments were already experimenting with new practices with
the support of academics like Munro herself and Barry Luckock at Sussex
University (Luckock et al. 2017), who had long advocated for alternative approaches. Munro's review obtained permission for four other local
authorities to relax some government regulations. This enabled them to

experiment with different approaches to a child-centred provision that supported social workers individually and collectively to develop their professional knowledge, reasoning and judgement. These pilots provided such compelling evidence that the government accepted all of the review's recommendations.

Munro (2012) reviewed progress on the four points in her report after one year. Several authorities were engaging in changes in social work professional practice and organisation. Government was changing its statutory guidance and Ofsted had already revolutionised its auditing and inspection system. Until these major changes had been fully implemented, local agencies were limited in their freedom to re-design their social work practices (Munro 2012: 7 §1.8). However, a newly appointed chief social worker had established a fund for local authorities to develop their social work practice and the whole-system changes recommended by Munro. Central government, Ofsted, local authority managers and social workers themselves were galvanised in a process of whole-system change.

The reforms by Brighton and Hove (2017) local authority exemplify this process. First, they focused on the relationship between the social worker and the child and family. Social workers, now treated as knowledgeable and fully trained professionals, used their expertise to construct a 'One Story' narrative detailing what happened in each interaction with the family. Other professions involved with the family also contributed to the One Story. Data still tracked the efficacy of social work interventions in improving outcomes for children, but the number of forms reduced from 78 to 12. Second, the focus was on creating an organisation that supported social workers in their often stressful and dangerous work. Organised into 'pods' (i.e. closely connected units), child protection social workers met regularly to share information about how they were working with their cases. This meant that each child had a designated social worker, but if one was absent, other pod members could maintain continuity.

Each social worker was also part of a cross-disciplinary group whose aim was to develop reflective practice (Lees 2017; McKeown et al. 2022). Their regular meetings followed a fixed procedure, whereby one person presented a case they were working on or struggling with. They then sat in silence while the others discussed the case and shared ideas. Formal evaluations showed that this process helped engender support and feelings of belonging to a collective (Lees 2017). They shared ideas and enhanced professional knowledge by reflecting on biases and assumptions and looking at situations from the child's or the parents' points of view (an approach called 'mentalisation'). There was a focus on 'containment' – ways for social workers to handle the emotions, distress and fears they faced when working in unpredictable situations and engaging with child cruelty and neglect.

The aim was to connect frontline experience to management change. Evaluations showed big changes from the previous 'blame culture', but the organisation was not yet fully 'learning' from frontline experience and making adjustments (Brighton and Hove 2017). The changes meant fewer children taken into care, more families working with a consistent social worker, and more children and parents satisfied with the service they received. Among social workers, there was less stress and sickness and, as the authority's standing improved, it attracted and retained more highly qualified and experienced social workers. This reduced the authority's reliance on expensive agency staff and generated better performance figures at lower cost, which pleased councillors and other policy makers.

This example shows how whole-system reform requires active and direct engagement by all actors in the sector. In this case it included social workers, academic researchers, lower-tier managers in social work departments, local authority leaders, ministry officials, Ofsted inspectors and politicians. The heart of the change was a focus on the child and on relationships, not performance figures and compliance with managerial procedures. This shows how other professional sectors could effectively dismantle the calculative and destructive logics of audit culture and reorganise themselves around their core function and professional aims and identities.

Reforming the International Audit Industry: Scale 3

The accounting industry itself is the third area needing initiatives to counter and dismantle audit culture. There are serious structural problems with the international audit market, but it is only subject to national regulations. At various points, the UK and US governments have legislated to regulate the industry, but these have been rolled back again. Following the collapse of Enron in 2001 and the demise of the international accounting firm Arthur Anderson, the US government passed the Sarbanes-Oxley Act (SOX) to protect shareholders, employees and the public against accounting errors and fraudulent financial practices. This introduced tougher accounting regulations, defined the rules for corporations' audit committees and external auditors, and set limits on the number of non-audit services a company's auditor could perform during audits. It also forced chief executive officers and chief finance officers to personally vouch for the accuracy of accounts, although the regulatory body, the Securities and Exchange Commission (SEC), did not take up a single case before 2007, and only 31 cases by 2013 (Morgenson 2013). The Sarbanes-Oxley Act was a major reform of the audit industry and between 2000 and 2002 EY, PwC and KPMG sold their consultancy practices. However, following the 2008 global financial crisis, some of the provisions of the act were relaxed, which led to the Big Four rebuilding their consultancy arms. By 2015 the Big Four held 'the biggest share of global consultancy income, with a combined 40% of the market' (Loxton 2015) and most of the systemic problems had returned.

In the UK the spectacular collapse of the construction and facilities management services company Carillion in 2018 (whose income came largely from PFI [private finance initiative] contracts) led to a £1.5 billion debt and 20,000 job losses. The retail firm BHS (British Home Stores) also suffered a scandalous collapse with 11,000 job losses and a £571 million pension deficit. These companies had long-term auditing relationships with KPMG and PwC respectively. The UK government and the Competition and Markets Authority (CMA) subsequently announced three separate reviews: The independent Kingman Review of the ineffectual Financial Reporting Council (FRC); the CMA's inquiry into the supply of statutory audit services in the UK; and the independent Brydon Review of the quality and effectiveness of audit. In 2018, the Shadow Labour Party Chancellor of the Exchequer, John McDonnell commissioned an independent report entitled 'Reforming the Auditing Industry' (Sikka et al. 2018). The following year, the House of Commons Business, Energy and Industrial Strategy Committee also published *The Future of Audit* (House of Commons 2019a). Between them, these reports identified the problems with the audit industry, and broadly agreed on solutions.

The first problem is that the Big Four oligopoly has become so powerful that it dominates the audit industry and ministries call on their expertise when drafting tax laws and regulations for the accounting industry. Despite the free market rhetoric, competition and choice are illusory and smaller accounting firms lack the resources to compete. KPMG, EY, Deloitte or PwC audit 98 per cent of FTSE 350 constituents (the largest companies on the UK market) and 99 per cent of Standard & Poor's top 500 publicly traded US companies (Marriage and Ford 2019). The CMA (2019) proposed capping the number of FTSE 350 companies that the Big Four can audit. The House Commons, CMA and Labour Party reports proposed mandatory joint audits of the kind successfully trialled in France, which required large firms to collaborate with smaller audit companies to enable challenger firms to gain a foothold in the market (House of Commons 2019a: 60–61). The Labour Party report also recommended that the state develop its own statutory body to provide audits for financial enterprises and 'become the fifth largest supplier of external audit in the UK' (Sikka et al. 2018: 73).

The second problem the reports highlighted was serious failures in company audits. The House of Commons listed BHS, Carillion, and ten other investigations into serious company audit failings (House of Commons 2019a: 7–8). The FRC also reported an unacceptable deterioration, with 27 per cent of audits not meeting its auditing standards. In the case of KPMG, that figure was 39 per cent (House of Commons 2019a: 9–10). As the House of Commons committee observed, few companies can afford such a rate of faulty products and 'we are not aware of other industries in which 27 per cent of products sold are defective' (House of Commons 2019a: 15). The Labour Party report's response to the FRC's figures went further:

Imagine if that routinely applied to the production of cars, aeroplanes, medicine or food. The producers would be sued and shut down and governments would step in. But that does not happen to auditing firms. They continue to be defended by regulator and government, and, in a so-called 'free market' economy enjoy the protection of a state-guaranteed market for auditing. (Sikka et al. 2018: 16)

Three of the heads of the Big Four acknowledged to the House of Commons committee that the quality of their audits was inadequate (2019a: 14). Systemic audit failure is also noted in the US-based Project on Government Oversight:

In the most recent annual inspections of the US arms of the Big Four for which the oversight board has reported results, inspectors found that Deloitte botched 20% of audits examined, PricewaterhouseCoopers botched 23.6%, Ernst and Young botched 27.3%, and KPMG botched 50%. (Hilzenrath 2019)

The reports called for tighter regulation, greater scepticism when dealing with company reports, and a redefinition of the meaning of audit. An exchange between David Dunckley, CEO of the audit company Grant Thornton, and the House of Commons committee, highlighted the need to redefine audit. Dunckley argued there was an 'expectation gap' between public and market understandings of audit, and what audit actually is:

> We are not looking for fraud. We are not looking at the future. We are not giving a statement that the accounts are correct. We are saying they are reasonable. We are looking in the past and we are not set up to look for fraud. That is the fundamental expectation gap in the market. (House of Commons 2019b)

Dunckley's argument was rejected by both the committee and the head of the FRC, who told the committee that 'a "mythology" had developed that auditors cannot detect fraud. The auditor is clearly responsible for pursuing fraud in the company' (House of Commons 2019a: 16). Technically defined, audit is a process to verify that 'the financial statements produced by a company's management provide a "true and fair view" of the company's assets, liabilities, financial position and profit or loss' (Companies Act 2006, section 393). Yet this wording is vague and open to interpretation. As a group of business school accountants point out, 'What constitutes a "true and fair" view is the subject of almost existential debate. It is rarely explicitly defined, and so has the capacity to summon quite different understandings of the purpose of accounting and auditing' (Leaver et al. 2020: 16). The House of Commons committee quoted the International Standard on Auditing's (ISA 200) definition:

> The purpose of an audit is to enhance the degree of confidence of intended users in the financial statements. This is achieved by the expression of an opinion by the auditor on whether the financial statements are prepared, in all material respects, in accordance with an applicable financial reporting framework. In the case of most general-purpose frameworks, that opinion is on whether the financial statements are presented fairly, in all material respects, or give a true and fair view in accordance with the framework. (House of Commons 2019a: 13)

The House of Commons committee pointed out that 'opinion' is not a fact or infallible guarantee, but audits should be evidence-based (House of Commons 2019a: 13). Furthermore, the concept of 'materiality' allows auditors to define which levels of reporting irregularity and fraud have material effects, and which can be ignored. The committee concluded that 'fraudulent reporting by directors is almost always material, by nature if not by size' (House of Commons 2019a: 84). The Labour Party report was also critical of the way:

> the industry sets its own auditing standards or benchmarks which are often the lowest common denominator. A mechanical checklist mentality dominates within the firms to the detriment of audit quality. A culture of profit maximisation has resulted in inadequate time budgets, irregular auditing practices, offshoring (or outsourcing) of audit work and reliance upon work performed by staff not under the direct control of the firms. (Sikka et al. 2018: 3)

It blamed audit companies' 'corrosive organisational culture', where, 'under time budget pressure, members of audit teams resort to irregular auditing practices and even falsification of audit work' (Sikka et al. 2018: 18). These problems are amplified when audit work is offshored to staff who are not under their control or supervision of those responsible for the veracity of the audit.

The third problem that all the reports highlighted is conflicts of interest when audit firms provide clients with both auditing and consultancy services. Auditing is used as a shop window to attract consultancy and financial advisory services. The massive growth in the Big Four's revenues from advisory services subsidises audit work. Such a cosy relationship between the auditors and the companies they audit disincentivises critical, sceptical and robust auditing for fear of losing valued clients. As Sikka says:

> audit firms have used audits as loss-leaders in the hope that having got a foot in the door, they will then secure lucrative non-auditing work. This is an abuse of the external audit function and disadvantages those businesses who cannot use audits as a market stall for selling other wares. (Sikka, cited in Marriage 2018b)

In the words of the House of Commons committee report:

> The opaque economics of audit undermine independence, erode trust and stifle competition. Audit can only be transparent and independent

when it is fully priced. It will only be fully priced when it is no longer subsidised. (House of Commons 2019a: 86)

The Labour Party report echoes the conclusions of other reports in asserting that:

- Statutory auditors of large companies and other entities must act exclusively as auditors
- The audit business of accounting firms must be legally separate from everything else, with no cross holdings
- Auditors and their associates cannot sell any non-auditing services, with the exception of delivering statutory returns, to audit clients
- It will be a criminal offence for statutory auditors of large companies and any entities related to them to offer or perform non-auditing services for audit clients
- Members of the audit team cannot join the staff of the audit client for five years after ceasing to be a member of the audit team. (Sikka et al. 2018: 4)

The fourth problem concerns the Big Four's role in helping the world's richest people avoid tax. The Luxembourg leaks in 2014 revealed how the world's largest companies negotiated special deals in the Grand Duchy, typically with the help of the Big Four. The leaking of thousands of documents in the 2016 Panama Papers and 2017 Paradise Papers provided further evidence of the Big Four's activities in facilitating tax avoidance schemes (ICIJ 2016, 2017). The Labour Party report condemned these ingenious tax-dodging schemes whose 'sole purpose is to deplete the UK public purse with the consequences that the elected government cannot deliver the social investment mandated through the ballot box. They exercise the ultimate veto on democratic choices' (Sikka et al. 2018: 9). The report pointed out that the courts have, on many occasions, declared these schemes unlawful, but not one of the Big Four firms has been investigated or disciplined. Despite this, the European Commission in 2018 awarded over €10.5 million to PwC, Deloitte and KPMG to help the European Union (EU) draft its taxation and customs policies. As Karthik Ramanna, professor at Oxford University's Blavatnik School of Governance said: 'Outsourcing tax expertise to tax avoidance enablers creates a clear conflict of interest' (in Marriage 2018c).

The fifth problem is the weakness of the FRC's regulatory system. The House of Commons committee report details repeated failures to investigate accounting scandals, from KPMG's audit of HBOS bank, which collapsed in 2008, to the FRC's decision to take no action against PwC for its lax auditing of Tesco in 2018. Two House of Commons committees came to the damning conclusion that the FRC was 'toothless' over the collapse of Carillion and reluctant to use its powers, declaring 'we have no confidence in the ability of these regulators' (House of Commons 2018: 195). The FRC itself was accused of being too close to these companies to carry out proper oversight. Many former Big Four accountants sat on the FRC's committees and panels, and the revolving door between government and the accountancy firms (see Chapter 3) had muted efforts at serious reform. The Kingman Report recommended that the FRC be 'replaced as soon as possible with a new independent regulator with clear statutory powers and objectives', which should be 'accountable to Parliament', have a 'duty to promote the interests of consumers of financial information, not producers', and 'should exercise significantly stronger ownership and oversight of the regulator's investigation and enforcement functions' (Kingman 2018: 5, 9).

With parliamentarians, academics and government all identifying the problems and proposing concrete solutions, why has the audit industry not been reformed? The government has accepted most of the recommendations, particularly Kingman's proposal for a new Audit, Reporting and Governance Authority. Meanwhile, under growing pressure, Ernst & Young has announced it will split its global audit and consulting practices. The other Big Four companies have been fearful and reluctant to concede to reforms that would threaten their market position and have lobbied strongly to block changes they deem harmful to their interests (Marriage 2018d). One Big Four partner said that splitting auditing from consultancy would create 'a low growth boring [audit] business next to a high growth consulting business' (O'Dwyer 2022a). As the Labour Party report noted, 'reforms of the auditing industry have been grudging, minimalist and ineffective and often on the terms specified by the Big Four accounting firms' (Sikka et al. 2018: 3).

The slow pace of reform can also be attributed to the cosy and collusive relationship between the Big Four, politicians, and the world's richest people. In the US, Republican Party leaders have consistently starved federal tax agencies of the funding, staffing and resources that they need to carry out their regulatory work (Bagchi 2016). Even out of office, Republican Party leaders have continued to oppose and block funding increases to the US tax agency (the Internal Revenue Service [IRS]), whose budget and staffing in 2022 were 20 per cent lower than their 2010 levels. As a result, their 'audit rate has dropped by 54 per cent for large companies and 71 per cent for millionaires' (Politi 2022: 4). In the UK, the revolving door between government and accountancy firms highlights similar problems. The EU could be an effective actor but has instead employed the Big Four, while some former EU leaders, including European Commission President Jean-Claude Juncker, have been criticised for promoting lucrative tax deals with multinationals when in office (Speigel 2014).

In Germany, a major accounting scandal did mobilise public opinion and led to actions from politicians. The country was shocked in 2020 by a €4 billion corruption scandal involving Wirecard, the Munich-headquartered financial services provider. The German government disbanded its ineffective financial regulator and replaced it with a powerful watchdog called the Federal Financial Supervisory Authority (BaFin) – with three times the staffing of its predecessor. The new watchdog has already warned the Big Four that they are 'too close' to clients and issued calls for more professional scepticism (Storbeck 2022).

All of the reports reviewed above indicate that governments know what measures are needed to reform the international audit industry. Some efforts by national governments have been effective, but they are always vulnerable to being watered down or reversed. These international accountancy firms are often better resourced than those trying to regulate them, and they can move country to take advantage of different jurisdictions and tax regimes. The Panama and Paradise Papers showed that there is a lack of political will to discipline them and restore the probity of audit. Although the EU's European Securities and Markets Authority has produced a directive on the regulation of public sector audits (EU 2014), the overall reform of this international private sector industry requires much more coordinated transnational effort and political enforcement – and a more rigorous and precise definition of what financial audits should entail.

Audit, Accountability and Democracy: Scale 4

The fourth scale where action is needed to challenge and reverse audit culture is with regard to the practice of accountability and democracy. Earlier chapters examined how the spread of audit from an instrument of financial accounting to a tool of management and governance undermines accountability. When audit reports are kept secret or identify problems but do not specify who is responsible, the public is denied the possibility of holding wrongdoers to account. When audit fails to give an accurate account of how resources have been used, it limits the possibility of 'stakeholders' and citizens engaging in meaningful political intervention and deliberating whether the resources could be used to better effect. How can accountability be reconceptualised in ways that promote public trust and halt audit culture's corrosive effects on democracy?

Philosophers, social scientists and critical accountants have also addressed these questions. There is a vast literature on the way that neoliberal rationality has colonised contemporary society so that '[a]ll conduct is economic conduct; all spheres of existence are framed and measured by economic terms and metrics, even when those spheres are not directly monetized' (Brown 2015: 9). As American philosopher, Wendy Brown, asks:

> What happens when the precepts and principles of democracy are remade by this order of reason and governance? When the commitment to individual and collective self-rule and the institutions supporting it are overwhelmed and then displaced by the encomium to enhance capital value, competitive positioning, and credit ratings? (Brown 2015: 10)

This is how, in her terms, neoliberal rationality is 'undoing the demos'. Despite her forensic analysis, however, she shies away from proposing any solutions stating that :

> My critique of neoliberalism does not resolve into a call to rehabilitate liberal democracy, nor, on the other hand, does it specify what kind of democracy might be crafted from neoliberal regimes to resist them. (Brown, 2015: 201)

In his book *Post-Democracy*, British sociologist Colin Crouch argues that while democratic institutions and processes may still exist, they have been reduced to a shell in which public debate and decision making is 'a tightly controlled spectacle, managed by rival teams of professional experts in the techniques of persuasion', and where the 'mass of citizens plays a passive, quiescent, even apathetic part' (Crouch 2004: 4). At the helm stands a self-referential business class that is more concerned with links to wealthy business interests than political programmes that benefit ordinary people. Crouch's proposed solution is to strengthen, and in many instances restore, the systems of regulation that governments have abandoned (Crouch 2020).

Scholars in the field of critical accounting have focused more on practical solutions for 'redoing the demos' by expanding audit to include civil society as well as social and environmental factors – capitalism's so-called 'externalities'. Critical accounting seeks to dislodge the 1970s 'Milton Friedman doctrine' that a company has no social responsibility to the public or society; that its only responsibility is to make a profit for its shareholders (Friedman 1970). Judy Brown and Jesse Dillard argue that the effects of a company's operations on the environment, climate, workforce and society must come within a company's audit purview. They see this as a democratically responsive and pluralistic approach to accounting that they call 'dialogic':

Rather than prioritize the perspectives, goals and values of business, investors and capital markets (e.g. profit maximization, economic growth) as in traditional accounting, dialogic accounting seeks to attend to a diverse range of – often conflicting and deeply contested – goals and values including, *inter alia*, efficiency, economic growth, sustainable livelihoods, labour rights, fair trade, cultural identity and social justice. (Brown and Dillard 2015: 248)

Their idea is to develop civil society-oriented accounts that foster critical reflection and debate organisational practices. For example, Brown and Tregidga (2017) criticise Social and Environmental Accounting (SEA) for being apolitical and having little impact on the dominant market paradigm or the capitalist assumptions that frame mainstream accounting. In formulating their ideas of dialogic accounting, they take agonistic and methodologically pluralistic approaches that include non-financial matters and bring the 'public' into the frame (Brown and Dillard 2021: 198; Bracci et al. 2021).

These critiques are important steps towards rethinking audit and challenging the hegemony of traditional accounting, but they are short on concrete proposals. However, some initiatives have challenged the logics of conventional auditing. For example, Christine Gilbert (2020) shows how the Ecuadorian government in 2008 was able to mobilise audit as a device of political resistance. Rafael Correa, Ecuador's then newly elected president, used his training as an economist to set up an independent audit of the country's public debt and determine which parts were illegitimate and therefore did not require the state to reimburse lenders. The Ecuadorian government invited independent national and international experts from civil society organisations, indigenous and social movements, and academia to conduct the audit and investigate the country's debt burden, loan-by-loan. It did not follow the international standard for auditing public debt established by the International Organization of Supreme Audit Institutions (INTOSAI), whose norms often tend towards 'reproducing the existing order rather than challenging it' (Gilbert 2020: 8). Despite external criticisms, Ecuador's government managed to reach an agreement with its creditors that reduced its public debt by some US $7 billion. Gilbert's conclusion is that audit, re-framed in social terms, can become a useful tool for resisting neoliberal hegemony. The activists redefined the language of audit to construct an alternative narrative, one that highlighted the illegitimacy of the external debt and showed how it 'violated liberal democratic values and institutions in Ecuador, such as universal human rights, as well as the state's sovereignty, constitution, and system of law' (Gilbert 2020: 17).

The importance of appropriating and recasting the language of audit to 'socialise' its meanings is also illustrated by Jane Andrew and Damien Cahill's (2016) study of local resistance to the proposed privatisation of two prisons in New South Wales (NSW), Australia. The NSW Department of Corrective Services presented the same economic rationale for privatisation of both prisons, saying it would produce efficiencies, give superior value for money, and offer savings to the taxpayer. For one prison, opponents tried to contest the proposals by showing how retaining public ownership would deliver better outcomes. Their argument used the same financial paradigm as the NSW government, and their resistance was unsuccessful. In the second, which succeeded, opponents adopted a different discourse, one that used a community-centred definition of costs. They highlighted the impact that privatisation would have on jobs, family income, community ties and the economic, cultural and social life of the region (Andrew and Cahill 2016: 22). The community was able to show convincingly how the social costs of family relocations, social isolation, ill health and unemployment would be borne by the community and the NSW taxpayer.

These examples of successfully reframing and reclaiming audit share four common features. First, while they echoed the dominant discourses and its keywords of audit, debt and costs, they cleverly used alternative concepts and calculations of value to redefine them. Second, they brought together a wider spectrum of the people who are affected by the outcome of audit, including communities, the poor and other voices that are usually muted and marginalised. Their consideration of the moral purpose and public responsibility of accounting countered that offered by the Friedman doctrine. Third, in creating the narrative about how resources had been or should be used, they clearly identified who was to be held to account to the community for any losses or injustice. Finally, they raised fundamental questions about how to mobilise existing institutions and processes to make them publicly accountable.

In Search of Solutions

This final chapter has provided suggestions about what can be done to take back control and reassert democratic forms of accountability and governance that the proliferation of audit culture has stripped away. In summary, we see audit as a technology that has multiple uses and meanings. It has been used as an instrument to promote neoliberal privatisation agendas, managerial control, and new sources of profit for accountancy firms and financial elites. For all the rhetoric about transparency and accountability, these factors, combined with its strong links to non-productive and entrepreneurial capitalism, have contributed significantly to the erosion of democracy. By this we mean the capacity of people to participate meaningfully in the decisions that affect their lives and to hold those with political and economic power to account. Yet audit *can* be used to create a genuinely accountable and democratic society. Rather than abandoning the concept as irredeemably failed and pernicious, our arguments are that, first, audit should be returned to its primary mandate of ensuring financial probity and providing trust. Chapters 1 and 2 showed, paradoxically, that the public sector has witnessed a massive expansion of surveillance, performance indicators and proxy measurements, while there has been far less scrutiny, regulation or accountability in the private and financial sectors. Second, as an instrument of public accountability, audits must include the full range of people who are affected by an organisation's decisions over its use of resources. In short, and as the example from Ecuador and our discussion of hospital PFIs showed (Chapter 5), public benefit cannot be measured simply in neoclassical economic terms. Third, as our examples of child protection, healthcare and higher education illustrated, systems of audit and accountability must re-focus on enabling professionals to develop their knowledge, skills and confidence so they can best exercise their own judgement and fulfil the core purpose of that sector, whether that be improving child protection, education or health. Fourth, because audit culture is so successful as a tool of multi-level governance – in that one measure can be used by government to reform a sector, by managers to steer their organisation, and by workers to know what is expected and what 'counts' – any serious reform requires changes at every level across a whole system.

To sum up, this book supports calls to reform the audit industry, rein in the power of the Big Four, and rethink public sector governance. We also concur with the argument to strengthen and redefine auditing standards and reporting responsibilities so that it is no longer possible for accounting firms to hide behind the vague terms 'true and fair'. Beyond these political-level actions, from our analysis we suggest five smaller steps for reducing audit's deleterious effects and opening up possibilities for more democratic forms of accountability.

Narratives, Not Just Numbers

While evaluations and assessments are necessary for good governance and management, accountability should be about giving an *account* – in the sense of telling a story. Audits should therefore be predominantly qualitative and discursive and avoid the reductionist logic that reduces qualities and complex realities to a single metric or score. Where numbers and indicators are necessary to measure performance, they should be placed in the service of qualitative evaluation, not the other way round.

Encouragement, Not Punishments

If audits reveal some organisations and individuals to be underperforming, they should be offered support rather than be blamed or punished. The divisive neoliberal ethos of the 1980s extolled cut-throat competition, rewarded the successful by redirecting resources from those less able to 'perform', and used naming and shaming to encourage struggling individuals and organisations to improve. This has intensified inequalities and stress, and encouraged greed, cheating and gaming behaviours which even the head of the UK audit regulator acknowledged constituted an 'unhealthy corporate culture' (O'Dwyer 2022c). Auditors and organisations should adopt an ethics of care (Bellacasa 2017), kindness and critical encouragement of the sort that is attentive to the fabric of social relations and enables individuals to become the best versions of themselves.

Stop Thinking of Organisations and People in Purely Economic Terms

Many of the problems of audit culture stem from its instrumental and calculative approach that treats human beings as units of economic resource. People are not simply 'human capital' and organisations, even in a capitalist society, should not define their prime purpose as maximising shareholder value. Rather, individual entrepreneurs and companies should recognise that profitability and success arise from their social embeddedness and collective endeavours. The principles of auditing need to be fundamentally re-evaluated so that any damage companies cause to society, the climate and the environment (such as water companies releasing sewage into rivers and seas; Laville 2022) or people (such as the exploitation and burnout of precarious workers; Ferreira and Gomes 2022) cannot be simply written off as 'externalities'.

Rebuilding Trust

Too many workplaces have become 'low-trust organisations'. Audit culture, which was supposed to promote trust, has substituted managerialism and external scrutiny for professional autonomy fuelling a spiral of mistrust. In a widespread 'blame culture', management and the public often assume the worst of those in public professional roles and colleagues no longer trust each other. This system of management by metricised objectives and governance through league tables must be replaced by one that builds confidence in professionals and their judgements. The challenge is to create and sustain more participatory and democratic forms of governance that restore trust.

Audibility, Not Hyper-visibility

Audit culture operates with an optics that James Scott (2008 [199]) famously described as 'seeing like a state'. This means imposing standardised taxonomies and measurements to make the world legible to the state so that it can be governed at a distance. Audit also operates in a similar way to Foucault's (1977) description of Bentham's panopticon, and produces what Marilyn Strathern (2000a) calls the 'tyranny of transparency'. These optics entail making people and organisations visible within preconceived and externally imposed models. Alternatives are needed that allow people to be heard and to express their own criteria of relevance. This would recast audit as 'audibility' rather than visibility, which would return audit to its original meaning of a public hearing. It might also encourage an ethics of *listening*, which would be a key step towards more deliberative, dialogic and socially responsive forms of accounting.

Bibliography

Acerete, Basilio, Stafford, Anne and Stapleton, Pamela. 2012. 'New development: New global health care PPP developments – a critique of the success story'. *Public Money & Management* 32(4): 311–314. https://doi.org/10.1080/0954096 2.2012.691315

Adams, Richard. 2016. 'Lauded academy chain to be stripped of schools after finances inquiry'. *Guardian*, 28 March. www.theguardian.com/education/2016/mar/28/perry-beeches-academy-chain-stripped-schools-critical-finance-report (accessed 9 August 2022).

Allen, John and Missirlis, Fanis. 2012. 'Queen Mary: Nobody expects the Spanish Inquisition'. *Lancet* 379(9828), 4 May. www.thelancet.com/journals/lancet/article/PIIS0140-6736(12)60697-7/fulltext (accessed 19 April 2019).

Al-Saggaf, Yeslam. 2015. 'The use of data mining by private health insurance companies and customers' privacy: An ethical analysis'. *Cambridge Quarterly of Healthcare Ethics* 24(3): 281–292.

Amsler, Mark and Shore, Cris. 2017. 'Responsibilisation and leadership in the neoliberal university: A New Zealand perspective'. *Discourse, Studies in the Cultural Politics of Education* 38(1): 123–137.

Anderson, Staffan and Heyward, Paul. 2009. 'The politics of perception: Use and abuse of Transparency International's approach to measuring corruption'. *Political Studies* 57(4): 746–767.

Andrew, Jane and Damien Cahill. 2016. 'Rationalising and resisting neoliberalism: The uneven geography of costs'. *Critical Perspectives on Accounting* 45: 12–28.

Andrews, Paul and eighty-four others. 2014. 'OECD and Pisa tests are damaging education worldwide – Academics'. *Guardian*, 6 May. www.theguardian.com/education/2014/may/06/oecd-pisa-tests-damaging-education-academics/ (accessed 23 August 2022).

Associated Press. 2017. 'Volkswagen fined $2.8bn in US diesel emission scandal'. *Daily Telegraph*, 21 April. www.telegraph.co.uk/business/2017/04/21/volkswagen-fined-28bn-us-diesel-emission-scandal/ (accessed 1 July 2023).

Audit Analytics. 2022. *2221 Financial Restatements a Twenty-one-year Review.* Sutton, MA: Audit Analytics. https://www.auditanalytics.com/doc/2021_Financial_Restatements_A_Twenty-One-Year_Review.pdf (accessed July 2023).

Audit Commission. 1984. *Report of Accounts for Year Ending 31 March 1984.* London: HMSO.

Bacchi, Carol. 2009. *Analysing Policy: What's the Problem Represented to Be?* Malaysia: Pearson.

Bagchi, Sutirtha. 2016. 'The political economy of tax enforcement: A look at the Internal Revenue Service from 1978 to 2010'. *Journal of Public Policy* 36(3): 335–380.

Bakan, Joel. 2005. *The Corporation: The Pathological Pursuit of Power and Profit*. New York: Free Press.

Basioudis, Ilias and Ellwoodan, Sheila. 2005. 'Empirical investigation of price competition and industry specialisation in NHS audit services'. *Financial Accountability & Management* 21(2): 219–248. https://doi.org/10.1111/j.1468-0408.2005.00216.x

BBC. 2013. 'Amazon workers face "increased risk of mental illness"'. *BBC News – Business*, 25 November. www.bbc.co.uk/news/business-25034598 (accessed 26 February 2023).

BBC. 2018. 'Wakefield City Academies Trust police probe closed'. *BBC News*, 10 April. www.bbc.com/news/uk-england-leeds-43713057 (accessed 9 August 2022).

BBC. 2019. 'WCAT to be wound up after schools lost £2m in collapse'. *BBC News*, 23 September. www.bbc.com/news/uk-england-leeds-49727901 (accessed 9 August 2022).

BBlaze. 2015. 'Comment on Grove: Newcastle University staff express fears over new "targets"'. *Times Higher Education*, 17 December. www.timeshighereducation.com/news/newcastle-university-staff-express-fears-over-new-targets (accessed 24 August 2022).

Bellacasa, Maria Puig de la. 2017. *Matters of Care: Speculative Ethics in More than Human Worlds*. Minnesota, MN: University of Minnesota Press.

Benjamin, Joel and Jones, Tim. 2017. 'The UK's PPPs disaster: Lessons on private finance for the rest of the world'. *Jubilee Debt Campaign* 3. https://debtjustice.org.uk/report/uks-ppps-disaster-lessons-private-finance-rest-world (accessed 14 June 2023).

Berger, Abi. 1998. 'Why doesn't audit work? Attempts are being made to revitalise audit'. *British Medical Journal* 316 (21 March): 875–876. https://doi.org/10.1136/bmj.316.7135.875

Bevan, Gwyn and Hood, Christopher. 2006. 'Have targets improved performance in the English NHS?' *British Medical Journal* 332 (18 February): 419–420. https://doi.org/10.1136/bmj.332.7538.419

Big Four. 2013. 'The 2012 Big Four firms performance analysis'. www.Big4.com. http://ww1.prweb.com/prfiles/2013/01/09/10318670/The%202012%20Big%20Four%20Firms%20Performance%20Analysis.pdf (accessed 3 May 2013).

Blyth, Peter and Cleminson, Arran. 2016. *Teaching Excellence Framework: Analysis of Highly Skilled Employment Outcomes*. Research report, September. London: Department for Education.

Bolton, Paul. 2022. 'Student loan statistics', House of Commons Library Briefing Paper, CBP01079, 2 December. London: House of Commons.

Booth, Lorna. 2018. 'Goodbye PFI'. House of Commons Library Report, 30 October. https://commonslibrary.parliament.uk/goodbye-pfi/ (accessed 25 September 2022).

Bovbjerg, Kirsten Marie (ed.). 2011. *Motivation og mismod* (Motivation and Despondency). Aarhus: Aarhus University Press.

Bowerman, Mary. 1995. 'Auditing performance indicators: The role of the Audit Commission in the Citizen's Charter Initiative'. *Financial Accountability & Management* 11(2): 171–183. https://doi.org/10.1111/j.1468-0408.1995.tb00403.x

Bowerman, Mary, Raby, Helen and Humphrey, Christopher. 2000. 'In search of the audit society: Some evidence from health care, police and schools'. *International Journal of Auditing* 4(1): 71–100. http://onlinelibrary.wiley.com/doi/10.1111/1099-1123.00304/abstract

Bracci, Enrico, Iris Saliterer, Mariafrancesca, Sicilia, and Ileana Steccolini. 2021. 'Accounting for (public) value (s): Reconsidering publicness in accounting research and practice'. *Accounting, Auditing & Accountability Journal* 34(7): 1513–1526.

Brankovic, Jelena. 2022. 'Why rankings appear natural (but aren't)'. *Business & Society* 61(4): 801–806.

Brenneis, Don, Shore, Cris and Wright, Susan. 2005. 'Getting the measure of academia: Universities and the politics of accountability'. *Anthropology in Action* 12(1): 1–10.

Brighton and Hove City Council. 2017. '*Empathy, Tenacity and Compassion*': An *Evaluation of Relationship-based Practice in Brighton & Hove*. Brighton: Brighton & Hove City Council in association with University of Sussex, Centre for Social Work Innovation and Research. https://brightonandhovelscb.org.uk/wp-content/uploads/Evaluation-of-relationship-based-practice-in-BH-July-2017.pdf (accessed 29 September 2022).

Brooks, Richard and Hughes, Solomon. 2016. 'Public servants, private paydays'. *Private Eye*. Revolving Doors Special Report, pp. 1–6. www.private-eye.co.uk/pictures/special_reports/revolving-doors.pdf (accessed 18 July 2022).

Brown, Jerry and Tarver, Jordan. 2021. 'Why did my credit score drop?' *Forbes Advisor*, 10 August. www.forbes.com/advisor/credit-score/why-did-my-credit-score-drop/

Brown, Judy and Dillard, Jesse. 2015. 'Opening accounting to critical scrutiny: Towards dialogic accounting for policy analysis and democracy'. *Journal of Comparative Policy Analysis: Research and Practice* 17(3): 247–268.

Brown, Judy, and Jesse Dillard. 2021. 'Accounting for non-financial matters: Technologies of humility as a means for developing critical dialogic accounting and accountability'. *Meditari Accountancy Research* 29(2): 197–218.

Brown, Judy and Tregidga, Helen. 2017. 'Re-politicizing social and environmental accounting through Rancière: On the value of dissensus'. *Accounting, Organizations and Society* 61: 1–21.

Brown, Wendy. 2015. *Undoing the Demos: Neoliberalism's Stealth Revolution*. New York: Zone Books.

Brumby, John. 2021. 'Foreign students are our fourth largest export, even with the pandemic'. *Sydney Morning Herald*, 19 February. www.smh.com.au/national/foreign-students-are-our-fourth-largest-export-even-with-the-pandemic-20210218-p573pz.html (accessed 24 August 2022).

Bruneau, William and Savage, Donald. 2002. *Counting Out the Scholars: How Performance Indicators Undermine Universities and Colleges*. Toronto: James Lorimer and Co.

BT. 2010. 'Our performance approach'. London: British Telecommunications plc. file:///C:/Users/au148152/Downloads/2011-01605-Agreement-BT-performance-management-agreement-booklet-Version-01-12-2011%20(2).pdf (accessed 15 January 2018).

Budaly, Najiyya. 2022. 'KPMG faces £14.4m sanction over Carillion, IT firm audits'. *Law 360*, 13 May. www.law360.com/articles/1493060/kpmg-faces-14-4m-sanction-over-carillion-it-firm-audits (accessed 1 July 2023).

Burchell, Graham. 1993. 'Liberal government and techniques of the self'. *Economy and Society* 22(3): 267–282.

Burnstein, L., Oakes, J. and Guiton, G. 1992. 'Education indicators', pp. 158–233 in Marvin C. Alkin (ed.) *Encyclopedia of Educational Research*, 6th edn. New York: Macmillan.

Burrows, Roger. 2012. 'Living with the H-Index? Metric assemblages in the contemporary academy'. *The Sociological Review* 60(2): 355–372.

Buxton, Martin. 1994. 'Achievements of audit in the NHS'. *Quality in Health Care*, 3 Supplement:S31–S34.

Cadwalladr, Carole. 2017. 'The great British Brexit robbery: How our democracy was hijacked'. *The Observer*, 7 May. www.theguardian.com/technology/2017/may/07/the-great-british-brexit-robbery-hijacked-democracy (accessed 19 August 2022).

Cadwalladr, Carole. 2018. '"I made Steve Bannon's psychological warfare tool": Meet the data war whistleblower'. *Guardian*, 18 March. www.theguardian.com/news/2018/mar/17/data-war-whistleblower-christopher-wylie-faceook-nix-bannon-trump (accessed 20 August 2022).

Çalışkan, Koray and Callon, Michel. 2009. 'Economization, Part 1: Shifting attention from the economy towards processes of economization'. *Economy and Society* 38(3): 369–398.

Carnegie, Garry and Napier, Christopher. 2010. 'Traditional accountants and business professionals: Portraying the accounting profession after Enron'. *Accounting, Organizations and Society* 35(3): 360–376.

Carvalho, Luís. 2014. 'The attraction of mutual surveillance performances: PISA as knowledge-policy instrument', pp. 58–72 in Tara Fenwick, Eric Mangez and Jenny Ozga (eds) *Governing Knowledge: Comparison, Knowledge-based Technologies and Expertise in the Regulation of Education*. London: Routledge.

CCTV America. 2016. 'Rating people controversy & a start-up ahead of the game'. *CGTN America*, uploaded 4 April on YouTube, video 3:07. www.youtube.com/watch?v=1WxuUxHxGLo. (accessed 24 August 2022).

Chakrabortty, Aditya. 2018. 'It's worse than Carillion: Our outsourced schools are leaving parents frozen out'. *Guardian*, 30 July. www.theguardian.com/commentisfree/2018/jul/30/outsourced-schools-parents-primary-academy-trusts (accessed 9 August 2022).

Chakrabortty, Aditya. 2019. '53,000 pupils in limbo after rise in "zombie" academy schools'. www.theguardian.com/education/2019/apr/15/53000-pupils-in-limbo-after-rise-in-zombie-academy-schools (accessed 9 August 2022).

Chan, Adrienne and Fisher, Donald (eds). 2008. *The Exchange University: Corporatization of Academic Culture*. Vancouver, BC: UBC Press.

Chandler Alfred D. 1977. *The Visible Hand*. Cambridge, MA: Harvard University Press.

Charlton, Bruce. 2001. 'Quality assurance auditing as a managerial technology: Clinical governance and the managerial regulation of NHS medical practice'. www.hedweb.com/bgcharlton/clingov.html (accessed 25 September 2022).

Cheng, Liying, Watanabe, Yoshinori and Curtis, Andy. 2004. *Washback in Language Testing*. Mahwah, NJ: Lawrence Erlbaum Associates.

Chong, Kimberly. 2012. *The Work of Financialisation: An Ethnography of a Global Management Consultancy in post-Mao China*. PhD thesis, Department of Anthropology, London School of Economics. http://etheses.lse.ac.uk/500/1/Chong_The%20work%20of%20financialisation%20(public).pdf (accessed 28 June 2023).

Christophers, Brett. 2020. *Rentier Capitalism: Who Owns the Economy, and Who Pays for It?* London: Verso.

Clarke, John, Newman, Janet, Smith, Nick, Vidler, Elizabeth and Westmarland, Louise. 2007. *Creating Citizen-Consumers: Changing Publics and Changing Public Services*. London: Sage.

Clatworthy, Mark A., Mellett, Howard J. and Peel, Michael J. 2003. 'The market for external audit services in the public sector: An empirical analysis of NHS trusts'. *Journal of Business Finance & Accounting*, 29(9–10): 1399–1439.

Clover, Charles. 2016. 'China: When Big Data meets Big Brother'. *Financial Times*, 19 January. www.ft.com/content/b5b13a5e-b847-11e5-b151-8e15c9a029fb (accessed 20 August 2022).

CMA (Competitions and Markets Authority). 2019. *Statutory Audit Services Market Study*. London: CMA.

Coffee Jr, John. 2002. 'Understanding Enron: "It's about the gatekeepers, stupid"'. *The Business Lawyer* 57(4): 1403–1420.

Coffee Jr, John. 2005. 'A theory of corporate scandals: Why the USA and Europe differ'. *Oxford Review of Economic Policy* 21(2): 192–211.

Colquhoun, David. 2012a. 'Is Queen Mary University of London trying to commit scientific suicide?' DC's Improbable Science blog, 29 June. www.dcscience.net/2012/06/29/is-queen-mary-university-of-london-trying-to-commit-scientific-suicide/ (accessed 13 February 2016).

Colquhoun, David. 2012b. 'Queen Mary, University of London in *The Times*. Does Simon Gaskell care?' DC's Improbable Science blog, 30 July. www.dcscience.net/2012/07/30/queen-mary-university-of-london-in-the-times-does-simon-gaskell-care/ (accessed 14 February 2016).

Comendeiro-Maaløe, Micaela, Manuel Ridao-López, Sophie Gorgemans and Enrique Bernal-Delgado. 2019. 'Public-private partnerships in the Spanish National Health System: The reversion of the Alzira model'. *Health Policy* 123(4): 408–411.

Committee of Vice-Chancellors and Principals of the Universities of the United Kingdom, Steering Committee for Efficiency Studies in Universities, and Sir Alex Jarratt. 1985. *Report of the Steering Committee for Efficiency Studies in Universities*. Committee of Vice-Chancellors and Principals.

Companies Act 2006. *UK Companies Act*, 46, Part 15, Accounts and reports. www.legislation.gov.uk/ukpga/2006/46/section/393?view=extent+interweave&timeline=false (accessed 30 September 2022).

Connell, Raewyn. 2013. 'The neoliberal cascade and education: An essay on the market agenda and its consequences'. *Critical Studies in Education* 54(2): 99–112.

Cook, Chris. 2016. 'Every school to become an academy, ministers to announce'. *BBC News*, 15 March. www.bbc.com/news/education-35814215 (accessed 8 August 2022).

Costanza, Robert, Kubiszewski, Ida, Giovannini, Enrico, Lovins, Hunter, McGlade, Jacqueline, Pickett, Kate et al. 2014. 'Time to leave GDP behind'. *Nature* 505(7483): 283–285.

Coughlan, Sean. 2016. 'PISA tests: UK lags behind in global school rankings'. *BBC News*, 6 December. www.bbc.com/news/education-38157811 (accessed 23 August 2022).

Couldry, Nick and Mejias, Ulises. 2020. *The Costs of Connection: How Data Are Colonizing Human Life and Appropriating It for Capitalism*. Stanford, CA: Stanford University Press

Covaleski, Mark, Dirsmith, Mark, Heian, James and Samuel, Sajay. 1998. 'The calculated and the avowed: Techniques of discipline and struggles over identity in Big Six public accounting firms'. *Administrative Science Quarterly* 43(2): 293–327.

Creemers, Rogier. 2018. 'China's Social Credit System: An evolving practice of control'. SSRN 3175792, 9 May. http://dx.doi.org/10.2139/ssrn.3175792 (accessed 20 July 2022).

Crouch, Colin. 2004. *Post-democracy*. Cambridge: Polity Press.

Crouch, Colin. 2020. *Post-democracy after the Crises*. London: John Wiley & Sons.

Cruikshank, Barbara. 1999. *The Will to Empower: Democratic Citizens and other Subjects*. Ithaca, NY: Cornell University Press.

Danechi, Shadi and Roberts, Nerys. 2019. 'FAQs: Academies and free schools'. House of Commons Library Briefing Paper No. 07059. London: House of Commons, 18 June. https://researchbriefings.files.parliament.uk/documents/SN07059/SN07059.pdf (accessed 9 August 2022).

Darling-Hammond, Linda. 2014. 'What can PISA tell us about US education policy?' *New England Journal of Public Policy* 26(1): 1–14.

Davies, Harry. 2015. 'Ted Cruz using firm that harvested data on millions of unwitting Facebook users'. *Guardian*, 11 December. www.theguardian.com/us-news/2015/dec/11/senator-ted-cruz-president-campaign-facebook-user-data (accessed 20 August 2022).

Dean, Mitchell. 1999. *Governmentality: Power and Rule in Modern Society*. London: Sage.

Deloitte. 2015. 'About Deloitte: Learn about our global network of member firms'. www2.deloitte.com/global/en/pages/about-deloitte/articles/about-deloitte.html (accessed 10 August 2022).

Deloitte. 2020 'The rise of healthcare companies. Applying best practices worldwide'. https://www2.deloitte.com/content/dam/Deloitte/global/Documents/Finance/gx-rise-global-health-care.pdf (accessed 1 July 2023).

Deloitte. 2022a. 'Our heritage. 175+ years of making an impact that matters'. www2.deloitte.com/global/en/pages/about-deloitte/articles/deloitte175.html (accessed 18 July 2022).

Deloitte. 2022b. *A Year of Connection, Action and Impact: 2021 Global Impact Report*. Deloitte Global. www2.deloitte.com/content/dam/Deloitte/global/Documents/About-Deloitte/about-deloitte-global-report-full-version-2021.pdf (accessed 18 July 2022).

Deloitte. 2022c. 'Deloitte organization structure'. www2.deloitte.com/global/en/pages/about-deloitte/articles/network-structure.html (accessed 18 July 2022).

Dennison, Richard. 2008. 'BT intranet strategy'. INSIDE OUT A view from deep inside the intestines of a global company. https://richarddennison.wordpress.com/2008/01/13/bt-intranet-strategy/ (accessed 3 July 2023).

Department for Education. 2012. *Academies Annual Report 2010/11*. London: The Stationery Office. https://assets.publishing.service.gov.uk/government/uploads/system/uploads/attachment_data/file/175360/academies_annual_report_2010-11.pdf (accessed 9 August 2022).

Department for Education. 2014. 'Transparency data: Open academies and academy projects in development. Information on all academies open in England, and those in the process of becoming academies'. 20 March. https://www.gov.uk/government/publications/open-academies-and-academy-projects-in-development (accessed 1 July 2023).

Department of Education. 1983. *A Nation at Risk: The Imperative for Educational Reform*. Washington, DC: US Department of Education.

Dewey, Caitlin. 2015. 'Everyone you know will be able to rate you on the terrifying "Yelp for people" – whether you want them to or not'. *Washington Post*, 30 September. www.washingtonpost.com/news/the-intersect/wp/2015/09/30/everyone-you-know-will-be-able-to-rate-you-on-the-terrifying-yelp-for-people-whether-you-want-them-to-or-not/ (accessed 17 August 2022).

Dixon, N. 1996. *Good Practice in Clinical Audit: A Summary of Selected Literature to Support Criteria for Clinical Audit*. London: National Centre for Clinical Audit.

Donnelly, Drew. 2023. 'China social credit system explained – What is it and how does it work?', *Horizons*, 3 January. https://nhglobalpartners.com/china-social-credit-system-explained/ (accessed 18 March 2023).

Durex. 2011. 'Sexual well-being around the world'. IndexMundi Blog. www.indexmundi.com/blog/index.php/2012/12/11/sexual-well-being-around-the-world/ (accessed 13 July 2022).

Eaton, Lynn. 2010. 'NHS may be forced to rely on private auditors, adding to costs'. *British Medical Journal* 341: c4526. https://doi.org/10.1136/bmj.c4526 (accessed 25 September 2022).

Education Research Centre. 2021. 'Who takes part in PISA?'. Education Research Centre website, 21 February. www.erc.ie/studies/pisa/who-takes-part-in-pisa/ (accessed 23 August 2022).

Edwards, Ivana. 1991. 'The essence of "Kafkaesque"'. *The New York Times*, 29 December, p. 12.

Espeland, Wendy and Sauder, Michael. 2007. 'Rankings and reactivity: How public measures recreate social worlds'. *American Journal of Sociology* 113(1): 1–40.

Espeland, Wendy and Sauder, Michael. 2016. *Engines of Anxiety: Academic Rankings, Reputation and Accountability*. New York: Russell Sage.

EU (European Union). 2014. 'Regulation No 537/2014 of the European Parliament and of the Council of 16 April 2014 on specific requirements regarding statutory audit of public-interest entities and repealing Commission Decision 2005/909/EC, 27.5.2014 EN Official'. *Journal of the European Union* L 158/77. https://eur-lex.europa.eu/legal-content/EN/TXT/PDF/?uri=CELEX:32014R0537&from=EN (accessed 30 September 2022).

Eurodad. 2018. *History RePPPted: How Public–Private Partnerships Are Failing.* Brussels: European Network on Debt and Development. www.right-to-education.org/sites/right-to-education.org/files/resource-attachments/Eurodad_history_repppeated_2018_ENG.pdf

EY (Ernst & Young). n.d. 'Legal statement'. www.ey.com. www.ey.com/en_gl/legal-statement (accessed 2 August 2022).

EY (Ernst & Young). 2015. 'Ernst & Young history'. www.zippia.com/ernst-young-careers-22739/history/ (accessed 10 August 2022).

EY (Ernst & Young). 2020. 'Global Code of Conduct'. April. https://assets.ey.com/content/dam/ey-sites/ey-com/en_gl/home-index/ey-global-code-of-conduct-english.pdf (accessed 10 August 2022).

EY (Ernst & Young). 2021. 'Audit'. www.ey.com. www.ey.com/en_se/audit (accessed 2 August 2022).

Eyles, Andrew and Machin, Stephen. 2015. 'The introduction of academy schools to England's education'. CEP Discussion Papers no. 1368. London: Centre for Economic Performance, London School of Economics. https://ideas.repec.org/p/cep/cepdps/dp1368.html (accessed 1 July 2023).

Falkvinge, Rick. 2015. 'In China, your credit score is now affected by your political opinions – and your friends' political opinions'. *Privacy News Online,* 3 October. www.privateinternetaccess.com/blog/in-china-your-credit-score-is-now-affected-by-your-political-opinions-and-your-friends-political-opinions/ (accessed 18 March 2023).

Farrell, Sean. 2018. 'Watchdog berates PwC over "misleading" BHS accounts'. *Guardian,* 15 August. www.theguardian.com/business/2018/aug/15/watchdog-berates-pwc-misleading-bhs-accounts (accessed 10 August 2022).

Fernyhough, James. 2022. 'KKR-led group launches $15bn bid for Australia's biggest hospital company'. *Financial Times,* 20 April.

Ferreira, Pedro and Gomes, Sofia. 2022. 'Temporary work, permanent strain? Personal resources as inhibitors of temporary agency workers' burnout'. *Administrative Sciences* 12(3): 87.

Fioramonti, Lorenzo. 2014. 'The world's most powerful number: An assessment of 80 years of GDP ideology'. *Anthropology Today* 30(2): 12–15.

Foley, Beth and Goldstein, Harvey. 2012. *Measuring Success: League Tables and the Public Sector.* London: British Academy Policy Centre.

Ford, Jonathan and Jack, Andrew. 2020. 'Number of academy trusts reporting deficit still rising'. *Financial Times,* 30 January. www.ft.com/content/516fa77c-42ab-11ea-a43a-c4b328d9061c (accessed 9 August 2022).

Foucault, Michel. 1977. *Discipline and Punish: The Birth of the Prison,* trans. Alan Sheridan. Harmondsworth: Penguin.

Foucault, Michel. 1979 [1976]. *The History of Sexuality,* vol. 1: *An Introduction.* London: Allen Lane.

Foucault, Michel. 1980 [1977]. 'The confession of the flesh', pp. 194–228 in Colin Gordon, (ed.) *Power/Knowledge: Selected Interviews and Other Writings.* New York: Pantheon.

Foucault, Michel. 1980. *Power/Knowledge: Selected Interviews and Other Writings,* 1972–79, ed. Colin Gordon. New York: Pantheon.

Foucault, Michel. 1982. 'The subject and power'. *Critical Inquiry* 8(4): 777–795.

Foucault, Michel. 1991. 'Governmentality', pp. 87–104 in Graham Burchell, Colin Gordon and Peter Miller (eds) *The Foucault Effect: Studies in Governmentality.* Chicago: University of Chicago Press.

Foucault, Michel. 1994. 'The politics of health in the 18th century', pp. 90–105 in James Faubion (ed.) *Power: Essential Works of Foucault, 1954–1984.* London: Penguin.

Foucault, Michel. 1998. *The History of Sexuality,* vol. 1: *The Will to Knowledge.* London: Penguin.

FRC (Financial Reporting Council). 2021. *Key Facts and Trends in the Accountancy Profession.* London: Financial Reporting Council Ltd.

Frelik, Bill. 2008. 'Bhutan's ethnic cleansing'. Human Rights Watch, 1 February. www.hrw.org/news/2008/02/01/bhutans-ethnic-cleansing.

Friedman, Milton, 1970. 'A Friedman doctrine – The social responsibility of business is to increase its profits'. *New York Times,* 13 September. www.nytimes. com/1970/09/13/archives/a-friedman-doctrine-the-social-responsibility-of-business-is-to.html (accessed 30 September 2022).

Fuchs, Christian and Chandler, David. 2019. 'Introduction: Big Data capitalism – Politics, activism, and theory', pp. 1–20 in Christian Fuchs and David Chandler (eds) *Digital Objects, Digital Subjects: Interdisciplinary Perspectives on Capitalism, Labour and Politics in the Age of Big Data,* London: University of Westminster Press.

Fullan, Michael and Scott, Geoff. 2009. *Turnaround Leadership for Higher Education.* Chichester: John Wiley and Sons.

Gapper, John. 2013. 'We should worry about the revolving door for jobs'. *Financial Times,* 29 May.

Garsten, Christina and Söborn, Adrienne. 2018. *Discreet Power: How the World Economic Forum Shapes Market Agendas.* Stanford, CA: Stanford University Press.

Gaskell, Simon. 2012. 'Academic research'. *The Times,* 3 August. www.thetimes. co.uk/article/academic-research-3gkp38c977v (accessed on 10 April 2019).

Gay, Oonagh. 1997. 'The accountability debate: Next steps agencies'. Research Paper 97/4. London: House of Commons Library, 24 January. www.civilservant. org.uk/library/1997_HoC_the%20acccountability%20debate_next%20 steps%20agencies.pdf (accessed 9 August 2022).

Gershon, Ilana. 2011. 'Neoliberal agency'. *Current Anthropology* 52(4): 537–555.

Gibson-Graham, J.K. 2006. *A Postcapitalist Politics.* Minneapolis, MN: University of Minnesota Press.

Gil, Lory. 2015. 'Numbers are in'. Wearable Website, 27 August. www.wareable. com/apple-watch/fitbit-top-seller-wearable-tech-1593 (accessed 20 August 2022).

Gilbert, Christine. 2020. 'The audit of public debt: Auditing as a device for political resistance in a neoliberal era'. *Critical Perspectives on Accounting* 85: 1–20.

Ginsberg, Benjamin. 2011. *The Fall of the Faculty. The Rise of the All-administrative University and Why it Matters.* Oxford: Oxford University Press.

Giroux, Henry. 2007. *University in Chains: Confronting the Military–Industrial–Academic Complex.* Boulder, CO: Paradigm Publishers.

Gjørup, Jes, Hjortdal, Henrik, Jensen, Tommy, Lerborg, Leon, Nielsen, Claus, Refslund, Niels et al. 2007. 'Tilgiv os – vi vidste ikke, hvad vi gjorde'. *Politiken*, 29 March. https://politiken.dk/debat/kroniken/art5480243/Tilgiv-os-vi-vidste-ikke-hvad-vi-gjorde (accessed 15 July 2022).

Gladwell, Malcolm. 2011. 'The order of things: What college rankings really tell us'. *New Yorker*, 6 February. www.newyorker.com/magazine/2011/02/14/the-order-of-things (accessed 24 August 2022).

Glenn, James and Florescu, Elizabeth. 2017. *State of the Future*. Washington: The Millennium Project.

Global Innovation Index. 2019. 'About the Global Innovation Index'. www.globalinnovationindex.org/about-gii (accessed 25 June 2019).

Goodhart, Charles. 1981 [1975]. 'Problems of monetary management: The UK experience', in Anthony Courakis (ed.) *Inflation, Depression and Economic Policy in the West*. Totowa, NJ: Barnes & Noble Books.

Goodman, Leah. 2015. 'Why Volkswagen cheated'. *Newsweek*, 15 December.

Gorman, Thomas. 2009. *Critical Issues in the Sarbanes–Oxley Act: Audit Committee*. San Francisco: LexisNexis Group. https://www.secactions.com/articles/Audit.pdf (accessed 2 March 2023).

Gorur, Radhika. 2011. 'ANT on the PISA trail: Following the statistical pursuit of certainty'. *Educational Philosophy and Theory* 43: 76–93.

Gorur, Radhika. 2016. 'Seeing like PISA: A cautionary tale about the performativity of international assessments'. *European Educational Research Journal* 15(5): 598–616.

Gray, Andrew and Jenkins, Bill. 1993. 'Codes of accountability in the new public sector'. *Accounting, Auditing and Accountability Journal* 6(3): 52–67.

Greenaway, John, Salter, Brian and Hart, Stella. 2007. 'How policy networks can damage democratic health: A case study in the government of governance'. *Public Administration* 85(3): 717–738.

Grek, Sotiria. 2009. 'Governing by numbers: The PISA "effect" in Europe'. *Journal of Education Policy* 24(1): 23–37.

Grove, Jack. 2015. 'Newcastle University staff express fears over new "targets"'. *Times Higher Education*, 17 December. www.timeshighereducation.com/news/newcastle-university-staff-express-fears-over-new-targets (accessed 24 August 2022).

Grove, Jack. 2017. 'National Student Survey 2017: Campuses omitted after NUS boycott'. *Times Higher Education*, 9 August. www.timeshighereducation.com/news/national-student-survey-2017-campuses-omitted-after-nus-boycott (accessed 9 March 2023).

Grove, Jack 2019. 'Strike action over "unrealistic" REF targets looms at Liverpool'. *Times Higher Education*, 14 March: 10–11.

Grove, Jack. 2020. 'Mark Griffiths: The professor who publishes a paper every two days'. *Times Higher Education*, 22 October. www.timeshighereducation.com/news/mark-griffiths-professor-who-publishes-paper-every-two-days (accessed 24 August 2022).

Gruber, Karl Heinz. 2006. 'The German "PISA-shock": Some aspects of the extraordinary impact of the OECD's PISA study on the German education system', pp. 195–208 in Hubert Ertl (ed.) *Cross-national Attraction in Education: Accounts from England and Germany*. Oxford: Symposium Books.

Hacking, Ian. 2004. 'Between Michel Foucault and Erving Goffman: Between discourse in the abstract and face-to-face interaction'. *Economy and Society* 33(3): 277.

Hacking, Ian. 2006. 'Making up people'. *London Review of Book* 28(16): 23–26.

Hall, Brian. 2003. 'Six challenges in designing equity-based pay'. *Journal of Applied Corporate Finance* 15(3): 21–33. https://onlinelibrary.wiley.com/doi/abs/10.1111/j.1745-6622.2003.tb00458.x (accessed 10 August 2022).

Hall, David. 2015. *Why Public–Private Partnerships Don't Work: The Many Advantages of the Public Alternative*. Public Services International Research Unit, first published 2014, updated 2015. www.worldpsi.org/sites/default/files/rapport_eng_56pages_a4_lr.pdf (accessed 16 June 2023).

Ham, Christopher. 2009. *Health Policy in Britain*. Basingstoke: Palgrave Macmillan.

Harney, Stefano and Moten, Fred. 2013. *The Undercommons: Fugitive Planning and Black Study*. New York: Minor Compositions.

Harvey, David. 1989. *The Condition of Postmodernity: An Enquiry into the Origins of Cultural Change*. Oxford: Blackwell.

Harvey, David. 2004. 'The new imperialism: Accumulation by dispossession'. *Socialist Register* 40: 63–87.

Hatton, Celia. 2015. 'China "social credit": Beijing sets up huge system'. *BBC News*, 26 October. www.bbc.co.uk/news/world-asia-china-34592186 (accessed 20 August 2022).

Havergal, Chris. 2015a. 'NSS "yea-saying": Is institutional zeal to blame?' *Times Higher Education*, 8 October: 11.

Havergal, Chris. 2015b. 'Standard tests: Giant leap or heading in wrong direction?' *Times Higher Education*, 8 October: 20–21.

Hayes, Adam. 2021. 'Special purpose vehicle'. *Investopedia*, 29 August. www.investopedia.com/terms/s/spv.asp (accessed 19 August 2022).

Hayward, Sarah and Fee, Elizabeth. 1992. 'More in sorrow than in anger: The British nurses' strike of 1988'. *International Journal of Health Services* 22(3): 397–415.

Hazelkorn, Ellen. 2008. 'Learning to live with league tables and ranking: The experience of institutional leaders'. *Higher Education Policy* 21(2): 193–215.

Hellowell, Mark and Pollock, Allyson. 2009. 'The private financing of NHS hospitals: Politics, policy and practice'. *Economic Affairs* 29(1): 13–19.

High Pay Commission. 2011. *Cheques with Balances: Why Tackling High Pay Is in the National Interest*. Final report of the High Pay Commission. London: High Pay Unit. https://highpaycentre.org/wpcontent/uploads/2020/10/Cheques_with_Balanceswhy_tackling_high_pay_is_in_the_national_interest.pdf (accessed 22 August 2022).

Hilzenrath, David. 2006. 'Fannie sues KPMG for approving bad numbers'. *Washington Post*, 13 December. www.washingtonpost.com/archive/business/2006/12/13/fannie-sues-kpmg-for-approving-bad-numbers/7764c99f-a2cc-42c0-906f-66c4128b1edc/ (accessed 10 August 2022).

Hilzenrath, David, 2019. 'Botched audits: Big Four accounting firms fail many inspections'. POGO (Project on Government Oversight), 5 September. www.

pogo.org/investigation/2019/09/botched-audits-big-four-accounting-firms-fail-many-inspections/ (accessed 29 August 2022).

Hinchliffe, David. 2002. 'NHS (private sector)'. *Hansard*, vol. 596, col. 309WH, 11 July. https://publications.parliament.uk/pa/cm200102/cmhansrd/v0020711/halltext/20711h01.htm (accessed 16 June 2023).

HM Treasury. 2019. 'Private finance initiative process'. gov.uk, 14 October. www.gov.uk/government/publications/private-finance-initiative-process (accessed 28 June 2023).

Hodge, Margaret. 2013. 'Treasury insiders help rich avoid tax, say MPs – video'. Interview with Margaret Hodge. ITN Productions, 26 April. www.theguardian.com/business/video/2013/apr/26/treasury-insiders-rich-tax-video (accessed 26 February 2015).

Hodson, Hal. 2015. 'Inside China's plan to give every citizen a character score'. *New Scientist*, 14 October. www.new scientist.com/article/dn28314-inside-chinas-plan-to-give-every-citizen-a-character-score/ (accessed 19 August 2022).

Hood, Christopher, James, Oliver, Jones, George, Scott, Colin and Travers, Tony. 1999. *Regulation Inside Government: Waste-watchers, Quality Police, and Sleazebusters*. Oxford: Oxford University Press.

Hornby, Lucy. 2017. 'China changes tack on "social credit" scheme plan'. *Financial Times*, 5 July. www.ft.com/content/f772a9ce-60c4-11e7-91a7-502f7ee26895 (accessed 20 August 2022).

Hoskin, Keith and Macve, Richard. 1988. 'The genesis of accountability: The West Point connections'. *Accounting, Organizations and Society* 13(1): 37–73.

House of Commons. 1990. National Health Service and Community Care Act 1990. https://www.legislation.gov.uk/ukpga/ (accessed 1 July 2023).

House of Commons. 2004. *Research Assessment Exercise: A Re-assessment*. Eleventh Report of Session 2003–4, Science and Technology Committee. London: House of Commons.

House of Commons. 2006. *The Refinancing of the Norfolk and Norwich PFI Hospital*. Committee of Public Accounts, HC694. London: The Stationery Office. https://publications.parliament.uk/pa/cm200506/cmselect/cmpubacc/694/694.pdf (accessed 1 July 2023).

House of Commons. 2011a. *Lessons from PFI and Other Projects*. Committee of Public Accounts, 1 September. London: London: The Stationery Office. https://publications.parliament.uk/pa/cm201012/cmselect/cmpubacc/1201/1201.pdf (accessed 16 June 2023).

House of Commons. 2011b. *Private Finance Initiative (Written Evidence)*. Treasury Committee, 17 May. www.parliament.uk/globalassets/documents/commons-committees/treasury/PFI-Evidence.pdf (accessed 16 June 2023).

House of Commons. 2018. 'Carillion'. Business, Energy and Industrial Strategy and Work and Pensions Committees. London: House of Commons, May. https://publications.parliament.uk/pa/cm201719/cmselect/cmworpen/769/76907.htm#_idTextAnchor168 (accessed 30 August 2022).

House of Commons. 2019a. *The Future of Audit*, Business Energy and Industrial Strategy Committee Report, HC 1718. London: House of Commons, 2 April. https://publications.parliament.uk/pa/cm201719/cmselect/cmbeis/1718/171802.htm (accessed 29 August 2022).

House of Commons. 2019b. *Oral Evidence: Future of Audit*, Business, Energy and Industrial Strategy Committee Report, HC 1718. London: House of Commons, 30 January 2019. http://data.parliament.uk/writtenevidence/committeeevidence. svc/evidencedocument/business-energy-and-industrial-strategy-committee/ future-of-audit/oral/95825.html (accessed 29 August 2022).

Huang, Zheping. 2015. 'All Chinese citizens now have a score based on how well we live, and mine sucks'. *QUARTZ*, 9 October. https://qz.com/519737/ all-chinese-citizens-now-have-a-score-based-on-how-well-we-live-and-mine-sucks/ (accessed 20 August 2022).

Hudson, Michael, Chavkin, Sasha and Mos, Bart. 2014. 'Big 4 audit firms play big role in offshore murk'. *International Consortium of Investigative Journalism*, 5 November. www.icij.org/project/luxembourg-leaks/big-4-audit-firms-play-big-role-offshore-murk/ (accessed 10 August 2022).

Humphris, Debra and Littlejohns, Peter. 1995. 'The development of multi-professional audit and clinical guidelines: Their contribution to quality assurance and effectiveness in the NHS'. *Journal of Interprofessional Care* 9(3): 207–225.

Hunt, Elle. 2015. 'Peeple review people: The user-review app you didn't dare ask for'. *Guardian*, 1 October. www.theguardian.com/technology/2015/oct/01/ peeple-review-people-the-user-review-app-you-didnt-dare-ask-for (accessed 20 August 2022).

Hunt, Jeremy. 2015. 'Hospital trusts (deficits)'. *Hansard*, vol. 596, debated on 2 June. https://hansard.parliament.uk/commons/20150602/debates/150602240 00023/HospitalTrusts(Deficits) (accessed 25 September 2022).

Iacone, Amanda and Skolnik, Sam. 2021. 'Big Four cut back federal lobbying amid pandemic'. *Bloomberg Tax*, 13 January. https://news.bloombergtax.com/ financial-accounting/big-four-cut-back-federal-lobbying-amid-pandemic (accessed 10 August 2022).

ICIJ (International Consortium of Investigative Journalists). 2016. 'The Panama Papers: Exposing the rogue offshore finance industry'. www.icij.org/ investigations/panama-papers/ (accessed 30 August 2022).

ICIJ (International Consortium of Investigative Journalists). 2017. 'Offshore trove exposes piggy banks of the wealthiest', 5 November. www.icij.org/investigations/ paradise-papers/ (accessed 30 August 2022).

IIM (International Institute of Management). 2005 (updated 2018). 'Gross National Happiness / Well-being (GNH / GNW) – A Policy White Paper'. www. iim-edu.org/grossnationalhappiness/ (accessed 25 June 2019).

Ingram, David and Aubin, Dena. 2012. 'Insight: Big 4 auditors spend more than ever on U.S. lobbying'. Reuters, 13 March. www.reuters.com/article/us-usa-accounting-big4-idUSBRE82C0JQ20120313 (accessed 26 February 2015).

Internal Revenue Service (IRS). 2005. 'KPMG to pay $456 million for criminal violations'. Press release, Department of Justice, Washington, DC, 29 August. www.justice.gov/archive/opa/pr/2005/August/05_ag_433.html (accessed 10 August 2022).

IT University. 2014. 'A model for measuring teaching and research contribution', draft internal document, IT University, Copenhagen.

Jack, Simon. 2016. 'The BHS scandal ... in 2 minutes'. *BBC News*, 6 May. www.bbc.com/news/av/business-36225914 (accessed 10 August 2022).

Jasy, Andy. 2023.'Amazon plans to cut 18,000 jobs to rein in costs'. *Financial Times*, 25 January. www.ft.com/content/0371225d-3131-4937-8af2-03582ca5e44d (accessed 1 July 2023).

Jenkins, Kate, Caines, Karen and Jackson, Andrew. 1988. *Improving Management in Government: The Next Steps*. Report to the Prime Minister (the Ibbs Report). February. London: HMSO.

Jones, Adam 2012. 'Grant Thornton wins quango audits', *Financial Times, Companies*, 5 March: 24.

Joseph Rowntree Foundation. 2021. *UK Poverty 2020/21*. Report, 13 January. www.jrf.org.uk/report/uk-poverty-2020-21 (accessed 9 August 2022).

Jump, Paul. 2014. 'Spike in NSS "yeah-sayers" could weaken survey data'. *Times Higher Education*, 3 July. www.timeshighereducation.com/news/spike-in-nss-yea-sayers-could-weaken-survey-data/2014290.article (accessed 24 August 2022).

Jump, Paul. 2015a. 'Grant income targets set at one in six universities, THE poll suggests'. *Times Higher* Education, 11 June. www.timeshighereducation.com/news/grant-income-targets-set-one-six-universities-poll-suggests (accessed 30 April 2016).

Jump, Paul. 2015b. 'Dismissal was unfair, but academic sparked it himself'. *Times Higher Education*, 25 June. www.timeshighereducation.com/dismissal-was-unfair-but-academic-sparked-it-himself (accessed 14 February 2016).

Kafka, Franz. 2009. *The Trial*, trans. David Wyllie. New York: Dover Thrift Editions.

Kantor, Jodi and Sundaram, Arya, 2022. 'The rise of the worker productivity score'. *The New York Times*, 14 August. www.nytimes.com/interactive/2022/08/14/business/worker-productivity-tracking.html (accessed 20 August 2022).

Kaplan, Robert and Norton, David. 1993. 'Putting the balanced scorecard to work'. *Harvard Business Review* Sept.–Oct.: 4–17.

Kaplan, Robert and Norton, David. 2004. *Focusing Your Organization on Strategy – With the Balanced Scorecard*. Cambridge, MA: Harvard Business School Publishing.

Kennedy, Ian. 2001. *Learning from Bristol: The Report of the Public Inquiry into Children's Heart Surgery at the Bristol Royal Infirmary 1984–95*. London: Stationery Office.

King, Lucy and Moutsou, Christina (eds). 2010. *Rethinking Audit Cultures*. Hertfordshire: PCCS Books.

Kingman, John. 2018. *Independent Review of the Financial Reporting Council*. London: HMSO.

Klein, Naomi. 2008. *The Shock Doctrine*. Harmondsworth: Penguin.

Komljenovic, Janja and Robertson, Susan L. 2016. 'The dynamics of "market-making" in higher education'. *Journal of Education Policy* 31(5): 622–636.

Kornberger, Martin, Justesen, Lise and Mouritsen, Jan. 2011. '"When you make manager, we put a big mountain in front of you": An ethnography of managers in a Big 4 accounting firm'. *Accounting, Organizations and Society* 36(8): 514–533.

KPMG. 2014. 'Former Federal Reserve Deputy Director Deborah Parker Bailey joins KPMG'. Press Release, 1 December. www.prnewswire.com/

news-releases/former-federal-reserve-deputy-director-deborah-parker-bailey-joins-kpmg-300002472.html (accessed 10 August 2022).

KPMG. 2015a. 'Explore our history'. https://home.kpmg/uk/en/home/about/150-years-supporting-the-uk/explore-our-history.html (accessed 10 August 2022).

KPMG. 2015b. 'KPMGs Code of Conduct'. www.kpmg.com/US/en/about/Pages/CodeOfConduct.aspx (accessed 26 Febuary 2015).

KPMG. 2021. 'KPMGs Code of Conduct'. 12 May. https://home.kpmg/uk/en/home/insights/2016/05/kpmg-uk-code-of-conduct.html (accessed 10 August 2022).

Laricchia, Federica. 2023. 'Smart wearable shipments forecast worldwide from 2016 to 2026'. *Statista*, 10 March. www.statista.com/statistics/878144/worldwide-smart-wristwear-shipments-forecast/ (accessed 18 March 2023).

Larner, Wendy and Walters, William (eds). 2004. *Global Governmentality: Governing International Spaces*. London: Routledge.

Lave, Jean and Wenger, Etienne. 1991. *Situated Learning: Legitimate Peripheral Participation*. Cambridge: Cambridge University Press.

Laville, Sandra. 2022. 'Raw sewage discharged into English rivers 375,000 times by water firms'. *Guardian*, 31 March. www.theguardian.com/environment/2022/mar/31/sewage-released-into-english-rivers-for-27m-hours-last-year-by-water-firms (accessed 24 March 2023).

Leaver, Adam, Seabrooke, Leonard, Staushom, Saila and Wigan, Duncan. 2020. *Auditing with Accountability: Shrinking the Opportunity Spaces for Audit Failure*. Sheffield: University of Sheffield and Copenhagen Business School. https://eprints.whiterose.ac.uk/163161/1/Auditing-with-Accountability.pdf (accessed 30 August 2022).

Lees, Amanda. 2017. *Evaluation of Reflective Practice Group project: Brighton & Hove Children's Services Preliminary Report*. London: Centre for Social Work Practice. https://cris.winchester.ac.uk/ws/portalfiles/portal/356526/824824_Lees_ReflectivePracticeGroupEvaluation_original.pdf (accessed 29 September 2022).

Leonhardt, David. 2022. 'Good morning. Employers have a new tool in the struggle with employees over workplace power: constant monitoring'. *The New York Times*, 15 August https://milled.com/nytimes/the-morning-youre-being-watched-oYYkUiJUKDxeE54Y (accessed 20 August 2022).

Lethbridge, Jane. 2015. *Health Care Reforms and the Rise of Global Multinational Health Care Companies*. London: Public Services International Research Unit, University of Greenwich. www.psiru.org/sites/default/files/2015-05-H-Healthcarereforms&riseofglobalhealthcarecompanies.pdf (accessed 25 September 2022).

Levine, Matt. 2018. 'Some accountants got caught in the revolving door'. *Bloomberg Opinion*, 23 January. www.bloomberg.com/opinion/articles/2018-01-23/some-accountants-got-caught-in-the-revolving-door (accessed 10 august 2022).

Levtzion-Korach, Osnat and Israeli, Avi. 2005. 'The British star rating system – Review and its implications for the Israeli health system'. *Harefuah* 144(12): 865–909. https://pubmed.ncbi.nlm.nih.gov/16400788/ (accessed 19 August 2022).

Lewis, Nicolas, Robertson, Susan, Lim, Miguel A., Komljenovic, Janja, Muellerleile, Christopher, Shore, Cris and Bajenova, Tatyana. 2022. 'Market making and the (re)production of knowledge in public universities'. *Learning and Teaching: International Journal of Higher Education in the Social Sciences (LATISS)* 15(3): 56–109.

Lewis, Nicolas and Shore, Cris. 2017. 'Managing the third mission: Reform or reinvention of the public university?', pp. 47–68 in Wright, Susan and Shore, Cris (eds) *Death of the Public University: Universities in the Knowledge Economy.* Oxford: Berghahn.

Lewis, Steven. 2017. 'Governing schooling through "what works": The OECD's PISA for schools'. *Journal of Education Policy* 32(3): 281–302.

Leys, Colin, 2001. *Market-driven Politics: Neoliberal Democracy and the Public Interest.* London: Verso.

LifeWay. 2021. 'Spiritual growth assessment process', http://blog.lifeway.com/ growingdisciples/files/2013/08/Spiritual_Growth_Assessment.pdf (accessed on 13 July 2022).

Lim, Miguel. 2016. *The Work of Global Rankers and the Building of Weak Expertise.* PhD thesis, Aarhus University, Denmark.

Lingard, Bon and Sellar, Sam. 2016. 'The changing organisational and global significance of the OECD's education work', pp. 357–373 in Karen Mundy, Andy Green and Antoni Verger (eds) *The Handbook of Global Education.* Chichester: John Wiley and Sons.

Lister, John. 2018. *Unhealthy Profits: PFI in the NHS – Its Real Costs and Consequences.* Leeds: Unison Mid-Yorkshire Health Branch.

Liu, Chuncheng. 2019. 'Multiple social credit systems in China'. *Economic Sociology: The European Electronic Newsletter* 21(1): 22–32.

Lock, Grahame and Martins, Herminio. 2011. 'Quantified control and the mass production of "psychotic citizens"'. *EspacesTemps.* https://www.espacestemps. net/articles/quantified-control-and-the-mass-production-of-ldquopsychotic-citizensrdquo/ (accessed 1 July 2023).

Loftus, Alex. 2006. 'RAE-ification and the consciousness of the academic'. *Area* 38(1): 110–112. www.jstor.org/stable/20004508 (accessed 24 August 2022).

London Economics. 2021. *The Costs and Benefits of International Higher Education Students to the UK Economy.* London: Universities UK International (UUKi) and the Higher Education Policy Institute (HEPI). https://londoneconomics.co.uk/ wpcontent/uploads/2021/09/LE-HEPI-UUKi-Impact-of-intl-HE-students-on-the-UK-economy-Summary-Report-September-2021.pdf (accessed 24 August 2022).

Loveday, Vik. 2021. 'Change management 101'. Goldsmiths Sociology blog, 28 September. https://sites.gold.ac.uk/sociology/change-management-101/ (accessed 22 October 2021).

Loveless, Tom. 2013. 'Attention OECD-PISA: Your silence on China is wrong'. *The Brown Center Chalkboard.* Washington, DC: Brookings Institute.

Loxton, Liz. 2015. 'How the Big Four have returned to consulting with a bang'. *Accountancy Age,* 15 September. www.accountancyage.com/2015/09/27/how-the-big-four-have-returned-to-consulting-with-a-bang/ (accessed 29 August 2022).

Lucas, Lisa. 2006. *The Research Game in Academic Life.* Maidenhead: McGraw-Hill, Open University Press.

Lucas, Lisa. 2017. 'Evaluating academic research ambivalence, anxiety and audit in the risk university', pp. 213–228 in Susan Wright and Cris Shore (eds) *Death of the Public University*. Oxford: Berghahn.

Luckock, Barry, Hickle, Kristine, Hampden-Thomson, Gillian and Dickens, Richard. 2017. *Islington 'Doing What Counts: Measuring What Matters'*. Children's Social Care Innovation Programme Evaluation Report 52. Sussex University and London: Department for Education. https://assets.publishing.service.gov.uk/government/uploads/system/uploads/attachment_data/file/625645/Islington_Doing_What_Counts_Measuring_What-Matters.pdf (accessed 29 September 2022).

Lund, Rebecca. 2012. 'Publishing to become an "ideal academic": An institutional ethnography and a feminist critique'. *Scandinavian Journal of Management* 28(3): 218–228.

Ma, Yihan. 2022. 'Number of annual active consumers across Alibaba's online shopping properties from 1st quarter 2017 to 1st quarter 2022 in China'. *Statista*, 13 June. www.statista.com/statistics/226927/alibaba-cumulative-active-online-buyers-taobao-tmall/ (accessed 19 August 2022).

MacAskill, Andrew. 2018. 'UK government questioned over Carillion contracts after profit warnings'. Reuters, 15 January. https://www.reuters.com/article/carillion-restructuring-government-idUKL3N1PA3W7 (accessed 1 July 2023).

MacMillan, Paul. 2012. 'Margaret Cole to join PwC'. *Money Marketin*,. 20 March. www.moneymarketing.co.uk/news/margaret-cole-to-join-pwc/ (accessed 10 August 2022).

Mansell, Warwick and Savage, Michael. 2018. 'Top academy schools sound alarm as cash crisis looms'. Guardian, 27 January. www.theguardian.com/education/2018/jan/27/schools-academy-trusts-warn-pay-staffing-public-spending (accessed 9 August 2022).

Marginson, Simon and Considine, Mark. 2000. *The Enterprise University: Power, Governance and Reinvention in Australia*. Cambridge: Cambridge University Press.

Marriage, Madison. 2018a. 'Big Four's extensive Carillion work sparks calls for action'. *Financial Times*, 13 February. www.ft.com/content/e67793a4-10e2-11e8-8cb6-b9ccc4c4dbbb (accessed 1 July 2023).

Marriage, Madison. 2018b. 'BDO call for greater restrictions on non-audit work'. *Financial Times*, 1 May. www.ft.com/content/342e6ae4-4c95-11e8-8a8e-22951a2d8493 (accessed 30 August 2022).

Marriage, Madison. 2018c. 'Big Four paid millions to advise Brussels on tax policy'. *Financial Times*, 10 July. www.ft.com/content/56f862ee-8392-11e8-96dd-fa565ec55929. (accessed 30 August 2022).

Marriage, Madison. 2018d. 'Biggest UK auditors hold secret talks to avert watchdog probe'. *Financial Times*, 13 July. www.ft.com/content/0605c1d8-86bc-11e8-96dd-fa565ec55929 (accessed 30 September 2022).

Marriage, Madison and Ford, Jonathan. 2019. 'An illusion of choice: The conflicts that mire the audit world'. *Financial Times*, 9 August. www.ft.com/content/2085cab2-9af3-11e8-9702-5946bae86e6d. (accessed 30 August 2022).

Marriott, Anna. 2014. *A Dangerous Diversion: Will the IFC's Flagship Health PPP Bankrupt Lesotho's Ministry of Health?* Oxford: Oxfam International.

Martin, Emily, 1997. 'Managing Americans: Policy and changes in the meanings of work and self', pp. 239–260 in C. Shore and S. Wright (eds) *Anthropology of Policy: Critical Perspectives on Governance and Power*. London: Routledge.

Martin, Keir. 2010. 'Robert McNamara and the limits of "bean counting"'. *Anthropology Today* 26(3):16–19.

McGaw, Barry. 2008. 'The role of the OECD in international comparative studies of achievement'. *Assessment in Education: Principles, Policy & Practice* 15(3): 223–243.

McGettigan, Andrew. 2013. *The Great University Gamble: Money, Markets and the Future of Higher Education*. London: Pluto Press. https://doi.org/10.2307/j.ctt183p3ns. (accessed 24 August 2022).

McGettigan, Andrew. 2021. 'Student loans: What counts as expenditure in national accounts'. *Critical Education* 5 March. https://andrewmcgettigan.org/2021/03/05/5971/ (accessed 21 October 2021).

McKee, Martin, Pollock, Allyson, Clarke, Aileen, McCoy, David, Middleton, John, Raine, Rosaline et al. 2011. 'In defence of the NHS: Why writing to the House of Lords was necessary'. *British Medical Journal* 343(11 October). www.bmj.com/content/343/bmj.d6535 (accessed 19 August 2022).

McKeown, Marie-Helene Lafleur and Yeung, Echo Yuet Wah. 2022. 'Deepening our understanding of reflective practice in a safeguarding child protection and welfare context'. *Practice: Social Work in Action* online, 13 February. www.tandfonline.com/action/showCitFormats?doi=10.1080%2F09503153.2022.2038124&area=0000000000000001 (accessed 29 September 2022).

McKinney Rogers, Damian. 2016. 'Mission statement accomplished'. www.mckinneyrogers.com/What_We_Do.aspx (accessed 5 August 2022).

Meikle, James. 2015. 'Focus on targets in NHS poses threat to patient care, says thinktank'. *Guardian*, 6 March. www.theguardian.com/society/2015/mar/06/focus-targets-threat-care-nhs-patients-thinktank (accessed 14 July 2022).

Meranze, Michael. 2014. 'The new brutalism in higher education'. Remaking the University blog, 4 September. http://utotherescue.blogspot.dk/2014/09/the-new-brutalism-in-higher-education.html (accessed 14 February 2016).

Merry, Sally Engle. 2011. 'Measuring the world: Indicators, human rights, and global governance'. *Current Anthropology* 52: S83–S95.

Merry, Sally Engle. 2016. *The Seductions of Quantification: Measuring Human Rights, Gender Violence, and Sex Trafficking*. Chicago: University of Chicago Press.

Meyer, Heinz-Dieter and Benavot, Aaron (eds). 2013. *PISA, Power, and Policy: The Emergence of Global Educational Governance*. Oxford: Symposium Books Ltd.

Miller, Peter. 1994. 'Accounting and objectivity: The invention of calculating selves and calculable spaces', pp. 239–264 in Allan Megill (ed.) *Rethinking Objectivity*. Durham, NC: Duke University Press.

Miller, Peter. 2001. 'Governing by numbers: Why calculative practices matter'. *Social Research* 68(2): 379–396.

Mitchell, Timothy. 1999. 'Society, economy and the state effect', pp. 76–97 in George Steinmetz (ed.) *State/Culture: State Formation after the Cultural Turn*. Ithaca, NY: Cornell University Press.

Monbiot, George. 2006. 'An easter egg hunt'. *The Guardian*, 9 May. http://www.monbiot.com/archives/2006/05/09/an-easter-egg-hunt/ (accessed 2 July 2023).

Monticello Kievlan, Patricia. n.d. 'Review of Peeple'. Common Sense Media. www. commonsensemedia.org/app-reviews/peeple (accessed 17 August 2022).

Morgan, Clara and Shahjahan, Riyad A. 2014. 'The legitimation of OECD's global educational governance: Examining PISA and AHELO test production'. *Comparative Education* 50(2): 192–205.

Morgenson, Gretchen, 2013. 'Clawbacks? They're still a rare breed'. *The New York Times*, 29 December. www.nytimes.com/2013/12/29/business/clawbacks-theyre-still-a-rare-breed.html (accessed 29 August 2022).

Morrish, Liz. 2019. *Pressure Vessels: The Epidemic of Poor Mental Health among Higher Education Staff.* HEPI Occasional Paper No. 20. Oxford: Higher Education Policy Institute.

Muller, Joann. 2014. 'Toyota admits misleading customers; Agrees to $1.2 billion criminal fine'. *Forbes Magazine*, 19 March. www.forbes.com/sites/ joannmuller/2014/03/19/toyota-admits-misleading-customers-agrees-to-1-2-billion-criminal-fine/#34c990216c1e (accessed 1 July 2023).

Munro, Eileen. 2005. 'A systems approach to investigating child abuse deaths'. *British Journal of Social Work* 35(4): 531–546.

Munro, Eileen. 2010a. 'LSE research: A new approach to child protection'. Uploaded 19 April. www.youtube.com/watch?v=E4wREr5dN_Q&list=RDCMUCK08_B5SZwoEUk2hDPMOijQ&index=1 (accessed 29 September 2022).

Munro, Eileen. 2010b. *The Munro Review of Child Protection, Part One: A Systems Analysis.* London: Department for Education. https://assets.publishing.service. gov.uk/government/uploads/system/uploads/attachment_data/file/624949/ TheMunroReview-Part_one.pdf (accessed 29 September 2022).

Munro, Eileen, 2011. *The Munro Review of Child Protection: Final Report. A Child-Centred System.* London: Department of Education. Cm 8062. https://assets. publishing.service.gov.uk/government/uploads/system/uploads/attachment_ data/file/175391/Munro-Review.pdf (accessed 29 September 2022).

Munro, Eileen, 2012. *Progress Report: Moving Towards a Child-Centred System.* London: Department of Education. www.gov.uk/government/publications/ progress-report-moving-towards-a-child-centred-system (accessed 29 September 2022).

Murphy, Richard. 2018. 'The PWC BHS audit failure reveals a system rotten to its very core'. 16 August. www.taxresearch.org.uk/Blog/2018/08/16/the-pwc-bhs-audit-failure-reveals-a-system-rotten-to-its-very-core/ (accessed 10 August 2022).

Nader, Laura. 1972. 'Up the anthropologist: Perspectives gained from studying up', pp. 284–311 in D. Hymes (ed.) *Reinventing Anthropology.* New York: Pantheon.

Nafus, Dawn and Sherman, Jamie. 2014. 'Big data, big questions – this one does not go up to 11: The Quantified Self movement as an alternative big data practice'. *International Journal of Communication* 8: 1784–1794.

NAO (National Audit Office). 1989. *The Next Steps Initiative,* HC 410, 1988–89. *Report by the Comptroller and Auditor General.* London: HMSO.

NAO (National Audit Office). 2005. *The Refinancing of the Norfolk and Norwich PFI Hospital: How the Deal Can be Viewed in the Light of the Refinancing.* London: House of Commons National Audit Office.

NAO (National Audit Office). 2011. *Lessons from PFI and Other Projects*, HC 920, 28 April. London: The Stationery Office. https://study.sagepub.com/sites/default/files/NAO%20on%20PFI.pdf (accessed 19 August 2022).

NAO (National Audit Office). 2018a. *Converting Maintained Schools to Academies*. Report by the Comptroller and Auditor General, HC 720, 20 February. London: National Audit Office. www.nao.org.uk/wp-content/uploads/2018/02/Converting-maintained-schools-to-academies.pdf (accessed 14 July 2022).

NAO (National Audit Office). 2018b. *PFI and PF2*. Report by the Comptroller and Auditor General, HC 716, 12 January. London: National Audit Office. www.nao.org.uk/wp-content/uploads/2018/01/PFI-and-PF2.pdf (accessed 19 August 2022).

Natsios, Andrew. 2011. *The Clash of the Counter-Bureaucracy and Development*. Washington, DC: Center for Global Development.

Nature. 2016. 'Macchiarini scandal is a valuable lesson for the Karolinska Institute'. *Nature* 537: 137. www.nature.com/articles/537137a (accessed 19 August 2022).

New Economics Foundation. 2018. 'About NEF'. http://happyplanetindex.org/about-nef/ (accessed 25 April 2018).

NHS (National Health Service). 2001. *Shifting the Balance of Power within the NHS – Securing Delivery*. July. London: Department of Health.

Nissan, Christian. 2007. 'Hvad er det, vi har gang i?' (What are we doing?) *Politiken*, 5 September. http://politiken.dk/debat/kroniken/ECE374233/hvad-er-det-vi-har-gang-i/ (accessed 19 August 2022).

Nye, Joseph S. 1990. 'Soft power'. *Foreign Policy* 80: 153–171.

O'Dwyer, Michael. 2022a. 'Auditors warn of "organisational culture crisis" at UK companies'. *Financial Times*, 28 February. www.ft.com/content/1e36321b-7cd1-4eae-82d2-a7068721cde5 (accessed 30 September 2022).

O'Dwyer, Michael. 2022b. 'KPMG faces £14.4mn fine for misleading UK regulators over Carillion audit'. *Financial Times*, 12 May. www.ft.com/content/ab3a30c6-4491-46fc-83cd-812c777c337a (accessed 1 July 2023).

O'Dwyer, Michael. 2022c. 'How to split a Big Four firm – And keep 13,000 partners happy'. *Financial Times*, 17 June. www.ft.com/content/d715734c-701c-4c97-b0b3-44050f48f6b1 (accessed 30 August 2022).

O'Dwyer, Michael. 2023. 'KPMG settles with Carillion liquidators over £1.3bn audit negligence claim'. *Financial Times*, 17 February. www.ft.com/content/5d0217af-cadf-4fd6-90e9-836fa9aead7a (accessed 1 July 2023).

OECD. n.d.a. 'Better Life Index'. www.oecdbetterlifeindex.org/#/11111111111 (accessed 25 June 2019).

OECD. n.d.b. 'PISA – The OECD Programme for International Student Assessment'. Paris: Organisation for Economic Cooperation and Development. www.oecd.org/pisa/pisaproducts/37474503.pdf (accessed 4 July 2019).

OECD. 2005. 'Is GDP a satisfactory measure of growth?'. *OECD Observer* No. 246–247. December 2004–January 2005. Paris: OECD. https://openlab.citytech.cuny.edu/environmentaleconomics-6709/files/2014/11/OECD-Observer_-Is-GDP-a-satisfactory-measure-of-growth_.pdf (accessed 14 July 2022).

OECD. 2014. 'PISA 2012 results in focus: What 15-year-olds know and what they can do with what they know'. Paris: OECD. www.oecd.org/pisa/keyfindings/pisa-2012-results-overview.pdf (accessed 20 July 2022).

OECD. 2016. *Low-performing Students. Why They Fall Behind and How to Help Them Succeed*. Paris: OECD. www.oecdilibrary.org/docserver/9789264250246en. pdf?expires=1661248523&id=id&accname=guest&checksum=oEC253596 C5117D376134C5AC52DEA55 (accessed 23 August 2022).

OECD. 2017. *How's Life? Measuring Well-being*. Paris: OECD. www.oecd-ilibrary. org/economics/how-s-life-2017_how_life-2017-en (accessed 25 June 2019).

OECD. 2018a. 'PISA 2018 global competence framework'. In *PISA 2018 Assessment and Analytical Framework*. Paris: OECD. www.oecd.org/pisa/innovation/global-competence/ (accessed 23 August 2022).

OECD. 2018b. 'PISA for Development' programme. Paris. OECD. www.oecd.org/ pisa/pisa-for-development/ (accessed 4 July 2019).

OECD, 2018c. 'PISA for Schools – FAQs'. Paris: OECD. www.oecd.org/pisa/ aboutpisa/pisa-based-test-for-schools-faq.htm. www.oecd.org/pisa/aboutpisa/ pisa-based-test-for-schools-faq.htm (accessed 11 November 2018).

OECD. 2021. 'Organisational Structure'. www.oecd.org/about/structure/ (accessed 23 August 2022).

OfS (Office for Students). 2018. 'Teaching Excellence and Student Outcomes: Guide to Subjectlevel Pilot Data'. 22 October. London: OfS 2018.44a.www. officeforstudents.org.uk/publications/teaching-excellence-and-student-outcomes-framework-subject-level-pilot-guide/ (accessed 24 August 2022).

Ofsted. 2022. *Inspection Report: Caversham Primary School 15 and 16 November*. Manchester: Office for Standards in Education, Children's Services and Skills.

Olds, Kris. 2010. 'Associations, networks, alliances etc. Making sense of the emerging global higher education landscape'. Discussion Paper presented to the IAU Conference, Mexico City.

Olssen, Mark and Peters, Michael. 2005. 'Neoliberalism, higher education and the knowledge economy: From the free market to knowledge capitalism'. *Journal of Education Policy* 20(3): 313–345.

O'Neill, Onora. 2002. *A Question of Trust: The BBC Reith Lectures*. Cambridge: Cambridge University Press.

OPHI. 2019. 'Bhutan's Gross National Happiness Index'. Oxford Poverty and Human Development Initiative, Oxford University. https://ophi.org.uk/policy/ national-policy/gross-national-happiness-index/ (accessed 25 June 2019).

Ørberg, Jakob. 2007. 'Who speaks for the university? Legislative frameworks for Danish university leadership 1970– 2003'. Working Papers on University Reform No. 5, May. Aarhus, Denmark. https://www.academia.edu/8331700/ Who_Speaks_for_the_University_Legislative_frameworks_for_Danish_ university_leadership_1970_2003 (accessed 25 August 2022).

Osborne, Samuel. 2015. 'China has made obedience to the State a game'. *The Independent*, 22 December. www.independent.co.uk/news/world/asia/china-has-made-obedience-to-the-state-a-game-a6783841.html (accessed 20 August 2022).

O'Sullivan, Isobel. 2022. 'Amazon's staff turnover is costing a quarter of its profits'. Tech.co, 18 October. https://tech.co/news/amazon-staff-turnover-costing-quarter-profits (accessed 22 October 2022).

Oxfam International. 2014. 'Working for the many: Public services fight inequality'. 3 April. Oxford: Oxfam International. wwwcdn.oxfam.org/s3fspublic/file_ attachments/bp182-public-services-fight-inequality-030414-en_1.pdf (accessed 19 August 2022).

Pai, Kalpana and Tolleson, Thomas D. 2012. 'The capture of government regulators by the Big 4 accounting firms: Some evidence'. *Journal of Applied Business and Economics* 13(1): 84–94.

Panchamia, Nehal and Thomas, Peter. 2014. *The Next Steps Initiative*. London: Institute for Government.

Paphitis, Nicholas. 2012. 'Greece debt crisis: Fitch downgrades country's credit rating'. *Huffington Post Business*, 22 February. www.huffingtonpost.com/2012/02/22/reece-debt-crisis-fitch-_n_1293167.html (accessed 2 December 2013).

Paterlini, Marta. 2018. 'Troubled rebuild of Stockholm's landmark hospital has cost twice as much as planned'. *British Medical Journal* 361:k1816. 25 April. www.bmj.com/content/361/bmj.k1816 (accessed 25 September 2022).

Peck, Jamie and Tickell, Adam. 2002. 'Neoliberalizing space'. *Antipode* 34(3): 380–404.

Perraudin, Frances. 2017a. '40,000 children trapped in "zombie" academy schools'. *Guardian*, 3 December. www.theguardian.com/education/2017/dec/03/thousand-pupils-trapped-in-zombie-academy-schools (accessed 14 July 2022).

Perraudin, Frances. 2017b. 'Collapsing academy trust "asset-stripped its schools of millions"'. *Guardian*, 21 October. www.theguardian.com/education/2017/oct/21/collapsing-wakefield-city-academies-trust-asset-stripped-schools-millions-say-furious-parents (accessed 9 August 2022).

Peters, Tom. 2001. 'Tom Peters's true confessions'. *Fast Company* 53: 80–92. www.fastcompany.com/44077/tom-peterss-true-confessions (accessed 12 July 2022).

Philips Living Health. 2015. 'The quantified self'. *New Scientists*, uploaded 30 November, video 2:20. www.youtube.com/watch?v=8wqC6ad1V_Q (accessed 20 August 2022).

Plimmer, Gill and Rovnick, Naomi. 2018. 'Accounting watchdog to probe KPMG over Carillion audits'. *Financial Times*, 29 January. www.ft.com/content/8edf5664-04ca-11e8-9650-9c0ad2d7c5b5/ (accessed 9 November 2023).

Pohjanpalo, Kati. 2022. 'World's happiest ranking goes to Finland for fifth year in a row', *Bloomberg UK*, 18 March. www.bloomberg.com/news/articles/2022-03-18/world-s-happiest-ranking-goes-to-finland-for-fifth-year-in-a-row?leadSource=uverify%20wall. (accessed 2 March 2023).

Politi, James. 2022. 'Republicans attack tax agency funding boost'. *Financial Times*, 22 August: 4.

Politics.co.uk. 2020. 'What are academies?' www.politics.co.uk/reference/academies/ (accessed 9 August 2022).

Pollitt, Christopher. 1993a. 'The politics of medical quality: Auditing doctors in the UK and the USA'. *Health Services Management Research* 6(1): 24–34. https://pubmed.ncbi.nlm.nih.gov/10124349/ (accessed 25 September 2022).

Pollitt, Christopher. 1993b. *Managerialism and the Public Services: Cuts or Cultural Change in the 1990s?* 2nd edn. Oxford: Blackwell Business.

Pollitt, Christopher, Bathgate, Karen, Caulfield, Janice, Smullen, Amanda, and Talbot, Colin. 2001. 'Agency fever? Analysis of an international policy fashion'. *Journal of Comparative Policy Analysis* 3(3): 271–290.

Pollock, Allyson. 2004. *NHS Plc: The Privatisation of Our Health Care*. London: Verso.

Pollock, Allyson. 2011. 'How the Secretary of State for Health proposes to abolish the NHS in England'. *British Medical Journal*, 22 March. www.bmj.com/content/342/bmj.d1695 (accessed 25 September 2022).

Pollock, Allyson, Dunnigan, Matthew, Gaffney, Decklan, Price, David and Shaoul, Jean. 1999. 'Planning the "new" NHS: Downsizing for the 21st century'. *British Medical Journal* 319(7203): 179–184.

Porter, Theodore. 1995. *Trust in Numbers: The Pursuit of Objectivity in Science and Public Life*. Princeton, NJ: Princeton University Press.

Porter, Theodore. 1996. 'Making things quantitative', pp. 36–56 in Michael Power (ed.) *Accounting and Science: Natural Inquiry and Commercial Reason*. New York: Cambridge University Press.

Power, Michael. 1994. *The Audit Explosion*. London: Demos.

Power, Michael. 1997. *The Audit Society: Rituals of Verification*. Oxford: Oxford University Press.

Power, Michael. 2005. 'The theory of the audit explosion', pp. 326–344 in Ewan Ferlie, Laurence Lynn and Christopher Pollitt (eds) *The Oxford Handbook of Public Management*. Oxford: Oxford University Press.

Press Association. 2016. 'Bradford free school founder jailed for defrauding government'. *Guardian*, 30 September. www.theguardian.com/education/2016/sep/30/bradford-free-school-founder-jailed-for-defrauding-government (accessed 9 August 2022).

Price, David, Pollock, Allyson and Brhlikova, Petra. 2011. 'Classification problems and the dividing line between government and the market: An examination of NHS Foundation Trust classification in the UK'. *Annals of Public and Cooperative Economics* 82(4): 455–473.

PwC (PricewaterhouseCoopers). 2010. *Build and Beyond: The ®evolution of Healthcare PPPs*. PwC Health Research Institute. December. www.pwc.se/sv/halso-sjukvard/assets/build-and-beyond-the-revolution-of-healthcare-ppps.pdf (accessed 25 September 2022).

PwC (PricewaterhouseCoopers). 2018. *PPPs in Healthcare: Models, Lessons and Trends for the Future*. Healthcare public–private partnership series, No. 4. San Francisco: The Global Health Group, Institute for Global Health Sciences, University of California, San Francisco and PwC. www.pwc.com/gx/en/healthcare/assets/ppps-in-healthcare.pdf (accessed 1 July 2023).

PwC (PricewaterhouseCoopers). 2022a. 'Our history and milestones'. www.pwc.com/us/en/about-us/pwc-corporate-history.html (accessed 10 August 2022).

PwC (PricewaterhouseCoopers). 2022b 'How we are structured'. www.pwc.com/gx/en/about/corporate-governance/network-structure.html (accessed 10 August 2022).

Ramanna, Karthik. 2018. 'The trouble with accounting's Big Four'. *CapX*. https://capx.co/the-trouble-with-accountings-big-four/ (accessed 19 July 2022).

RateMyProfessors. 2019. 'About RateMyProfessors'. www.ratemyprofessors.com/About.jsp. (accessed 25 June 2019).

Reed, Kevin. 2012. 'Big firms scoop up Audit Commission work'. *Accountancy Age*, 5 March. www.accountancyage.com/2012/03/05/big-firms-scoop-up-audit-commission-work/ (accessed 10 August 2022).

REF (Research Excellence Framework) 2021. 'Index of revisions to the "Panel criteria and working methods" (2019/02)'. www.ref.ac.uk/media/1084/ref-2019_02-panel-criteria-and-working-methods.pdf (accessed 21 August 2022).

Reich, Robert. 1991. *The Work of Nations: Preparing Ourselves for 21st-century Capitalism*. New York: Knopf Publishing.

Reilly, Jessica, Lyu, Muyao and Robertson, Megan. 2021. 'China's Social Credit System: Speculation vs. reality'. *The Diplomat*, 30 March.

Reyes, Angela. 2014. 'Linguistic anthropólogy in 2013: Super-new-big'. *American Anthropologist* 116(2): 366–378.

Richardson, Scott, Tuna, Irem and Wu, Min. 2002. 'Predicting earnings management: The case of earnings restatements'. May. Ann Arbor, MI: University of Michigan Business School. http://d1c25a6gwz7q5e.cloudfront.net/papers/1072.pdf (accessed 10 August 2022).

Richardson, Thomas, Elliott, Peter, Roberts, Ron and Jansen, Megan. 2017. 'A longitudinal study of financial difficulties and mental health in a national sample of British undergraduate students'. *Community Mental Health Journal* 53(3): 344–352.

Ringarp, Johanna and Rothland, Martin. 2010. 'Is the grass always greener? The effect of the PISA results on education debates in Sweden and Germany'. *European Educational Research Journal* 9(3): 422–430.

Robertson, Susan, Dale, Roger, Moutsios, Stavros, Nielsen, Gritt, Shore, Cris and Wright, Susan. 2012. 'Globalisation and regionalisation in higher education: Toward a new conceptual framework'. Working Papers in University Reform No. 20. Aarhus: Danish School of Education and Aarhus University. http://edu.au.dk/fileadmin/www.dpu.dk/forskning/forskningsprogrammer/epoke/workingpapers/WP_20_-_final.pdf (accessed 10 December 2013).

Rose, Nikolas. 1999. *Powers of Freedom*. Cambridge: Cambridge University Press.

Rose, Nikolas and Miller, Peter. 1992. 'Political power beyond the state: Problematics of government'. *British Journal of Sociology* 43(2): 173–205.

Ruckert, Arne and Labonté, Ronald. 2014. 'Public–private partnerships (PPPs) in global health: The good, the bad and the ugly'. *Third World Quarterly* 35(9): 1598–1614.

Russell, Ian and Wilson, Brenda. 1992. 'Audit: The third clinical science'. *Qualitiy in Health Care* 1(51): 5.

Rutkowski, David. 2015. 'The OECD and the local: PISA-based test for schools in the USA'. *Discourse: Studies in the Cultural Politics of Education* 36(5): 683–699.

Sachs, Jeffrey, Layard, Richard and Helliwell, John. 2018. *World Happiness Report 2018*. https://worldhappiness.report/ed/2018/ (accessed 16 June 2023).

Sainato, Michael. 2022. 'Amazon could run out of workers in the US in two years, internal memo suggests'. *Guardian*, 22 June. www.theguardian.com/technology/2022/jun/22/amazon-workers-shortage-leaked-memo-warehouse.

Samans, Richard. 2017. *Global Competitiveness Report 2017–18*. Geneva: World Economic Forum. www3.weforum.org/docs/GCR20172018/05FullReport/The GlobalCompetitivenessReport2017–2018.pdf (accessed 23 August 2022).

Sampson, Steven. 2005. 'Integrity warriors: Global morality and the anti-corruption movement in the Balkans', pp. 103–130 in Dieter Haller and Cris Shore (eds) *Corruption: Anthropological Perspectives*. London: Pluto Press..

Sauder, Michael and Espeland, Wendy. 2009. 'The discipline of rankings: Tight coupling and organisational change'. *American Sociological Review* 74(1): 63–82.

Savage, M. n.d. 'Strategic HR briefings and case studies: British Telecom'. *Businessintelligence*. http://ss393.fusionbot.com/b/ss_cache?cch=1890447&ck=7920972933&sn=157430325&k= (accessed 15 January 2018).

Schleicher, Andreas. 2012. 'Use data to build better schools'. TED Talk, uploaded 21 February, video 19:47. www.youtube.com/watch?v=7Xmr87nsl74 (accessed 23 August 2022).

Schleicher, Andreas and Zoido, Pablo. 2016. 'The policies that shaped PISA, and the policies that PISA shaped', pp. 374–384 in Karen Mundy, Andy Green, Bob Lingard and Antoni Verger (eds) *The Handbook of Global Education Policy*. London: John Wiley & Sons.

Scholz, Susan. 2014. *Financial Restatement: Trends in the United States, 2003–2012*. Washington DC: Centre for Audit Quality. www.thecaq.org/wp-content/uploads/2019/03/financial-restatement-trends-in-the-united-states-2003-2012.pdf (accessed 10 August 2022).

Schwittay, Anke. 2021. *Creative Universities: Re-imagining Education for Global Challenges and Alternative Futures*. Bristol: Bristol University Press.

Scott, Geoff, Coates, Hamish and Anderson, Michelle. 2008. *Learning Leaders in Times of Change: Academic Leadership Capabilities for Australian Higher Education*. Sydney: University of Western Sydney and Australian Council for Educational Research.

Scott, James C. 2008 [1999]. *Seeing Like a State: How Certain Schemes to Improve the Human Condition Have Failed*. New Haven, CT: Yale University Press.

Scott, Peter. 2013. 'Why research assessment is out of control'. *Guardian*, 4 November. www.theguardian.com/education/2013/nov/04/peter-scott-research-excellence-framework (accessed 25 August 2022).

Secretaries of State for Health, Wales, Northern Ireland and Scotland. 1989. *Working for Patients*. London: HMSO (Cmnd 555).

Secretary of State for Health. 1997. *The New NHS: Modern, Dependable*. London: HMSO.

Secretary of State for Health. 2002. *Delivering the NHS Plan*. London: Stationary Office.

Securities and Exchange Commission (SEC). 2011. 'SEC charges India-based affiliates of PWC for role in Satyam accounting fraud', 4 May. www.sec.gov/news/press/2011/2011-82.htm (accessed 10 August 2022).

Seglen, Per. 1997. 'Why the impact factor of journals should not be used for evaluating research'. *British Medical Journal* 314 (15 February): 497. https://doi.org/10.1136/bmj.314.7079.497.

Sellar, Sam and Lingard, Bob. 2013. 'Looking east: Shanghai, PISA 2009 and the reconstitution of reference societies in the global education policy field'. *Comparative Education* 49(4): 464–485.

Senate and House of Representatives. 2001. No Child Left Behind Act of 2001. Washington, DC: Senate and House of Representatives of the United States of America.

Serco. 2022. 'About Serco'. www.serco.com/about (accessed 11 July 2022).

Sevillana, Elena, Abril, Guillermo and Prats, Jaime. 2012. 'The revolving door'. *El País*, 11 December. https://english.elpais.com/elpais/2012/12/10/inenglish/1355160134_388674.html (accessed 25 September 2022).

Sharma, Alkesh. 2022. 'Global Smartwatch shipments up 24% in 2021 on strong demand'. *The National News*, 15 March. https://www.thenationalnews.com/business/technology/2022/03/15/global-smartwatch-shipments-up-24-in-2021-on-strong-demand/ (accessed 1 July 2022).

Shaw, Charles and Costain, David. 1989. 'Guidelines for medical audit: Seven principles'. *British Medical Journal* 299(6697): 498–499.

Shore, Cris. 2008. 'Audit culture and illiberal governance: Universities and the politics of accountability'. *Anthropological Theory* 8(3): 278–299.

Shore, Cris. 2021. 'Audit failure and corporate corruption: Why Mediterranean patron–client relations are relevant for understanding the work of international accountancy firms'. *Focaal* 2021(90): 91–105.

Shore, Cris and McLauchlan, Laura. 2012. '"Third Mission" activities and academic entrepreneurs: Commercialization and the remaking of the university'. *Social Anthropology / Anthropologie Sociale* 20(3): 267–286.

Shore, Cris and Taitz, Mira. 2012. 'Who owns the university? Institutional autonomy and academic freedom in an age of knowledge capitalism'. *Globalisation, Societies and Education* 10(2): 201–219.

Shore, Cris and Wright, Susan. 1997a. 'Policy: A new field of anthropology', pp. 3–39 in Cris Shore and Susan Wright (eds) *Anthropology of Policy: Critical Perspectives on Governance and Power*. London: Routledge.

Shore, Cris and Wright, Susan (eds). 1997b. *Anthropology of Policy: Critical Perspectives on Governance and Power*. London: Routledge.

Shore, Cris and Wright, Susan. 1999. 'Audit culture and anthropology: Neoliberalism in British higher education'. *Journal of the Royal Anthropological Institute* 5(4): 557–575.

Shore, Cris and Wright, Susan. 2000. 'Coercive accountability: The rise of audit culture in higher education', pp. 57–89 in Marilyn Strathern (ed.) *Audit Cultures: Anthropological Studies in Accountability, Ethics and the Academy* (EASA Series). London: Routledge.

Shore, Cris and Wright, Susan. 2004, 'Whose accountability? Governmentality and the auditing of universities'. *Parallax* 10(2): 101–117.

Shore, Cris and Wright, Susan (eds). 2011. *Policy Worlds: Anthropology and the Analysis of Contemporary Power*. Oxford: Berghahn.

Shore, Cris and Wright, Susan. 2015a. 'Governing by numbers: Audit culture, rankings and the new world order'. *Social Anthropology/Anthropologie Sociale* 23(1): 22–28.

Shore, Cris and Wright, Susan. 2015b. 'Audit culture revisited: Rankings, ratings, and the reassembling of society'. *Current Anthropology* 56(3): 431–432.

Shore, Cris and Wright, Susan 2021 'The Kafkaesque pursuit of "world class": Audit culture and the reputational arms race in academia', in Sharon Rider,

Michael A. Peter, Mats Hyvönen and Tina Besley (eds) *World Class Universities*. Singapore: Springer Singapore.

Shumar, Wesley. 1997. *College for Sale: A Critique of the Commodification of Higher Education*. Abingdon: Routledge.

Sikka, Prem. 2009. 'Financial crisis and the silence of the auditors'. *Accounting, Organizations and Society* 34: 868–873.

Sikka, Prem. 2013. 'The uncompetitive culture of auditing's Big Four remains undented'. *Guardian*, 23 February. www.theguardian.com/commentisfree/2013/feb/23/uncompetitive-culture-auditing-big-four-undented (accessed 24 February 2015).

Sikka, Prem. 2014. 'The professor's view: Number's up for Big Four accountants behind tax avoidance schemes and duff audits of banks'. *This is the Money*, 9 November. www.thisismoney.co.uk/money/comment/article-2827741/Number-s-Big-Four-accountants-tax-avoidance-schemes-duff-audits-banks.html (accessed 10 August 2022).

Sikka, Prem. 2016. 'Big Four accounting firms: Addicted to tax avoidance'. In Jim Haslam and Sikka, Prem (eds) *Pioneers of Critical Accounting: A Celebration of the Life of Tony Lowe*. London: Palgrave Macmillan.

Sikka, Prem, Haslam, Colin, Cooper, Christine, Haslam, James, Christensen, John, Driver, Deepa et al. 2018. *Reforming the Auditing Industry*. Report commissioned by John McDonnell MP, Shadow Chancellor of the Exchequer, December. http://betterfinance.eu/wp-content/uploads/LabourPolicymaking-AuditingReformsDec2018.pdf (accessed 10 August 2022).

Simola, Hannu. 2005. 'The Finnish miracle of PISA: Historical and sociological remarks on teaching and teacher education'. *Comparative Education* 41(4): 455–470.

Sinmaz, Emine. 2023. 'Headteacher killed herself after news of low Ofsted rating, family says'. *Guardian*, 17 March. https://amp.theguardian.com/education/2023/mar/17/headteacher-killed-herself-after-news-of-low-ofsted-rating-family-says (accessed 24 March 2023).

Slater, Don. 1997. *Consumer Society and Modernity*. Cambridge: Polity Press.

Slaughter, Sheila and Leslie, Larry. 1999 *Academic Capitalism: Politics, Policies, and the Entrepreneurial University*. Baltimore, MD: Johns Hopkins University Press.

Slaughter, Sheila and Rhoades, Gary. 2004. *Academic Capitalism and the New Economy: Markets, State, and Higher Education*. Baltimore, MD: Johns Hopkins University Press.

Smith, Gavin. 2014. *Intellectuals and (Counter-) Politics: Essays in Historical Realism (Dislocations)*. Oxford: Berghahn.

Smith, Gavin. 2015. 'Comments on "Audit culture revisited: Rankings, ratings and the reassembling of society"'. *Current Anthropology* 57(3): 537–538.

Social Progress Imperative. 2018. 'Social Progress Index 2018'. www.socialprogress.org/ (accessed 25 June 2019).

Sodha, Sonia. 2018. 'The great academy schools scandal'. *Observer*, 22 July. www.theguardian.com/education/2018/jul/22/academy-schools-scandal-failing-trusts (accessed 9 August 2022).

Somers, Bailey. 2006. 'KPMG off the hook in Hollinger scandal'. *Law 360*, 25 January. www.law360.com/articles/5108/kpmg-off-the-hook-in-hollinger-scandal (accessed 10 August 2022).

Speigel, Peter. 2014. 'Jean-Claude Juncker regrets failing to reform tax law'. *Financial Times*, 27 November. www.ft.com/content/4b87f3f0-7637-11e4-a777-00144feabdc0 (accessed 30 August 2022).

Spence, Crawford and Carter, Chris. 2014. 'An exploration of the professional habitus in the Big 4 accounting firms'. *Work, Employment and Society* 28(6): 946–962.

Stasha, Smiljanic. 2022. 'The state of healthcare industry – Statistics for 2022'. *Policy Advice*, 5 March (accessed 20 August 2022).

Statista, 2021. 'Revenue of the Big Four accounting / audit firms worldwide in 2020, by function'. Statista Research Department, 16 February. https://www.statista.com/statistics/250935/big-four-accounting-firms-breakdown-of-revenues/ (accessed 2 July 2023).

Statista, 2023a. 'Number of employees of the Big Four accounting / audit firms worldwide in 2022'. www.statista.com/statistics/250503/big-four-accounting-firms-number-of-employees/ (accessed 12 July 2023).

Statista, 2023b. 'Number of Deloitte employees worldwide 2006–2022'. Statista Research Department, 10 January. www.statista.com/statistics/269014/number-of-employees-at-deloitte-worldwide/ (accessed 2 March 2023).

Statista, 2023c. 'Revenue of the Big Four accounting / audit firms worldwide in 2022, by function'. www.statista.com/statistics/250935/big-four-accounting-firms-breakdown-of-revenues/ (accessed 13 July 2023).

Staufenberg, Jess. 2018. 'Perry Beeches Academy Trust closes after schools move to new sponsors'. *Schools Week*, 11 January. https://schoolsweek.co.uk/perry-beeches-academy-trust-closes-after-schools-move-to-new-sponsors/ (accessed 9 August 2022).

Steiner-Khamsi, Gita and Draxler, Alexandra. 2018. 'Seeing like the state, calculating like a business: Public–private partnerships in education revisited'. *Norrag*, 11 January. www.norrag.org/seeing-like-state-calculating-like-business-public-private-partnerships-education-revisited-gita-steiner-khamsi-alexandra-draxler/ (accessed 23 August 2022).

Storbeck, Olaf. 2022. 'New German watchdog says auditors too close to clients'. *Financial Times*, 22 August: 7.

Storm, Darlene. 2015. 'ACLU: Orwellian citizen score, China's credit score system, is a warning for Americans'. *Computerworld*. www.computerworld.com/article/2990203/security/aclu-orwellian-citizen-score-chinas-credit-score-system-is-a-warning-for-americans.html (accessed 20 August 2022).

Strathern, Marilyn. 2000a. 'The tyranny of transparency'. *British Educational Research Journal* 26(3): 309–321.

Strathern, Marilyn. 2000b. 'Introduction', pp. 1–18 in Marilyn Strathern (ed.) *Audit Cultures: Anthropological Studies in Accountability, Ethics and the Academy* (EASA Series). London: Routledge.

Strathern, Marilyn. 2000c. *Audit Cultures: Anthropological Studies in Accountability, Ethics and the Academy*. Abingdon: Routledge.

Sweney, Mark. 2022. 'Alibaba founder Jack Ma hiding out in Tokyo, reports say'. *Guardian*, 29 November. www.theguardian.com/business/2022/nov/29/alibaba-founder-jack-ma-hiding-out-in-tokyo-reports-say (accessed 1 July 2023).

Sweney, Mark. 2023. 'China to take "golden shares" in tech firms Alibaba and Tencent'. *Guardian*, 13 January. www.theguardian.com/world/2023/jan/13/china-to-take-golden-shares-in-tech-firms-alibaba-and-tencent (accessed 1 July 2023).

Syal, Rajeev. 2018. 'Taxpayers face £200 billion bill for PFI'. *Guardian* weekly, 26 January.

Syrett, Michael. 2007. *The Economist: Successful Strategy Execution: How to Keep Your Business Goals on Target*. London: Profile Books.

Tabuchi, Hiroko and Bradsher, Keith. 2011. 'Global business: The culture was corrupt at Olympus, panel finds'. *New York Times*, 6 December. www.nytimes.com/2011/12/07/business/global/banks-aided-in-olympus-cover-up-report-finds.html (accessed 10 August 2022).

Takayama, Keita. 2009. 'Politics of externalization in reflexive times: Reinventing Japanese education reform discourses through "Finnish PISA success"'. *Comparative Education Review* 54(1): 51–75.

Tao, Hu. 2017. 'Zhima Credit does not share user scores or data'. *Financial Times*, 17 November. www.ft.com/content/ec4a2a46-c577-11e7-a1d2-6786f39ef675 (accessed 19 August 2022).

Taylor, Frederik. 1913. *The Principles of Scientific Management*. New York: Harper and Bros.

Tett, Gillian. 2009. *Fool's Gold: How the Bold Dream of a Small Tribe at JP Morgan was Corrupted by Wall Street Greed and Unleashed a Catastrophe*. New York: Simon and Schuster.

The Economist. 2012a. 'The quantified self: Counting every moment'. 3 May. www.economist.com/node/21548493/print (accessed 20 August 2022).

The Economist. 2012b. 'The Big Four accounting firms: Shape shifters'. 29 September. www.economist.com/node/21563726 (accessed 24 February 2015).

The Economist. 2014. 'Accounting scandals: The dozy watchdogs'. 11 December. www.economist.com/news/briefing/21635978-some-13-years-after-enron-auditors-still-cant-stop-managers-cooking-books-time-some (accessed 25 February 2015).

The Independent. 2003. 'The fat cat list 2003, part one'. 19 May. www.independent.co.uk/news/business/analysis-and-features/the-fat-cat-list-2003-part-one-105372.html (accessed 20 August 2022).

Thedvall, Renita. 2006. *Eurocrats at Work: Negotiating Transparency in Postnational Employment Policy*. PhD dissertation, Department of Social Anthropology, Stockholm University.

Thomas, Chris. 2019. 'The "make do and mend" health service: Solving the NHS' capital crisis'. London: Institute for Public Policy Research. www.ippr.org/research/publications/the-make-do-and-mend-health-service (accessed 20 August 2022).

Topendsports. 2019. 'The most demanding sports'. www.topendsports.com/world/lists/fittest-sport/espn.htm (accessed 25 June 2019).

Treanor, Jill. 2013. 'Hector Sants resigns from Barclays: Compliance chief and former head of the FSA quits just weeks after being signed off work with exhaustion'. *Guardian*, 13 November. www.theguardian.com/business/2013/nov/13/hector-sants-resigns-from-barclays#:~:text=Sir%20Hector%20Sants%2C%20one%20of,sick%20with%20exhaustion%20and%20ostress. (accessed 10 August 2022).

Trouillot, Michel-Rolph. 2001. 'The anthropology of the state in the age of globalization: Close encounters of the deceptive kind'. *Current Anthropology* 42(1): 125–138.

Tsing, Anna. 2006 (22–24 May). 'Figures of capitalist globalization: Firm models and chain links'. Keynote to the Danish Research School of Anthropology and Ethnography's Megaseminar 'Holism in Anthropological and Ethnographic Research', Hindsgavl Castle, Denmark.

Tuchman, Gaye. 2011. *Wannabe U: Inside the Corporate University*. Chicago: University of Chicago Press.

UK Cabinet Office. 1993. 'Realising our potential: A strategy for science, engineering and technology', Policy paper. 26 May. https://assets.publishing.service.gov.uk/government/uploads/system/uploads/attachment_data/file/271983/2250.pdf (accessed 25 August 2022).

UK Government. 2013. 'Healthcare: Public–private partnerships'. 18 December. www.gov.uk/government/publications/public-private-partnerships/public-private-partnerships (accessed 20 August 2022).

University of Auckland (UoA). 2013. *Guide to the University of Auckland Leadership Framework*. Staff and Organisational Development Unit. https://cdn.auckland.ac.nz/assets/auckland/about-us/equity-at-the-university/about-equity/what-is-equity/guide-to-the-leadership-framework-capabilities-defined.pdf (accessed 20 August 2022).

University of Auckland (UoA). 2016. *Academic Standards: The University of Auckland HR Policy*. www.auckland.ac.nz/en/about/the-university/how-university-works/policy-and-administration/human-resources1/academic-processes-and-standards/academic-standards/academic-standards-other.html (accessed 20 August 2022).

Ura, Kama, Alkire, Sabina, Zangmo, Tshoki and Wangdi, Karma. 2012. *An Extensive Analysis of GNH Index*. Thimphu: Centre for Bhutan Studies. https://opendocs.ids.ac.uk/opendocs/handle/20.500.12413/11818 (accessed 13 July 2022).

U.S. News & World Report. 2016. www.usnews.com/news/articles/2016-02-16/ranking-countries-by-the-worst-students (accessed 25 August 2022).

Välijärvi, Jouni, Linnakylä, Pirjo, Kupari, Pekka, Peinikainen, Pasi and Arffman, Inga. 2002. *The Finnish Success in PISA – And Some Reasons Behind It*. Jyväskylä: Institute for Educational Research. University of Jyväskylä.

Waldow, Florian. 2009. 'What PISA did and did not do: Germany after the "PISA-shock"'. *European Educational Research Journal* 8(3): 476–483.

Warin, Robbie and McCann, Duncan. 2018. 'Who watches the workers? Power and accountability in the digital economy (Part 2)'. London: New Economics Foundation.

Warner, Marina. 2014. 'Diary'. *London Review of Books* 36, no. 17 (11 September): 42–43. www.lrb.co.uk/v36/n17/marina-warner/diary (accessed 25 August 2022).

Washburn, Jennifer. 2005. *University, Inc.: The Corporate Corruption of Higher Education*. New York: Basic Books.

Weber, Max. 2013 [1903]. *The Protestant Ethic and the Spirit of Capitalism*, trans. Stephen Kalberg. London: Routledge.

Wedel, Janine. 2009. *Shadow Elite: How the World's New Power Brokers Undermine Democracy, Government, and the Free Market*. New York: Basic Books.

WEF (World Economic Forum). 2018a. *The Global Risks Report 2018*. Geneva: WEF www.weforum.org/reports/the-global-risks-report-2018/ (accessed 24 September 2022).

WEF (World Economic Forum). 2018b. 'The Forum of Young Global Leaders'. www.weforum.org/communities/young-global-leaders (accessed 23 August 2022).

White, Aoife and Miller, Hugo. 2020. 'Big Four face big split as watchdog sets separation deadline'. *Bloomberg*, 6 July. www.bloomberg.com/news/articles/2020-07-06/u-k-asks-big-four-firms-to-separate-auditing-units-by-june-2024#xj4y7vzkg (accessed 10 August 2022).

Whitfield, Dexter. 2011. *The £10bn Sale of Shares in PPP Companies: New Source of Profits for Builders and Banks*. ESSU Research Report No. 4. Tralee, Ireland: European Services Strategy Unit. www.european-services-strategy.org.uk/wp-content/uploads/2011/01/10bn-sale-of-ppp-shares.pdf

Whitfield, Dexter. 2017a. *PPP Profiteering and Offshoring: New Evidence. PPP Equity Database 1998-2016 (UK)*. ESSU Research Report No. 10. Tralee, Ireland: European Services Strategy Unit.

Whitfield, Dexter. 2017b. *PFI/PPP Buyouts, Bailouts, Terminations and Major Problem Contracts in UK*. ESSU Research Report No. 9. Tralee, Ireland: European Services Strategy Unit. www.european-services-strategy.org.uk/wp-content/uploads/2017/02/pfi-ppp-buyouts-bailouts-and-terminations.pdf

Whitson, Jennifer. 2013. 'Gaming the quantified self'. *Surveillance and Society* 11(1–2): 163–176.

WHO (World Health Organization). 2020. *Global Spending on Health: Weathering the Storm*. Geneva: WHO. https://apps.who.int/iris/rest/bitstreams/1322903/retrieve (accessed 20 August 2022).

Wild, Kate. 2014. 'KPMG denies role in alleged theft from Australia's richest Aboriginal land trust'. *ABC News*, 11 November. www.abc.net.au/news/2014-11-11/kpmg-denies-role-in-alleged-theft-from-groote-eylandt-land-trust/5882920 (accessed 26 February 2015).

Wilks-Heeg, Stuart. 2015. 'Revolving-door politics and corruption', pp. 135–144 in David Whyte (ed.) *How Corrupt Is Britain?* London: Pluto.

Willett, Gudrun. 2013. 'Beyond pedagogy: Community feeling, educational development and power in a U.S. liberal arts college'. *Learning and Teaching: International Journal of Higher Education in the Social Sciences* 6(1): 47–71.

Wittgenstein, Ludvig. 1953 [1967]. *Philosophical Investigations*, trans, Gertrude Anscombe, 3rd edn. Oxford: Blackwell.

Wolf, Gary. 2010. 'An interview with Gary Wolf on the quantified self'. Institute For The Future (IFTF). www.iftf.org/future-now/article-detail/an-interview-with-gary-wolf-on-the-quantified-self/ (accessed 20 August 2022).

Wolf, Gary. 2011. 'TEDx Amsterdam 2011 – Gary Wolf'. TEDx Talks, uploaded 25 November, video 10:33. www.youtube.com/watch?v=YN_MjyNq3Z8 (accessed 23 August 2022).

Wright, Susan. 2004. 'Politically reflexive practitioners', in D. Drackle and I. Edgar (eds) Current Policies and Practices in European Social Anthropology Education (EASA series). Oxford: Berghahn, pp. 34–52.

Wright, Susan. 2008. 'Governance as a regime of discipline', pp. 75–98 in Noel Dyck (ed.) Exploring Regimes of Discipline: The Dynamics of Restraint (EASA Series). Oxford: Berghahn.

Wright, Susan. 2009 'What counts? The skewing effects of research assessment systems'. Nordisk Pedagogik/Journal of Nordic Educational Research 29: 18–33.

Wright, Susan. 2011. 'Viden der tæller [Knowledge that counts]', pp. 211–236 in Kirsten Marie Bovbjerg (ed.) Motivation og mismod (Motivation and Despondency). Aarhus Universitetsforlag.

Wright, Susan. 2012. 'Ranking universities within a globalised world of competition states: To what purpose, and with what implications for students?' pp. 79–100 in Hanne Andersen and Jens Jacobsen (eds) Uddannelseskvalitet i det 21. århundrede (Quality in Higher Education in the 21st Century). Frederiksberg: Samfundslitteratur.

Wright, Susan. 2014. 'Knowledge that counts: Points systems and the governance of Danish universities', pp. 294–337 in Dorothy Smith and Alison Griffith (eds) Under New Public Management: Institutional Ethnographies of Changing Front-line Work. Toronto: University of Toronto Press.

Wright, Susan. 2016. 'The imaginators of English university reform', pp. 127–150 in Sheila Slaughter and Barrett Jay Taylor (eds) Higher Education, Stratification, and Workforce Development: Competitive Advantage in Europe, the US, and Canada. Switzerland: Springer.

Wright, Susan. 2020. 'University reform: International policy making through a Danish prism', pp. 55–85 in Susan Wright, Stephen Carney, John Krejsler, Gritt Nielsen and Jakob Ørberg, Enacting the University: Danish University Reform in an Ethnographic Perspective. Dordrecht: Springer.

Wright, Susan and Ørberg, Jakob. 2017. 'Universities in the competition state: Lessons from Denmark', pp. 69–89 in Susan Wright and Cris Shore (eds) Death of the Public University? Uncertain Futures for Higher Education in the Knowledge Economy. New York: Berghahn.

Wright, Susan, Curtis, Bruce, Lucas, Lisa and Robertson, Susan. 2014. Research Assessment Systems and their Impacts on Academic Work in New Zealand, the UK and Denmark: Summative Working Paper for URGE Work Package 5. Working Papers in University Reform 24. Copenhagen Danish School of Education, Aarhus University. http://edu.au.dk/fileadmin/edu/Forskning/URGE/WP_24.pdf (accessed1 July 2023).

Zak, Paul. 2013. 'Measurement myopia'. Drucker Institute, 4 July. www.drucker.institute/thedx/measurement-myopia/ (accessed 20 August 2022).

Zuboff, Shoshana. 2019. The Age of Surveillance Capitalism: The Fight for a Human Future at the New Frontier of Power. London: Profile Books.

Index